DUTCH OVEN COOKBOOK

300 Home Recipes For Indoor Cooking
Easy One-Pot Ideas For Beginners

Zoey Taylor

DUTCH OVEN COOKBOOK

DUTCH OVEN COOKBOOK

© Copyright 2021 - All rights reserved.

The content contained within this book may not be reproduced, duplicated or transmitted without direct written permission from the author or the publisher.

Under no circumstances will any blame or legal responsibility be held against the publisher, or author, for any damages, reparation, or monetary loss due to the information contained within this book. Either directly or indirectly.

Legal Notice:

This book is copyright protected. This book is only for personal use. You cannot amend, distribute, sell, use, quote or paraphrase any part, or the content within this book, without the consent of the author or publisher.

Disclaimer Notice:

Please note the information contained within this document is for educational and entertainment purposes only. All effort has been executed to present accurate, up to date, and reliable, complete information. No warranties of any kind are declared or implied. Readers acknowledge that the author is not engaging in the rendering of legal, financial, medical or professional advice. The content within this book has been derived from various sources. Please consult a licensed professional before attempting any techniques outlined in this book.

By reading this document, the reader agrees that under no circumstances is the author responsible for any losses, direct or indirect, which are incurred as a result of the use of information contained within this document, including, but not limited to, errors, omissions, or inaccuracies.

Table of Contents

INTRODUCTION **15**

CHAPTER 1. BASICS OF DUTCH OVEN **16**

    1. What Is a Dutch oven? 16
    2. Cooking With a Dutch Oven 18

CHAPTER 2. 1-WEEK MEAL PLAN **21**

CHAPTER 3. BREAKFAST RECIPES **22**

    1. Dutch Oven Bread 22
    2. Bread Pudding 23
    3. Basic Dutch Oven Breakfast 24
    4. Dutch Oven Pizza 25
    5. Irish Soda Bread 26
    6. Breakfast Wassail 27
    7. Raisin and Almond Granola 27
    8. Syrupy Pear Oatmeal 28
    9. Apple Quinoa 29
    10. Butter Toast Casserole 30
    11. Cheesy Broccoli Casserole 31
    12. Cheese Egg Scramble with Salsa 32
    13. Bacon and Cheese Potato 33
    14. Apple Dutch Baby Pancake 34
    15. Bacon and Cheese Frittata 35
    16. Bacon n' Eggs Breakfast 36
    17. Baked Fruit Oatmeal 37
    18. Congee with Eggs and Herbs 38
    19. Cherry Almond Breakfast Scones 39
    20. Baked Oatmeal with Blueberries and Apples 40
    21. Dutch Baby with Lemon Glaze 41
    22. Middle Eastern Shakshuka 42
    23. Breakfast Chicken Casserole 43
    24. Classic Bacon and Eggs 44
    25. Ham Cheese Omelet 45
    26. Sausage-Hash Morning 46

27.	Breakfast Sausage Casserole	47
28.	Biscuits and Gravy	48
29.	Dutch Oven Tater Tot Casserole	49
30.	Baked Oatmeal	50

CHAPTER 4.   CHILIES, STEWS, SOUPS 51

31.	Hearty Vegetarian Chili	51
32.	Chickpea Tortilla Soup	52
33.	Seafood Bisque	53
34.	Cheese Chicken Soup	54
35.	Pork Noodle Soup	54
36.	Italian White Bean Soup	55
37.	Turkey and Noodle Tomato Soup	56
38.	Taco Soup	57
39.	Chicken Meatball and Zucchini Noodle Soup	58
40.	Chicken Zoodle Soup	59
41.	Cauliflower Soup	60
42.	Italian Sausage Soup	61
43.	Italian Wedding Soup	62
44.	Sausage Minestrone	64
45.	Minestrone with Turkey	65
46.	Orzo Shrimp Stew	66
47.	Spicy Chicken Stew	67
48.	Kale and White-Bean Stew	67
49.	Chicken Mushroom Soup	68
50.	Creme Potato Chicken Soup	69
51.	Beef and Cabbage Soup	70
52.	Quinoa Chickpea Corn Soup	71
53.	Sweet Potato Soup	72
54.	Pork and Bean Soup	73
55.	Tomato Cream Soup with Basil	74
56.	Chicken Bean Barley Soup	75
57.	Collard Green White Bean Soup with Sausages	76
58.	Bacon and Potato Soup	77
59.	Tomato Bisque with Shrimp	78
60.	Creamy Broccoli Soup	79

61.	Vegetable and Lentil Soup	80
62.	Cauliflower-Leek Potage	81
63.	Pork Green Chili	82
64.	Black Bean Soup with Citrus	83
65.	Turmeric Vegetable Soup	84

CHAPTER 5. VEGETABLES AND VEGETARIAN 86

66.	Beans with Chard	86
67.	Savory Beans Rice	87
68.	Corn and Bean Succotash	88
69.	Panko Eggplant	89
70.	Navy Beans and Zucchini	91
71.	Butternut Squash Risotto	92
72.	Cheese Mushrooms Bake	93
73.	Cream Mushroom Pasta Bake	95
74.	Tomato and Peas Korma	96
75.	Rice with Kale and Lentils	97
76.	Lentils and Tomato over Rice	98
77.	Tofu with Cashews and Spinach	99
78.	Kidney Bean and Tomato Pasta Soup	101
79.	Peas and Carrot Fried Rice	102
80.	Cabbage Noodles	103
81.	Asparagus Peas Risotto with Cheese	104
82.	Cheesy Spinach Ziti Bake	105
83.	Chickpeas Pasta with Cheese	106
84.	Cheesy Butter Pasta	107
85.	Spaghetti with Cheese	108
86.	White Bean and Tomato Chili	109
87.	Baked Cheese Pizza	110
88.	Rice and Quinoa Stuffed Pepper	111
89.	Barley Butternut Squash Risotto	112
90.	Barley and Mushroom Casserole	113
91.	Corn and Black Bean Couscous	114
92.	Roast Chickpeas and Zucchini	115
93.	Lentils with Carrot and Turnip	116
94.	Cauliflower with Chickpeas	117

95.	Spinach and Mushroom Curry	118
96.	Okra Corn and Tomato Stew	119
97.	Ratatouille with Tomato	120

CHAPTER 6. SIDE AND APPETIZER DISHES 121

98.	Korean Fried Chicken	121
99.	Scallion Baked Beans	122
100.	Old Bay French Fries	123
101.	Crab Hush Puppies	124
102.	Chicken Pesto with Pasta	125
103.	Peas with Collard Greens	125
104.	Creamed Corn	126
105.	Buffalo Sloppy Joes	127
106.	Garlic Mashed Potatoes	128
107.	Almond and Herb Couscous	129
108.	Golden Onion Rings	130
109.	Tomato and Cauliflower Antipasto	131
110.	Egg and Butter Spaetzle	132
111.	Buffalo Style Cauliflower	133
112.	Crispy Asian Green Beans	134
113.	Riederalp Swiss Fondue	135
114.	Crunchy Parmesan and Garlic Zucchini	136
115.	Garlicky-Lemon Zucchini	137
116.	Ginger-Infused Kabocha Squash	138
117.	Glazed Carrots	139
118.	Herbed Focaccia Bread	140
119.	Pancetta and Asparagus with Fried Egg	141
120.	Laqua Family Slow-Cooked Beans	142
121.	Golden Hash Brown Cake	143

CHAPTER 7. PASTA, PIZZA AND RICE 144

122.	Ginger-Scented Rice	144
123.	Lemony Quinoa and Kale Salad	145
124.	Spanakorizo	146
125.	Salmon Congee with Sesame	147
126.	Rigatoni with Pumpkin Seed Pesto	148

127.	Parmesan Polenta with Thyme-Roasted Mushrooms	149
128.	Italian Beef and Tomato Goulash	150
129.	Beef Stroganoff	151
130.	Sesame-Ginger Soba Noodle Salad	153
131.	Gouda-Cheddar Mac and Cheese	154
132.	Meat Overload Pizza	155
133.	Classic Pepperoni	156
134.	Meat with Bell Pepper & Mushrooms	156
135.	Barbecue Pizza	157
136.	Meat with Mushrooms, Bell Pepper & Olives	158
137.	Meatball Pizza	159
138.	Spicy Italian Sausage Pizza	160
139.	Brussels Sprouts & Pancetta Pizza	161
140.	Hawaiian Pizza	162
141.	Breakfast Sausage Pizza	163
142.	Philly Cheesesteak Pizza	164
143.	Veggie Pizza	165
144.	Neopolitan Apollonia Pizza	166
145.	Chicago-Style Deep-Dish Pizza	167
146.	Sicilian Pizza	168

CHAPTER 8. CHICKEN **170**

147.	Chicken Cacciatore with Tomato	170
148.	Carrot Chicken With Pea	171
149.	Rice With Chicken & Sausage	172
150.	Chicken Pot with Tomato Sauce	173
151.	Bamboo Shoot Chicken	174
152.	Lemony Chicken with Tomato	175
153.	Cheese Lemon Chicken Pasta Bake	176
154.	Lemony Chicken with Parsnip	177
155.	Cheese–Stuffed Chicken Breasts	178
156.	Chicken and Potato Broccoli Casserole	179
157.	Chicken Fricassee with Onion	180
158.	Broccoli Chicken with Almond	181
159.	Golden Fried Chicken Tenders	182
160.	Fried Chicken	183

161.	Roast Chicken with Lemon	185
162.	Roast Chicken Drumsticks	186
163.	Chicken Thighs with Mushroom	187
164.	Mushroom Chicken a la King	188
165.	Creamy Broccoli Chicken Noodles	189
166.	Pineapple Chicken	190
167.	Dutch Oven Chicken	191
168.	Roast Chicken with Garlic and Truffles	192
169.	Chinese-Style One Pot Chicken	194
170.	Moroccan Stew	195
171.	Chicken Risotto	196

CHAPTER 9. TURKEY AND DUCK 198

172.	Grilled Turkey	198
173.	Peppers with Turkey Stuffing	199
174.	Artichoke Turkey with Spinach Casserole	200
175.	Turkey Pilaf with Cheese	201
176.	Turkey Breast with Asparagus	202
177.	Savory Turkey Breast	203
178.	Duck Breast with Olive	204

CHAPTER 10. BEEF, PORK AND LAMB 205

179.	Jerk Pork Chops with Plantains	205
180.	Pork with Rice & Beans	206
181.	Cajun Riblets	208
182.	Pork Rib Casserole	209
183.	Beef Bourguignon	210
184.	Herb-Crusted Roast Beef & Potatoes	211
185.	Beef Tenderloin	212
186.	Roast Beef with Root Vegetables	214
187.	Stuffed Meatballs	215
188.	Lamb Shanks with Vegetables	216
189.	Braised Beef Ribs	218
190.	Dutch Oven Corned Beef	219
191.	Braised Pork Ribs	220
192.	Pork BBQ Burger	221

193.	Mushroom Sausage Pizza	222
194.	Lentil Sausage Pasta	223
195.	Beef Carrot Meal	224
196.	Bacon Ranch Pasta	225
197.	Zucchini Beef Meal	226
198.	Cheddar Beef Gnocchi Bake	227
199.	Pork Chops Potatoes	228
200.	Bulgur Sausage Bean Meal	229
201.	Succulent Braised Pork	230
202.	Roasted Pork Loin in Mushroom Sauce	231
203.	Korean Style Pork Chops	232
204.	Slow Roasted Pork Shoulder with Rosemary	233
205.	Sunday Pork Roast	234
206.	Pulled Pork	235
207.	Classic Beef Stew	236
208.	Braised Short Ribs	237
209.	Dutch Oven Chili	238
210.	Lemony Rib Lamb Chops	239

CHAPTER 11. SEAFOOD AND FISH RECIPES 240

211.	Shrimp and Wild Rice in a Pot	240
212.	Baked Trout	241
213.	Poached Fish	241
214.	Chili Catfish	242
215.	Beer Batter Shrimp	243
216.	Pasta with Clams and Pancetta	244
217.	Beer Mustard Shrimp	245
218.	Tilapia Nuggets	246
219.	Lobster Bisque	247
220.	Baked Salmon with Herbs	249
221.	Baked Trout with Cherry Tomatoes	250
222.	Tilapia Cacciatore	251
223.	Seafood Risotto	252
224.	Calamari Fra Diavolo	253
225.	Seafood Stew	254
226.	Lemony Salt Snapper	255

227.	Baked Salmon Fillet	256
228.	Lemon Halibut with Salsa	256
229.	Quick Swordfish Steaks	257
230.	Salmon with Spinach	258
231.	Buttery Grouper	259
232.	Whitefish and Oyster Bouillabaisse	260
233.	Lemon Halibut with Tomato	261
234.	Roast Fish with Lemon	262
235.	Beer Catfish Fillet	263
236.	Cod Fillet with Beer	264
237.	Salmon Fillet with Lemon	265
238.	Arugula Cod with Cherry Tomato	266
239.	Olive Cod with Lemon	267
240.	Mussels with Bacon	268
241.	Chives Mussels	269
242.	Shrimp and Mussels Paella	270
243.	Crab and Clam Cioppino	271
244.	Breaded Crab Fish Cheese Casserole	272
245.	Panko Shrimp Scampi	273
246.	Creamy Shrimp Mushrooms Stroganoff	274
247.	Oysters and Shrimp Cream Salad	275
248.	Shrimp and Tomato Provencal	276
249.	Savory Calamari	277
250.	Buttery Tomato Shrimp	278
251.	Mango Shrimp	279
252.	Panko Crab Cakes	279
253.	Sausage Corn Chowder	280

CHAPTER 12. BREADS AND ROLLS 282

254.	No-Knead Bread	282
255.	Sourdough Bread	283
256.	5 Seeds Bread	284
257.	Focaccia	285
258.	Oven Tomato and Olive Focaccia	286
259.	Cheddar Sage Bread	287
260.	Chocolate, Walnut, and Cranberry Bread	288

261.	Honey Sunflower Bread	289
262.	Rosemary and Lemon Bread	290
263.	Rosemary Cheese Bread	291
264.	Rosemary Bread	293
265.	Zucchini Bread	294
266.	Cornbread with Green Chiles	295
267.	Buttermilk Cornbread	296
268.	Sweet Honey Corn Bread	297
269.	Corn Muffins	298
270.	Breadsticks	299
271.	Buttermilk Biscuits	300
272.	Cinnamon Bread	300
273.	Cashew Bread	301
274.	Sesame Seeds Bread	302

CHAPTER 13. SAUCES 304

275.	Cream and Butter Sauce	304
276.	Honey and Soy Sauce	304
277.	Syrupy Sauce with Ketchup	305
278.	Tomato Marinara Sauce	305
279.	Enchilada Tomato Sauce	306
280.	Cream Sauce with Lemon	307
281.	Chile and Cheese Sauce	308

CHAPTER 14. DESSERTS 309

282.	Heavenly Peach Cobbler	309
283.	Chocolate Cake	310
284.	Pecan Pralines	311
285.	Quick and Easy Pop Brownies	312
286.	Chocolate Chip Cookies	312
287.	Dutch Oven Brownies	313
288.	Cinnamon Rolls	314
289.	Very Berry Swirl	315
290.	Peach Cobbler	316
291.	Apple Crisp	317
292.	All in One Apple Cake	318

293.	Dutch Oven Chocolate Chip Cookies	319
294.	Fruity Doughnuts	319
295.	Cobbler	321
296.	Apple Cobbler	322
297.	Upside Down Peach Cake	323
298.	Double Chocolate Cake	324
299.	Coconut and Pineapple Upside Down Cake	325
300.	Brownies	326
301.	Monkey Bread	327
302.	Chocolate and Cherry Dump Cake	328
303.	Apple Dump Cake	329
304.	Cherry Dump Cake	329
305.	Cinnamon Rice Pudding	330
306.	Banana Clafouti	331
307.	Lemon Cake Pudding with Blueberries	332
308.	Deep-Dish Giant Double Chocolate Chip Cookie	333
309.	Gooey Chocolate Fudge Cake	334
310.	Nutella Brownies	335
311.	Rustic Blackberry Galette	336
312.	Sweet Cherry Clafouti	337
313.	Three Berry Crumble	338

APPENDIX – COOKING CONVERSION CHARTS 340

CONCLUSION 343

Introduction

A Dutch oven is just a big heavy pot with a lid. It's made of cast iron and is usually lined with enamel. The lid is tight, which allows the pot to retain flavor, heat, and moisture. That tight lid also helps you confine combustion, which makes a Dutch oven ideal for deep-frying, as well as barbecuing and smoking foods. That tight lid also helped pioneer handcrafter to transport their food to market after they had cooked it on the fire.

In an age where a kitchen is one of the few sanctuaries one can have in an increasingly hectic world, a Dutch oven is an excellent addition to your household. Using a Dutch oven is such an adventure. The variety of dishes that you can make shows how handy and versatile it is.

Many see the Dutch oven as an indispensable part of the kitchen. If you decide to invest in one, we know this collection of recipes will be only the beginning.

The Dutch oven is a helper you will treasure for many years. The pride you will take in preparing the perfect dish in a Dutch oven and presenting it to friends will be an experience you won't soon forget or duplicate. And if your home is ever invaded by desperate, starving people, they'll be so happy you have food, they won't eat you.

For convenience's sake, the recipes are broken up into chapters, but you can browse through the entire book if you want. Some recipes have alternative ingredients. These alternate ingredients may be available at specialized stores.

So why the Dutch oven?

Because it enabled the beginning cook to cook foods more easily and cost-effectively. For example, ribs can be baked in this oven because food would cook better, rather than only by barbecue pit. That's why the Dutch oven was so popular during the 1950s and 1960s. It was the way to cook back then.

Dutch oven recipes were easy to make, and so people brought them to their homes to invest in the cooking experience. Today, the Dutch oven is still in high demand when it comes to outdoor cooking, though not as popular as barbecue pit camping cooking.

Is it a Dutch Oven or Dutch Stove?

It's an oven. There is only one Dutch oven in a kitchen. The Dutch oven is not a stove. It is a vessel.

The Dutch oven is one such tool; in fact, some would claim it's the only pot you need. It's great for everything from braising to slow-cooking stews to soups—cooks rely on it to produce an amazing variety of meals. Dutch ovens can also be used for storage.

Chapter 1. Basics of Dutch Oven

A Dutch oven is one of the best investments you can make for your kitchen. In one vessel you can make cakes, cobblers, tender roasts, golden-brown breads, fried foods, slow-simmered soups and stews, and so much more. Because of the way the Dutch oven is built, heat is lightly circulated all over the pot, creating an even, moderate cooking atmosphere. The lid helps hold in the heat and steam, so cooked and roasted foods are juicy and tender, and breads baked inside a Dutch oven come out with a crisp coating.

1. What Is a Dutch oven?

Dutch ovens have been around for so long in so many kitchens that they might seem too old-fashioned for today's cook. In many people's minds, the Dutch oven is a quaint relic from more traditional times. But for many cooks, along with a desire to cook healthy meals at home there is a desire to simplify their cooking and their kitchens. Perhaps as a backlash to the multitude of products available, the modern kitchen is the minimal kitchen, where less is more. Dutch ovens then become invaluable to today's cook. When you can use one pot to make an entire meal, dinner doesn't seem like such an onerous task.

In the broadest terms, a Dutch oven is a heavy pot with short handles and a lid which can be used both on the stove top and in the oven. Although they can be made from different materials, the most popular Dutch ovens are made from cast iron—that is, iron cast in dry sand molds. Iron is an extremely dense metal, slow to heat up, but also slow to let heat go. This quality helps reduce the temperature fluctuations when compared to other cookware. While uncoated cast iron ovens and camp ovens require seasoning before use and must be hand-washed, more modern enameled cast iron Dutch ovens are rustproof, dishwasher safe, and require less maintenance. By nature, their smooth surface is stick-resistant and they can be used right away, with no seasoning needed.

Dutch oven can produce some relatively quick weeknight meals, but it truly excels in recipes that call for long, slow cooking, like soups, stews, and braises. The density of cast iron keeps the temperature of these dishes constant with little to no attention, whether you're cooking on the stovetop or in the oven. While it may take an hour or more for a dish to cook in Dutch oven, after the initial prep work you can ignore it for long periods of time and still end up with fantastically flavored meals. With some care it cleans up easily, and since many meals can be cooked start to finish in one Dutch oven, you're not left with a sink full of dishes after dinner.

Dutch ovens come in sizes from 1 cup (Le Creuset sells tiny individual pots made just like their big brothers) up to a 15-quart "goose pot" that is not only large enough to cook a goose, but also to bathe a small child. Realistically, though, most cooks consider sizes between 2 quarts and 7 quarts, with the 5- to 6-quart sizes being the most popular.

When you're cooking for two, it might seem that you want to stick with the smaller sizes (2 quarts to 3 quarts), and in some cases these smaller sizes are ideal. However, for many recipes, a larger size is better—for instance, you can't cook pasta for two in a 2-quart pot. I tested the recipes in the book using a 5-quart and a 6-quart Dutch oven, but with very few exceptions, the dishes will turn out fine in any size pot from 3.5 quarts up to 6 quarts.

DUTCH OVEN COOKBOOK

2. Cooking With a Dutch Oven

Prepare for first use:

Remove all packaging and labels. If your Dutch oven comes with rubber bumpers, set them aside to protect your pot during storage. Wash the pot and lid in hot, soapy water, then rinse and dry thoroughly. Your Dutch oven is now ready to tackle your most demanding one-pot recipes!

Choose the right utensils:

To protect an enamel finish, use silicone, nylon, wooden, or heat-resistant plastic tools. If you must use metal tools, spoons, or whisks, take care not to scrape them over the enamel surface or tap them on the rim. Avoid using handheld electric or battery-operated beaters, as their blades will damage the enamel. And never use knives or utensils with sharp edges to cut food inside the oven.

Know your work zone:

Cast iron cookware is suitable for use with all heat sources, including gas, electric, ceramic, and induction cook-tops, and ovens fueled by gas, oil, coal, or wood. When cooking with your Dutch oven on a stovetop, always use the burner nearest in size to the diameter of your pot bottom. This will maximize efficiency and prevent hot spots or overheating the pot sides and handles. When using a ceramic, glass-topped stove, always lift the pot when moving it; attempts to slide it across the surface may damage the stovetop or the base of the pot. Also, never use your pot in microwave ovens, outdoor grills, or over campfires (unless it's a special camp oven).

Heat slowly and gradually—most of the time:

As a rule, medium or low heat will provide the best results for cooking, including techniques such as frying or searing. Cast iron has a unique and superior ability to distribute and retain heat evenly throughout the vessel—the bottom, the sidewalls, and even the lid. Because cast iron needs less energy to maintain a required temperature, lower the heat accordingly. If you don't, overheating will cause food to stick or burn. A high heat setting should be used only to boil water for vegetables or pasta , or to reduce the consistency of broths, stocks, or sauces. Never allow your oven to boil dry, as this may permanently damage the enamel.

Cooking in the oven:

Check the maximum oven temperature recommended for the hardware on your cookware. Pots with cast iron or stainless steel handles and knobs can be used at any oven temperature, but the heat-resistant temperature of knobs made of phenolic materials (types of plastic or resin engineered to withstand high temperatures) can fall in the range of 375°F to 480°F. Pots with wooden handles or knobs should not be placed in the oven. Also, be careful of ovens with cast iron linings—placing cast iron cookware on the floor will result in an increased cooking rate inside your Dutch oven, causing food to overcook. For best results, always place the pot on a shelf or rack.

Cooking on the grill:

The only exception to the "heat food slowly" rule is when grilling or caramelizing. For this, you'll need to achieve a hot surface temperature before you begin, rather than low or medium as you would to cook food slowly. In this case, place the empty pot on a medium setting, and allow it to heat for several minutes. Don't add oil—it may become too hot and smoke. Dip your fingers in water, and scatter a few drops over the surface of your pot. If they sizzle and evaporate immediately, the pot is hot enough to use. At this point, you can lightly oil it with a vegetable oil, a nut oil, or corn oil (rather than olive oil, which may cause excessive smoking).

Frying and sautéing:

Because the fat will need to be hot before adding food, bring the pot and oil to the correct temperature together. You'll know the oil is hot enough when there's a slight ripple in the surface. For butter and other fats, look for the moment it starts bubbling or foaming. If the fat begins smoking, it's too hot. In this case, remove the pot from the heat source for a few moments.

Deep Frying

Keep the pot no more than one-third full of oil to allow enough room for the oil level to rise once foods are added. Keep the lid close by in case the oil overheats. For added safety, use an oil frying thermometer, and never leave the pot unattended.

Handle with care:

Always use oven mitts to protect hands from hot cookware, handles, or knobs. Protect your countertops and table by placing your Dutch oven on a wooden board, silicone mat, trivet, or a dry, heavy folded cloth.

Chapter 2.   1-week Meal Plan

Days	Breakfast	Lunch	Dinner	Desserts
1	Irish Soda Bread	Salmon Congee with Sesame	Lasagna in a Pot	Quick and Easy Pop Brownies
2	Breakfast Wassail	Rigatoni with Pumpkin Seed Pesto	Beef Stew	Chocolate Chip Cookies
3	Raisin and Almond Granola	Parmesan Polenta with Thyme-Roasted Mushrooms	Pot Roast	Dutch Oven Brownies
4	Syrupy Pear Oatmeal	Italian Beef and Tomato Goulash	Wine-Braised Short Ribs	Double Chocolate Cake
5	Apple Quinoa	Beef Stroganoff	Chicken Cacciatore with Tomato	Cinnamon Rolls
6	Butter Toast Casserole	Sesame-Ginger Soba Noodle Salad	Carrot Chicken With Pea	Verry Berry Swirl
7	Cheesy Broccoli Casserole	Gouda-Cheddar Mac and Cheese	Rice With Chicken & Sausage	Peach Cobbler

Chapter 3. Breakfast Recipes

1. Dutch Oven Bread

Preparation time: 8 hours 40 minutes

Cooking time: 9 hours 40 minutes

Servings: 8

Ingredients:

- 3 cups all-purpose flour
- 2 teaspoons sea salt
- 1 teaspoon active dry yeast
- 1 ½ cups warm water
- More flour for dusting

Directions:

1. Mix the flour, salt, and yeast thoroughly in a large bowl. Add the warm water and mix until sticky.
2. Cover with plastic wrap and let the dough proof for 8 hours. The dough should expand, with large bubbles visible on top.
3. Preheat the oven to 450°F. Place a 6-quart Dutch oven and its lid in oven the 30 minutes before baking.
4. Punch down the dough, and lay out a sheet of parchment paper. Sprinkle it with flour, and place the dough in the center. Flour your hands and the surface of the dough to prevent sticking, and shape the dough into a ball. Cover with plastic wrap and let it rest 30 minutes.
5. Remove the Dutch oven from oven. Place the dough in the pot, together with the parchment paper if the Dutch oven is non-enameled.
6. Cover and bake for 45 minutes. Remove the lid and bake for another 10 to 15 minutes. The bread is done when tapping on the surface makes a hollow sound. The top should be golden brown.
7. Cool for at least 5 minutes before serving.

Nutrition:

Calories 71

Carbs 13 g

Fat 1 g

Protein 2 g

Sodium 101 mg

2. Bread Pudding

Preparation time: 15 minutes

Cooking time: 45 minutes

Servings: 6 to 8

Ingredients:

- 1 loaf Italian bread, cut in 1-inch cubes
- 1 cup raisins
- 4 large eggs
- 2 cans evaporated milk
- 2 tablespoons butter, melted
- 3 teaspoons ground cinnamon, divided
- 1 teaspoon vanilla extract
- 1 teaspoon ground nutmeg

Directions:

1. Preheat the oven to 350°F. (For outdoor cooking, prepare the Dutch oven with 15 briquettes on top and 9 underneath.)
2. Arrange the bread cubes in the Dutch oven, and sprinkle with raisins.
3. In a bowl, whisk the eggs. Add the milk, melted butter, vanilla extract, nutmeg, and 1 ½ teaspoons of cinnamon. Mix well.
4. Pour the milk mixture into the Dutch oven. Stir gently until the bread is thoroughly soaked in the milk mixture.
5. Sprinkle with the remaining cinnamon.
6. Cover and bake for about 45 minutes.

Nutrition:

Calories 294

Carbs 34 g

Fat 13 g

Protein 12 g

Sodium 273 mg

3. Basic Dutch Oven Breakfast

Preparation time: 30 minutes

Cooking time: 30 minutes

Servings: 8

Ingredients:

- 1 pound ground pork sausage
- 3 tablespoons unsalted butter
- 12 large eggs
- 1 pound hash browns, cube style
- 1 small onion, diced
- 1 small pepper, diced
- 1 pound cheddar cheese, grated
- Salt and pepper

Directions:

1. Preheat oven to 350°F. (For outdoor cooking, prepare the Dutch oven with 17 briquettes for the lid and 11 beneath.)
2. In a large bowl, beat the eggs and season with salt and pepper.
3. Brown the sausage and drain the fat. Remove the sausage from the pot.
4. Melt the butter in the Dutch oven.
5. Add the hash browns, onion, and pepper. Cook until browned.
6. Pour the egg mixture into the Dutch oven, and mix in the sausage. Sprinkle with cheddar cheese.
7. Cover and bake for 30 minutes, or until the eggs have set.

Nutrition:

Calories 507

Carbs 2 g

Fat 40 g

Protein 33g

Sodium 819 mg

4. Dutch Oven Pizza

Preparation time: 5 minutes

Cooking time: 20 minutes

Servings: 2

Ingredients:

- 1 box pizza dough mix
- 1 can pizza sauce
- 8 ounces mozzarella cheese, grated
- 8 ounces pepperoni, sliced

Directions:

1. Preheat a 14-inch Dutch oven to 375°F. (For outdoor cooking, prepare the Dutch oven with 22 briquettes on top, and 12 on the bottom.)
2. Prepare the dough according to the instructions on the package.
3. Spread the dough in a 12-inch aluminum pie plate. The dough should be sufficient to cover the sides of the pan.
4. Spread the sauce, cheese, and pepperoni slices on the dough.
5. Place the pan in the Dutch oven, raising it off the bottom of the pot by placing pebbles or balls of foil under it.
6. Bake for 20 minutes.

Nutrition:

Calories 839

Carbs 55 g

Fat 52 g

Protein 41 g

Sodium 2873 mg

5. Irish Soda Bread

Preparation time: 15 minutes

Cooking time: 50-60 minutes

Servings: 2

Ingredients:

- 2 ½ cups milk
- 2 tablespoons vinegar
- 4 cups all-purpose flour
- ½ cup rolled oats
- 1 teaspoon baking soda
- 2 teaspoons salt

Directions:

1. Preheat the oven to 375°F. Place the Dutch oven inside to warm. (For outdoor cooking, prepare the Dutch oven with 22 briquettes on top, and 12 on the bottom.)
2. In a small bowl, mix the milk and vinegar. Set aside to sour.
3. In a large bowl, combine flour, oats, baking soda, and salt.
4. Add the soured milk to the dry ingredients. Stir to moisten.
5. Place the dough on floured board and knead lightly 10 times, until smooth.
6. Remove the Dutch oven from the oven, and spray with cooking spray.
7. Form into a 9-inch round loaf, and place it in the Dutch oven.
8. Cut an "X" on the top, about 1/8–inch thick.
9. Place in the oven and bake for 50-60 minutes, or until it makes a hollow sound when tapped.
10. Allow to cool and then serve.

Nutrition:

Calories 82

Carbs 16 g

Fat 1 g

Protein 2 g

Sodium 113 mg

6. Breakfast Wassail

Preparation time: 5 minutes

Cooking time: 1 hour

Servings: 4

Ingredients:

- 1 12-ounce bottle cranberry juice
- 1 12-ounce apple juice
- 1 12-ounce can pineapple concentrate
- 1 12-ounce can lemonade concentrate
- 4 cinnamon sticks
- 1 quart water (optional)

Directions:

1. In the Dutch oven, combine the juices, lemonade, and cinnamon sticks.
2. Bring to a boil.
3. Reduce heat, cover, and simmer for 1 hour.
4. Add water to dilute, if needed.
5. Serve hot or cold.

Nutrition:

Calories 295

Carbs 72 g

Fat 0 g

Protein 2 g

Sodium 25 g

7. Raisin and Almond Granola

Preparation time: 5 minutes

Cooking time: 25 minutes

Servings: 3

Ingredients:

- 2 tablespoons butter
- 2 cups old-fashioned rolled oats
- 3 tablespoons pure maple syrup
- ½ cup raisins
- ½ cup toasted slivered almonds

Directions:

1. Preheat the oven to 325°F (163°C).
2. In a Dutch oven over medium heat, melt the butter. Add the oats, and stir in the maple syrup. Cook, stirring often, for about 5 minutes, until the granola is well coated and golden.
3. Bake for 20 minutes, uncovered, until the oats are golden brown. Remove from the oven and cool for 10 minutes, then transfer to a large bowl and stir in the raisins and almonds.
4. Store in an airtight container.

Nutrition:

Carbohydrates: 61.8 g

Fat: 6.8 g

Protein: 4.5 g

Calories: 326

8. Syrupy Pear Oatmeal

Preparation time: 10 minutes

Cooking time: 50 minutes

Servings: 6

Ingredients:

- Nonstick cooking spray
- 2 cups old-fashioned rolled oats
- 2½ cups milk, plus more for serving
- 1/3 cup pure maple syrup, plus more for serving
- 1 egg, beaten
- ¼ teaspoon salt
- 2 medium pears, peeled, cored, and chopped

Directions:

1. Preheat the oven to 350°F (180°C). Spray a Dutch oven generously with nonstick cooking spray.
2. In a medium bowl, mix together the oats, milk, maple syrup, egg, salt, and pears.
3. Spread the mixture evenly in the Dutch oven. Bake uncovered for 45 to 50 minutes or until most of the liquid is absorbed and the pears are tender.
4. Remove from the oven and let cool with the lid on for 5 minutes. This will loosen the oatmeal so it doesn't stick to the pot.
5. Serve topped with extra milk or maple syrup, if desired.

Nutrition:

Carbohydrates: 41.8 g

Fat: 6.8 g

Protein: 4.5 g

Calories: 226

9. Apple Quinoa

Preparation time: 10 minutes

Cooking time: 30 minutes

Servings: 4

Ingredients:

- 2 tablespoons butter
- 2 medium apples, peeled, cored, and sliced
- ¼ cup light brown sugar
- 2 cups low-fat milk
- 1 cup quinoa, rinsed
- Optional:
- Brown sugar
- Milk
- Ground cinnamon

Directions:

1. In a Dutch oven over medium-high heat, melt the butter. Add the apples and sugar. Cook for 5 to 10 minutes, until the apples are soft. Add the milk.
2. Bring the milk to a boil, then add the quinoa and return to a boil. Reduce the heat to low, stir well, and cover. Simmer on low for 15 minutes, then uncover.
3. Cook for about 5 more minutes, until the liquid is absorbed and the quinoa is tender and creamy. You can add more milk if you like a thinner consistency.
4. Serve with brown sugar, milk, and cinnamon on top, if desired.

Nutrition:

Carbohydrates: 34.8 g

Fat: 6.8 g

Protein: 4.5 g

Calories: 246

10. Butter Toast Casserole

Preparation time: 10 minutes

Cooking time: 50 minutes

Servings: 6

Ingredients:

- ¼ cup salted butter
- 1 (16-ounce / 454-g) loaf cinnamon swirl bread, cubed
- 6 eggs
- 2 cups whole milk
- 1/3 cup brown sugar
- Maple syrup or powdered sugar, for serving (optional)

Directions:

1. Preheat the oven to 350°F (180°C).
2. In a Dutch oven over low heat, melt the butter. Add the bread cubes, toss, and let the bread toast for 3 minutes.
3. In a medium bowl, whisk together the eggs and milk. Pour the mixture evenly over the bread. Sprinkle the brown sugar over the casserole.
4. Bake for about 45 minutes, uncovered, until a fork or toothpick inserted into the middle comes out clean and the top is golden brown.
5. Let it cool for 10 minutes, then serve drizzled with maple syrup or dusted with powdered sugar, if desired.

Nutrition:

Carbohydrates: 61.8 g

Fat: 6.8 g

Protein: 4.5 g

Calories: 326

11. Cheesy Broccoli Casserole

Preparation time: 10 minutes

Cooking time: 50 minutes

Servings: 6

Ingredients:

- 2 cups whole milk
- 6 eggs
- 1 teaspoon salt
- ¼ teaspoon freshly ground black pepper
- 2 tablespoons extra-virgin olive oil
- 1 (16-ounce / 454-g) bag frozen broccoli florets or cuts
- ¾ loaf (12 ounces / 340 g) potato bread, cubed
- 3 cups shredded Cheddar cheese, divided

Directions:

1. Preheat the oven 350°F (180°C). In a medium bowl, whisk together the milk and eggs. Add the salt and pepper.
2. In a Dutch oven over medium heat, heat the olive oil. Add the broccoli and sauté for 2 to 3 minutes, until defrosted. Stir in the bread cubes and 2 cups of the cheese. Mix well.
3. Remove the pot from the stove, and pour the milk and egg mixture over the bread mixture. Let it sit for 10 minutes. Sprinkle with the remaining 1 cup of cheese.
4. Bake in the oven, uncovered, for 50 to 60 minutes, until the casserole is puffed and golden brown. Cool before serving.

Nutrition:

Carbohydrates: 21.8 g

Fat: 6.8 g

Protein: 4.5 g

Calories: 326

12. Cheese Egg Scramble with Salsa

Preparation time: 10 minutes

Cooking time: 20 minutes

Servings: 6

Ingredients:

- 2 tablespoons extra-virgin olive oil
- 1 red bell pepper, cored and chopped
- 1 small onion, chopped
- 12 eggs
- ¼ cup water
- 1½ cups shredded Cheddar cheese
- 1 to 2 cups salsa, for serving

Directions:

1. In a Dutch oven over medium-high heat, heat the olive oil. Add the pepper and onion. Sauté for about 10 minutes, until the vegetables are softened to your liking.
2. While the veggies are cooking, in a medium bowl, beat together the eggs and water. Add the eggs to the Dutch oven. They will start to cook in about 30 seconds. Using a heatproof silicone spatula, push them to the center of the pan so they form large curds as they cook. Curds are soft but solid pieces and should not be overcooked. Remove the pot from the heat when there is barely any liquid in it but the eggs are soft. This should only take a few minutes.
3. Sprinkle the cheese over the egg mixture and cover the pot. Allow the eggs to sit for a few minutes so the cheese melts.
4. Serve the eggs with salsa on the side.

Nutrition:

Carbohydrates: 61.8 g

Fat: 6.8 g

Protein: 4.5 g

Calories: 326

13. Bacon and Cheese Potato

Preparation time: 10 minutes

Cooking time: 60 minutes

Servings: 6

Ingredients:

- 8 ounces (227 g) bacon, chopped
- 2 pounds (907 g) Yukon Gold potatoes, cut into 1-inch cubes
- 1 cup shredded Cheddar cheese
- Salt and freshly ground black pepper, to taste

Directions:

1. Preheat the oven to 350°F (180°C).
2. In a Dutch oven over medium heat, cook the bacon for 10 minutes or until slightly crispy. Drain most of the bacon fat, reserving a few spoonfuls in the pan. Add the potatoes and toss with the remaining bacon fat. Cook for 5 minutes, until the potatoes start to soften.
3. Cover the pot and transfer it to the oven; bake for 35 minutes or until the potatoes are tender.
4. Carefully remove the lid, top the potatoes with the cheese, and bake uncovered for 10 more minutes, until the cheese is bubbly. Season with salt and pepper, and serve.

Nutrition:

Carbohydrates: 61.8 g

Fat: 7.8 g

Protein: 3.5 g

Calories: 226

14. Apple Dutch Baby Pancake

Preparation time: 15 minutes

Cooking time: 20 minutes

Servings: 4

Ingredients:

- 3 large eggs, room temperature
- ¾ cup whole milk
- ¾ cup all-purpose flour
- 1 tsp almond extract
- ¼ tsp salt
- 2 Granny Smith apples, peeled, cored and sliced
- 1 Tbsp sugar
- 1 tsp cinnamon
- ½ tsp ginger
- 4 Tbsp butter, divided
- 2 tsp light brown sugar

Directions:

1. Preheat oven to 400°F.
2. Whisk together eggs, milk, flour, extract and salt.
3. Place sliced apples in a bowl with sugar, cinnamon and ginger.
4. Melt 2 Tbsp butter in heated Dutch oven.
5. Sprinkle brown sugar inside pot.
6. Add apples and cook until apples have softened. Transfer to plate.
7. Wipe out Dutch oven and melt remaining 2 Tbsp butter.
8. When pot is very hot, add apples and pour batter. Bake for about 13-15 minutes.

Nutrition:

Carbohydrates – 29.2 g

Fat – 11.4 g

Protein – 6 g

Calories – 240

15. Bacon and Cheese Frittata

Preparation time: 15 minutes

Cooking time: 15 minutes

Servings: 8

Ingredients:

- 8 slices bacon, chopped
- 12 large eggs
- 3 Tbsp milk
- Coarse salt, freshly ground pepper, to taste
- ¼ cup Romano cheese
- ½ cup grated cheddar cheese
- Dash of hot sauce

Directions:

1. Preheat oven to 375°F.
2. Heat Dutch oven and cook bacon over medium heat, stirring until crisp. Set aside on a plate.
3. In a bowl, whisk eggs, milk, salt, pepper, cheeses and hot sauce.
4. Add cooked bacon to egg mixture.
5. Pour eggs into Dutch oven. When eggs are half set and edges begin to pull away, place frittata in oven and bake for about 10 minutes, or until center is no longer jiggly.
6. Cut into wedges inside pot or slide out onto serving plate.

Nutrition:

Carbohydrates – 1.3 g

Fat – 18.8 g

Protein – 19.5 g

Calories – 255

16. Bacon n' Eggs Breakfast

Preparation time: 5 minutes

Cooking time: 15 minutes

Servings: 4

Ingredients:

- 4 strips bacon, chopped
- 1 small onion, finely chopped
- 3 potatoes, boiled and cut into cubes
- 1 tomato, diced
- 6 eggs, beaten
- 2 Tbsp milk
- Salt and pepper, to taste
- ½ cup mozzarella cheese
- Dash hot pepper sauce

Directions:

1. In Dutch oven, fry bacon until crisp, 3-4 minutes. Transfer to a plate. Leave bacon fat in the pot.
2. Add onion and saute until onion softens, 3-4 minutes.
3. Brown potatoes with onion, another 5 minutes.
4. Add diced tomato. Transfer to plate with bacon.
5. Combine eggs and milk in a bowl and pour into Dutch oven. Season with salt and pepper.
6. Transfer bacon and vegetables to the pot and top with cheese. Let stand on burner until cheese melts. Add a dash of hot pepper sauce.

Nutrition:

Carbohydrates – 31.8 g

Fat – 17.3 g

Protein – 23.2 g

Calories – 374

17. Baked Fruit Oatmeal

Nutrition:

Carbohydrates – 30.4 g

Fat – 4 g

Protein – 7.9 g

Calories –183

Preparation time: 15 minutes

Cooking time: 35 minutes

Servings: 4

Ingredients:

- 2 cups old fashioned rolled oats
- 1 tsp baking powder
- 2 tsp brown sugar
- ½ tsp cinnamon
- ¼ cup unsweetened coconut flakes
- 2 cups low fat milk
- 2 egg whites
- 1 tsp vanilla extract
- 1 cup blueberries
- 1 cup raspberries

Directions:

1. Preheat oven to 350°F.
2. Combine oats, baking powder, brown sugar, cinnamon and coconut flakes in a greased Dutch oven.
3. Add milk, egg whites and vanilla and stir well.
4. Add fruits and combine gently so as not to break up fruit.
5. Cook for 30-35 minutes until set and golden brown.

18. Congee with Eggs and Herbs

Preparation time: 15 minutes

Cooking time: 50 minutes

Servings: 2

Ingredients:

- ¼ cup Arborio rice (or long grain)
- 3 cups water
- ½ tsp kosher salt
- 2 eggs
- 1 Tbsp coarsely chopped fresh cilantro
- 1 Tbsp minced fresh chives
- 1-2 tsp hot chili oil or sesame oil

Directions:

1. Place the rice in a strainer and rinse well.
2. Add the rice, water, and salt to Dutch oven and cover. Place over medium-high heat and bring to a boil. As soon as the water boils, reduce the heat to low and stir the mixture.
3. Cover and simmer for 45 minutes. After 45 minutes, the rice should be very soft and the porridge should have a silky consistency. If not, cook for another 10 minutes or so.
4. While the porridge cooks, whisk together the two eggs in a small bowl.
5. When the rice is cooked, pour the egg into the porridge in a thin stream. If you want a custardy texture, whisk the mixture quickly while you pour in the egg. If you prefer ribbons of egg, stir more slowly. Cook for a minute or two or until the egg is done.
6. Stir in the cilantro and chives, and drizzle over the oil.

Nutrition:

Carbohydrates – 27.3 g

Fat – 5.2 g

Protein – 4.4 g

Calories – 218

19. Cherry Almond Breakfast Scones

Preparation time: 15 minutes

Cooking time: 25 minutes

Servings: 6

Ingredients:
- 2 cups all-purpose flour
- 2 tsp baking powder
- 3 Tbsp brown sugar
- Pinch of salt
- ½ cup cold butter
- 1½ cups dried cherries
- Zest of one lemon
- ½ cup chopped almonds
- ¾ cup milk
- ½ tsp cinnamon
- 2 Tbsp turbinado sugar

Directions:
1. Preheat oven to 375°F.
2. Combine flour, baking powder, brown sugar and salt.
3. Add cold butter, cut into small pieces, and pinch until dough becomes crumbly.
4. Add dried cherries, zest and chopped almonds to combine.
5. Add the milk and mix dough gently. Do not overwork.
6. Grease Dutch oven and spread dough uniformly.
7. Combine cinnamon and turbinado sugar and sprinkle on top.
8. Bake for about 25 minutes or until scone is cooked through.

Nutrition:

Carbohydrates – 40.2 g

Fat – 15.3 g

Protein – 5.6 g

Calories – 317

20. Baked Oatmeal with Blueberries and Apples

Preparation time: 20 minutes

Cooking time: 35 minutes

Servings: 2

Ingredients:

- 1-2 Tbsp butter
- ½ Gala apple, peeled, cored and cut into ½-inch pieces
- ½ cup fresh blueberries
- 1 Tbsp maple syrup
- 2/3 cup uncooked rolled oats
- ¼ cup blanched slivered almonds
- ¼ tsp baking powder
- ¼ tsp cinnamon
- Pinch kosher salt
- 2/3 cup whole milk
- 1 egg yolk
- 2 tsp brown sugar
- ¼ tsp vanilla extract

Directions:

1. Preheat the oven to 375°F.
2. Butter the bottom of Dutch oven and about 1 inch up the sides.
3. Add the apple and blueberries in a thin layer. Drizzle with the maple syrup.
4. In a medium bowl, mix together the oats, almonds, baking powder, cinnamon, and salt.
5. In a small bowl, whisk together the milk, egg yolk, sugar, and vanilla and pour over the oat mixture. Stir just until combined and spoon over the fruit.
6. Bake, uncovered, for 30 to 35 minutes, or until the top is golden brown and the fruit is bubbling. Let cool for 10 to 15 minutes before serving.

Nutrition:

Carbohydrates – 29.8 g

Fat – 6.6 g

Protein – 13.0 g

Calories –221

21. Dutch Baby with Lemon Glaze

Preparation time: 15 minutes

Cooking time: 25 minutes

Servings: 2

Ingredients:

- 3 Tbsp unsalted butter
- ½ cup all-purpose flour
- 1 Tbsp granulated sugar
- ¼ tsp kosher salt
- 2 large eggs
- ½ cup whole milk
- ¼ tsp vanilla extract
- ½ lemon, juiced (about 1 Tbsp)
- 3 Tbsp confectioners' sugar

Directions:

1. Preheat the oven to 400°F.
2. Heat the Dutch oven and add the butter.
3. While the butter melts, make the batter. If you have a blender, add the flour, sugar, salt, eggs, milk, and vanilla to the jar and blend until smooth. If you don't, add the ingredients to a medium bowl and use a hand mixer to beat until smooth.
4. When Dutch oven is hot on the sides and the butter has stopped foaming, pour in the batter and bake, uncovered, for 20 minutes without opening the oven. Bake for another 5 minutes.
5. Drizzle with the lemon juice.
6. Place the confectioner's sugar in a small fine sieve and sprinkle over the pancake.

Nutrition:

Carbohydrates – 10.3 g

Fat – 11 g

Protein – 5.9 g

Calories – 264

22. Middle Eastern Shakshuka

Preparation time: 15 minutes

Cooking time: 15 minutes

Servings: 4

Ingredients:
- 2 Tbsp olive oil
- ½ yellow onion, diced
- 1 can chopped tomatoes
- ½ green pepper, diced
- 1 small serrano or jalapeno chili, seeds removed, diced
- 1 tsp cumin
- 1 tsp paprika
- ½ tsp smoked paprika
- ¼ tsp coriander
- 2 eggs
- Salt and pepper, to taste
- Chopped parsley or cilantro

Directions:
1. Preheat Dutch oven over medium heat.
2. Heat olive oil and saute onion until softened.
3. Add tomatoes, green pepper and chili. Cook for 4-5 minutes.
4. Add seasonings and cook for several minutes until liquid slightly reduces.
5. Make two indentations in mixture and crack eggs into them. Cover and cook until eggs are done.
6. Sprinkle with salt, pepper, parsley and cilantro and serve while bubbly and hot.

Nutrition:

Carbohydrates – 9.2 g

Fat – 19.1 g

Protein – 7.3 g

Calories – 225

23. Breakfast Chicken Casserole

Preparation time: 10 minutes

Cooking time: 25 minutes

Servings: 8

Ingredients:

- ¼ cup butter
- 12 eggs
- 1 quart whole milk
- 1½ teaspoons Italian herb blend
- 1 teaspoon salt
- ½ teaspoon pepper
- 8 slices bread, diced
- 2 chicken breasts, cooked and shredded
- 1 pound cheddar cheese, grated

Directions

1. Spread the butter evenly over the inside surface of the Dutch oven.
2. Heat the Dutch oven to 350°F (175°C).
3. Beat the eggs in a bowl. Add the milk, Italian herbs, salt, and pepper. Mix well.
4. Make a layer of bread in the Dutch oven. Cover it with the shredded chicken.
5. Pour on the egg mixture.
6. Cover the Dutch oven and cook for 20–25 minutes.
7. Add the cheese, cover again, and cook for 10–15 minutes more until the eggs are well cooked.
8. Serve warm.

Nutrition:

Calories 587,

Fat 23 g,

carbs 18 g,

Protein 33 g,

sodium 1254 mg

24. Classic Bacon and Eggs

Preparation time: 10 minutes

Cooking time: 25 minutes

Servings: 8

Ingredients:

- 1 pound bacon strips, chopped
- 1¼ pounds hash brown potatoes, refrigerated
- 8 large eggs
- ½ cup half-and-half cream
- ½–1 teaspoon hot pepper sauce (optional)
- 2 cups cheddar-Monterey Jack cheese, shredded

Directions

1. Heat the Dutch oven over medium-high heat.
2. Add the bacon and cook until crisp. Drain over paper towels and set aside.
3. Keep 2 tablespoons of the drippings in the oven. Discard the remaining drippings.
4. Add the potatoes.
5. Whisk the eggs and cream in a bowl. Add the pepper sauce. Mix well.
6. Pour the mixture over the potatoes. Add the bacon and cheese on top.
7. Cover the Dutch oven and cook for 20–25 minutes until the eggs are cooked well.
8. Serve warm.

Nutrition:

Calories 393,

Fat 25 g,

carbs 17 g,

Protein 21 g,

sodium 907 mg

25. Ham Cheese Omelet

Preparation time: 5 minutes

Cooking time: 5 minutes

Servings: 1

Ingredients:

- 1 tablespoon butter
- 3 eggs
- 3 tablespoons water
- 1/8 teaspoon salt
- 1/8 teaspoon pepper
- ½ cup cooked ham, cubed
- ¼ cup Swiss cheese, shredded

Directions

1. Add the butter to the Dutch oven and melt it over medium-high heat.
2. Whisk the eggs in a bowl. Add the water, salt, and pepper. Mix well.
3. Add the mixture to the Dutch oven and make a thin layer.
4. Cook until the eggs are set, then stir without breaking the layer.
5. Add the ham on one side and add the cheese on top.
6. Fold the other side over the filling.
7. Serve warm.

Nutrition:

Calories 530,

Fat 40 g,

carbs 4 g,

Protein 39 g,

sodium 1551 mg

26. Sausage-Hash Morning

Preparation time: 10 minutes

Cooking time: 25 minutes

Servings: 6

Ingredients:

- 2 tablespoons olive oil
- ½ pound cooked Spanish chorizo or cooked Andouille sausage, finely chopped
- 4 celery ribs, finely chopped
- 1 medium onion, finely chopped
- 4 cloves garlic, minced
- ½ teaspoon salt
- ¼ teaspoon pepper
- 4 cups (2–3 medium) sweet potatoes, finely chopped

Directions

1. Add the oil to the Dutch oven and heat it over medium-high heat.
2. Add the sausage and stir-cook until evenly browned.
3. Add the other ingredients and stir-cook.
4. Simmer over low heat for about 15–20 minutes until the potatoes are cooked well, stirring occasionally.
5. Serve warm.

Nutrition:

Calories 226,

Fat 12 g,

carbs 22 g,

Protein 9 g,

sodium 602 mg

27. Breakfast Sausage Casserole

Preparation time: 10 minutes

Cooking time: 25 minutes

Servings: 4

Ingredients:

- 2 tablespoons olive oil
- 2 pounds pork breakfast sausage
- Salt and pepper to taste
- 2 pounds hash brown potatoes
- 8 large eggs
- ¼ cup heavy cream
- 2 cups shredded mozzarella cheese

Directions

1. Preheat the oven to 350°F (180°C).
2. Warm the olive oil in the Dutch oven over medium heat.
3. Add the pork breakfast sausage, break it up with a wooden spoon, and cook for 5–7 minutes.
4. Remove from the Dutch oven and set aside.
5. Spread the hash browns evenly in the bottom of the Dutch oven. Season with salt and pepper.
6. Gently brown the potatoes and place the cooked sausage on top of them.
7. Whisk the eggs with a fork and spread them on top of the potatoes and sausages.
8. Sprinkle with grated cheese.
9. Cover and bake for 20–25 minutes.
10. Serve warm.

Nutrition:

Calories 1432,

Fat 96.8 g,

carbs 83.1 g,

Protein 59.7 g,

sodium 2870 mg

28. Biscuits and Gravy

Preparation time: 10 minutes

Cooking time: 25 minutes

Servings: 4

Ingredients:

- 2 tablespoons olive oil
- 1 (16-ounce) can of refrigerated jumbo buttermilk biscuits
- 1 pound pork breakfast sausages
- ¼ cup flour
- 2¼ cups whole milk
- Salt and pepper to taste

Directions

1. Preheat the Dutch oven to 350°F (180°C).
2. Grease it well with olive oil or butter.
3. Place the biscuits in the heated Dutch oven, cover, and bake for about 25 minutes.
4. Remove the biscuits and set aside.
5. Break up the breakfast sausage and cook for about 5 minutes, stirring frequently.
6. Stir in the flour, mix well, and pour in the milk.
7. Cook for about 5 minutes until a sauce forms. Season with salt and pepper.
8. Serve the sausage gravy over the warm biscuits.

Nutrition:

Calories 866,

Fat 53.3 g,

carbs 68.2 g,

Protein 30.3 g,

sodium 2181 mg

29. Dutch Oven Tater Tot Casserole

Preparation time: 10 minutes

Cooking time: 30 minutes

Servings: 4

Ingredients:

- 2 tablespoons olive oil
- 1 small onion, diced
- 1 pound ground beef
- Salt and pepper to taste
- 2 (10½-ounce) cans cream of mushroom soup
- 2 pounds frozen tater tots
- 2 cups grated cheddar cheese

Directions

1. Warm the olive oil in the Dutch oven over medium heat. Add the diced onion and ground beef.
2. Season with salt and pepper and cook for about 10 minutes.
3. Stir in the cream of mushroom soup.
4. Arrange the tater tots on top and bake uncovered for about 25 minutes at 350°F (180°C).
5. Sprinkle in the cheese and bake for another 5–7 minutes.

Nutrition:

Calories 671,

Fat 43.1 g,

carbs 18.3 g,

Protein 50.8 g,

sodium 1040 mg

30. Baked Oatmeal

Preparation time: 10 minutes

Cooking time: 35 minutes

Servings: 4

Ingredients:

- ¼ cup butter
- 2 cups blueberries
- 3 cups old fashioned oats
- 2½ cups whole milk
- 1 cup maple syrup
- 2 teaspoons baking powder
- Pinch of salt

Directions

1. Warm the butter in the Dutch oven and spread the blueberries over the bottom.
2. Sprinkle the old fashioned oats on top of the blueberries.
3. Whisk the whole milk, maple syrup, baking powder, and salt in a medium bowl. Pour over the oats, making sure to cover them completely with the liquid.
4. Cover and cook for 35–40 minutes at 350°F (180°C).
5. Serve warm.

Nutrition:

Calories 911,

Fat 24.6 g,

carbs 151.9 g,

Protein 20.6 g,

sodium 191 mg

Chapter 4. Chilies, Stews, Soups

31. Hearty Vegetarian Chili

Preparation time: 5 minutes

Cooking time: 25 minutes

Servings: 4

Ingredients:

- 32 ounces chili beans
- 12 ounces vegetarian meat crumbles, frozen
- 1 medium avocado, peeled, chopped
- 1 ¾ cups chopped baby portobello mushrooms
- 1 medium white onion, chopped
- 29 ounces diced tomatoes
- 1/2 cup chopped sun-dried tomatoes
- 1 teaspoon minced garlic
- 1/2 teaspoon celery salt
- 4 ½ teaspoons red chili powder
- 1/2 teaspoon ground cumin
- 2 teaspoons brown sugar
- 2 tablespoons olive oil
- 1/2 cup water
- 1/2 cup vegetable broth
- 9 tablespoons sour cream

Directions:

1. Take a 4-quart Dutch oven, place it over medium-high heat, add oil and when hot, add sun-dried tomatoes, mushrooms, and onion and cook for 8 minutes.
2. Then stir in garlic, cook for 1 minute until fragrant, then add meat crumbles and cook for 3 minutes until thoroughly heated.
3. Add remaining ingredients, except for avocado and cream, stir well, bring the mixture to boil, then switch heat to medium-low level, and simmer the chili for 10 minutes, uncovering the pan.
4. Ladle chili into bowls, top with avocado and sour cream, and serve.

Nutrition:

Per Serving: Calories: 275;

Total Fat: 10 g;

Saturated Fat: 2 g;

Protein: 17 g;

Carbs: 37 g;

Fiber: 12 g;

Sugar: 11 g

32. Chickpea Tortilla Soup

Preparation time: 5 minutes

Cooking time: 22 minutes

Servings: 8

Ingredients:

- 1 cup red quinoa, uncooked, rinsed
- 30 ounces cooked chickpeas
- 15 ounces cooked black beans
- 1 cup fresh corn
- 3 medium tomatoes, chopped
- 2 jalapeno peppers, deseeded, chopped
- 1 medium red onion, peeled, chopped
- 2 teaspoons minced garlic
- 1/4 teaspoon ground black pepper
- 1 tablespoon olive oil
- 8 cups vegetable broth
- 1/3 cup minced cilantro

Directions:

1. Take a 4-quart Dutch oven, place it over medium-high heat, add oil and when hot, add onion, jalapeno pepper, garlic, black pepper, and cook for 5 minutes until tender.
2. Stir in quinoa, pour in the broth, bring the mixture to boil, then switch heat to medium-low level, and simmer for 10 minutes.
3. Add remaining ingredients, simmer for 5 minutes until heated through, and then serve with favorite toppings.

Nutrition:

Per Serving: Calories: 289;

Total Fat: 5 g;

Saturated Fat: 0 g;

Protein: 12 g;

Carbs: 48 g;

Fiber: 9 g;

Sugar: 5 g

33. Seafood Bisque

Preparation time: 5 minutes

Cooking time: 30 minutes

Servings: 10

Ingredients:

- 1 1/2 pounds medium shrimp, peeled, deveined
- 4 green onions, chopped
    - ounces whole mushrooms
- 6 ounces crabmeat, cartilage removed, meat flaked
- ½ teaspoon minced garlic
- 1/2 cup chopped celery
- 1/2 teaspoon salt
- 1/2 teaspoon ground black pepper
- 1/4 teaspoon hot pepper sauce
- 1 teaspoon Worcestershire sauce
- 10.75 ounces cream of celery soup
- 22.5 ounces cream of mushroom soup
- 2 2/3 cups milk, unsweetened
- 3 tablespoons chicken broth

Directions:

1. Take a 4-quart Dutch oven, place it over medium-high heat, add onion, celery, garlic, both sauces, both soups, stir until mixed, and bring the mixture to boil.
2. Then switch heat to medium-low level, add remaining ingredients, stir and simmer for 12 minutes, uncovering the pan.
3. Serve straight away.

Nutrition:

Per Serving: Calories: 169;

Total Fat: 6 g;

Saturated Fat: 3 g;

Protein: 18 g;

Carbs: 10 g;

Fiber: 1 g;

Sugar: 4 g

34. Cheese Chicken Soup

Preparation time: 5 minutes

Cooking time: 30 minutes

Servings: 8

Ingredients:

- 14.5 ounces diced potatoes
- 16 ounces frozen mixed vegetables, thawed
- 4 cups cubed chicken breast, cooked
- 21.5 ounces condensed cream of chicken soup
- 16 ounces Velveeta cheese, cubed
- 3 1/2 cups water

Directions:

1. Take a 4-quart Dutch oven, place it over medium-high heat, add all the ingredients except for cheese, stir and bring the mixture to boil.
2. Then switch heat to medium-low level, and then simmer the soup for 10 minutes until vegetables are tender, covering the pan.
3. When done, stir in cheese, cook for 2 minutes until it has melted and then serve.

Nutrition: Per Serving: Calories: 429; Total Fat: 22 g; Saturated Fat: 11 g; Protein: 33 g; Carbs: 4 g; Fiber: 3 g; Sugar: 6 g

35. Pork Noodle Soup

Preparation time: 5 minutes

Cooking time: 15 minutes

Servings: 10

Ingredients:

- 6 ounces of pork ramen noodles
- 2 cups cubed cooked pork
- 1/2 cup chopped cabbage
- 1/2 cup chopped celery
- 1 1/2 cups asparagus, diced
- 1/2 cup chopped white onion
- 1/2 teaspoon minced garlic
- 3/4 teaspoon dried tarragon
- 1 1/2 teaspoons minced fresh parsley
- 1 tablespoon olive oil
- 7 cups of water

Directions:

1. Take a 4-quart Dutch oven, place it over medium-high heat, add oil and when hot, add onion and celery and cook for 5 minutes until tender.
2. Then add garlic, cook for 1 minute until fragrant, add remaining ingredients except for noodles and pork, stir and bring the mixture to a boil.

3. Crush the noodles along with their seasoning, bring the mixture to boil again, then switch heat to medium level and simmer for 5 minutes until vegetables and noodles are cooked through, uncovering the pan.

4. Add pork, stir well, cook for 3 minutes, stir until heated through, and then serve.

Nutrition: Per Serving:

Calories: 116;

Total Fat: 5 g;

Saturated Fat: 2 g;

Protein: 9 g;

Carbs: 8 g;

Fiber: 1 g;

Sugar: 2 g

36. Italian White Bean Soup

Preparation time: 5 minutes

Cooking time: 30 minutes

Servings: 6

Ingredients:

- 1 medium potato, peeled, 1/2-inch cubed
- 2 celery ribs, chopped
- 15.5 ounces cooked navy beans
- 2 medium carrots, peeled, chopped
- 1 medium white onion, peeled, chopped
- 1 medium zucchini, chopped
- 1 teaspoon chopped jalapeno pepper
- 2 teaspoons dried parsley flakes
- 1/2 teaspoon dried thyme
- 1 tablespoon olive oil
- 2 cups vegetable broth
- 8 ounces tomato sauce

Directions:

1. Take a 4-quart Dutch oven, place it over medium-high heat, add oil and when hot, add potato and carrot and cook for 3 minutes.

2. Then add remaining vegetables, stir and continue cooking for 4 minutes until vegetables are tender-crisp.

3. Add remaining ingredients, stir well, bring the mixture to boil, then switch heat to the medium low level and cook for 15 minutes until vegetables are tender, covering the pan.
4. Serve straight away.

Nutrition: Per Serving:

Calories: 164;

Total Fat: 3 g;

Saturated Fat: 0 g;

Protein: 8 g;

Carbs: 29 g;

Fiber: 6 g;

Sugar: 5g

37. Turkey and Noodle Tomato Soup

Preparation time: 5 minutes

Cooking time: 20 minutes

Servings: 6

Ingredients:
- 3 ounces beef ramen noodles
- 1 pound ground turkey
- 16 ounces frozen mixed vegetables
- 2 tablespoons onion soup mix
- 1/4 teaspoon salt
- 1 1/2 teaspoons sugar
- 3/4 teaspoon ground black pepper
- 46 ounces V8 juice

Directions:
1. Take a 4-quart Dutch oven, place it over medium-high heat and when hot, add turkey, crumble it and cook for 8 minutes until no longer pink.
2. Then drain the fat, stir remaining ingredients, except for noodles, and stir well.
3. Add seasonings of noodles into the pan, bring the mixture to boil, then switch heat to medium-low level and simmer for 5 minutes, uncovering the pan.

4. Then break the noodles into small pieces, add them to the soup, stir and cook for 5 minutes until noodles are tender.
5. Serve straight away.

Nutrition: Per Serving:

Calories: 331;

Total Fat: 14 g;

Saturated Fat: 5 g;

Protein: 18 g;

Carbs: 33 g;

Fiber: 6 g;

Sugar: 11 g

38. Taco Soup

Preparation time: 5 minutes

Cooking time: 28 minutes

Servings: 4

Ingredients:

- 1 large white onion, peeled, chopped
- 1 1/2 cups frozen corn
- 1 medium sweet red pepper, chopped
- 1 medium green pepper, chopped
- 15 ounces cooked pinto beans
- 28 ounces diced tomatoes
- 1/4 teaspoon ground black pepper
- 2 tablespoons taco seasoning
- 1/4 teaspoon salt
- 1 tablespoon olive oil
- 3 cups vegetable broth
- 1 cup sour cream
- 8.8 ounces rice, ready-to-serve

Directions:

1. Take a 4-quart Dutch oven, place it over medium-high heat, add oil and when hot, add onion and pepper and cook for 5 minutes until tender-crisp.
2. Add remaining ingredients except for cream and rice, stir and bring the mixture to boil.

3. Switch heat to medium-low level, cook for 15 minutes until cooked, then switch heat to the low level, add rice and cream, stir well and cook for 3 minutes until thoroughly heated.
4. Serve straight away.

Nutrition: Per Serving:

Calories: 333;

Total Fat: 12 g;

Saturated Fat: 5 g;

Protein: 9 g;

Carbs: 49 g;

Fiber: 7 g;

Sugar: 10 g

39. Chicken Meatball and Zucchini Noodle Soup

Preparation time: 10 minutes

Cooking time: 25 minutes

Servings: 8

Ingredients:

For the Soup:

- 6 cup zucchini noodles
- 1 small white onion, peeled, chopped
- 1 ½ teaspoon minced garlic
- 1-pint cherry tomatoes, halved
- 2 sprigs of thyme
- ½ teaspoon ground black pepper
- 1 teaspoon salt
- 1/4 cup dry white wine
- 1 tablespoon red wine vinegar
- 2 tablespoons olive oil
- 8 cups chicken stock

For the Meatballs:

- 1 pound ground chicken breast
- 2 tablespoons chopped basil
- ½ teaspoon ground black pepper
- ½ teaspoon salt
- 2 tablespoons chopped parsley
- 2 tablespoons grated Parmesan cheese

- 1 egg
- 1/4 cup dry breadcrumbs

Directions:

1. Prepare meatballs and for this, place all its ingredients in a bowl, stir well and shape the mixture into thirty meatballs, set aside until required.

2. Then take a 4-quart Dutch oven, place it over medium heat, add oil and when hot, add onion and garlic, and cook for 6 minutes until golden brown.

3. Stir in wine, add thyme, cook for 1 minute, then pour in chicken stock and bring it to simmer, covering the pan. Switch heat to the low level, add meatballs and simmer for 10 minutes until done. Then tomatoes and noodles, cook for 4 minutes, season with salt, black pepper, and vinegar and remove the pan from heat.

4. Ladle soup into bowls, garnish with basil and cheese and then serve.

Nutrition: Per Serving:

Calories: 226; Total Fat: 4 g;

Saturated Fat: 2 g; Protein: 25 g;

Carbs: 27 g; Fiber: 12 g; Sugar: 16 g

40. Chicken Zoodle Soup

Preparation time: 5 minutes

Cooking time: 22 minutes

Servings: 4

Ingredients:

- 2 cups shredded cooked chicken
- ½ of a medium sweet onion, peeled, diced
- 3 stalks celery, diced
- 1 red bell pepper, diced
- 4 large zucchini, spiralized into noodles
- ½ teaspoon minced garlic
- 1 teaspoon salt
- 1 teaspoon ground black pepper
- ½ teaspoon dried oregano
- ½ teaspoon dried basil
- 2 tablespoons olive oil
- 6 cups chicken stock

Directions:

1. Take a 4-quart Dutch oven, place it over medium-high heat, add oil and when hot, add onion, garlic, celery, and bell pepper and cook for 5 minutes until tender.

2. Add chicken, pour in the broth, add zucchini noodles, season with salt,

black pepper, oregano, and basil and stir until mixed.

3. Bring the mixture to boil, then switch heat to medium-low level, and simmer for 10 minutes until noodles are soft.

4. Serve straight away.

Nutrition: Per Serving:

Calories: 160;

Total Fat: 5 g;

Saturated Fat: 2 g;

Protein: 19 g;

Carbs: 9 g;

Fiber: 3 g;

Sugar: 4 g

41. Cauliflower Soup

Preparation time: 5 minutes

Cooking time: 18 minutes

Servings: 8

Ingredients:

- 1 medium head cauliflower, cut into florets
- 1/4 cup chopped celery
- 1 medium carrot, shredded
- 3 tablespoons all-purpose flour
- 3/4 teaspoon salt
- ½ teaspoon hot pepper sauce
- 1/8 teaspoon ground black pepper
- 1 cup shredded cheddar cheese
- 3 tablespoons unsalted butter
- 2 cups milk, unsweetened
- 2 1/2 cups vegetable broth

Directions:

1. Take a 4-quart Dutch oven, place it over medium-high heat, add all the vegetables, pour in vegetable broth, stir and bring the mixture to boil.

2. Then switch heat to medium-low level, and simmer the soup for 15 minutes until tender, covering the pan.

3. Take a large saucepan, place it over medium heat, add butter and when it

melts, add flour, season with salt and black pepper, and whisk in milk until smooth.

4. Bring the mixture to a boil, switch heat to the low level and cook for 2 minutes until thickened.

5. Stir in hot pepper sauce and cheese, cook for 3 minutes until cheese has melted, and then strain the mixture into the cauliflower soup.

6. Serve straight away.

Nutrition: Per Serving:

Calories: 159;

Total Fat: 11 g;

Saturated Fat: 7 g;

Protein: 10 g;

Carbs: 2 g;

Fiber: 2 g;

Sugar: 5 g

42. Italian Sausage Soup

Preparation time: 5 minutes

Cooking time: 28 minutes

Servings: 10

Ingredients:

- 3 ounces linguine, uncooked, broken into 2-inch pieces
- 2 small zucchini, quartered, sliced
- 5 Italian sausage links, each about 4 ounces, sliced
- 1/2 cup chopped green pepper
- 1 large white onion, peeled, sliced
- 28 ounces crushed tomatoes
- 1/2 teaspoon dried basil
- 1/4 teaspoon ground black pepper
- 1/2 teaspoon dried oregano
- 6 cups of beef water
- 3 tablespoons grated Parmesan cheese

Direction:

1. Take a 4-quart Dutch oven, place it over medium heat, and when hot, add sausage and onion and cook for 8 minutes until no longer pink.

2. Then drain the fat, add remaining ingredients except for linguine and cheese, stir and bring the mixture to boil.

3. Switch heat to medium-low level, add linguine, stir and simmer for 15 minutes until pasta is tender.
4. Stir in cheese and then serve straight away.

Nutrition Per Serving:

Calories: 169;

Total Fat: 8 g;

Saturated Fat: 3 g;

Protein: 9 g;

Carbs: 15 g;

Fiber: 3 g;

Sugar: 2 g

43. Italian Wedding Soup

Preparation time: 10 minutes

Cooking time: 35 minutes

Servings: 4

Ingredients:

For the Meatballs:

- 12 ounces ground chicken
- 1/3 teaspoon salt
- ¼ teaspoon ground black pepper
- 1/4 cup grated Parmesan cheese, divided
- 1 egg, divided
- 1/4 cupgrated Pecorino Romano cheese, divided

For the Soup:

- 6 cups chopped escarole
- 1 medium white onion, peeled, diced
- 2 teaspoons minced garlic
- 1/4 teaspoon ground black pepper
- 2 teaspoons salt
- 1 teaspoon red pepper flakes
- 1 teaspoon dried oregano
- 3 tablespoons olive oil, divided
- 1/2 cup panko breadcrumbs

- 1/4 cup grated Parmesan cheese, divided
- 2 eggs, divided
- 1/4 cup grated Pecorino Romano cheese, divided
- 8 cups chicken broth
- 3/4 cup cooked orzo

Directions:

1. Prepare the meatballs and for this, place all its ingredients in a bowl, stir until mixed and shape the mixture into ¾ inch balls, set aside until required.
2. Take a skillet pan, place it over medium-high heat, add 2 tablespoons oil and when hot, add meatballs in a single layer and cook for 5 minutes until browned on all sides.
3. Transfer meatballs to a plate lined with paper towels and then cook remaining meatballs in batches in the same manner, set aside until required.
4. Take a 4-quart Dutch oven, place it over medium-high heat, add remaining oil and when hot, add onion and garlic and cook for 5 minutes until softened.
5. Pour in broth, bring it to boil, then add escarole, switch heat to the low level, and simmer for 10 minutes, covering the pan.
6. Then add meatballs into the soup and continue cooking for 5 minutes.
7. Meanwhile, crack eggs in a bowl, add both cheese and beat well until blended.
8. Pour the egg-cheese mixture slowly into the soup, stirring in one direction and simmer for 30 seconds until eggs are set.
9. Add pasta, season with black pepper, salt, and pepper flakes, cook for 3 minutes and then serve.

Nutrition: Per Serving:

Calories: 120;

Total Fat: 3.5 g;

Saturated Fat: 1.5 g;

Protein: 7 g;

Carbs: 15 g;

Fiber: 2 g;

Sugar: 3 g

44. Sausage Minestrone

Preparation time: 5 minutes

Cooking time: 22 minutes

Servings: 8

Ingredients:

- 32 ounces cooked kidney beans
- 2 medium carrots, chopped
- 1 medium white onion, peeled, chopped
- 1 pound Italian sausage
- 2 celery ribs, chopped
- 1/4 teaspoon garlic powder
- 43.5 ounces diced tomatoes with basil, oregano, and garlic
- 1 teaspoon salt
- 1/4 teaspoon ground black pepper
- 29 ounces chicken broth
- 1 cup orzo pasta, uncooked

Directions:

1. Take a 4-quart Dutch oven, place it over medium heat and when hot, add sausage, crumble it, then add carrot, onion, and celery and cook for 10 minutes until meat is no longer pink.
2. Drain the fat, add beans and tomatoes, season with garlic, black pepper, and salt, stir and bring the mixture to boil.
3. Switch heat to the low level, add pasta, stir and cook for 8 minutes until pasta is tender.
4. Serve straight away.

Nutrition: Per Serving:

Calories: 372;

Total Fat: 13 g;

Saturated Fat: 4 g;

Protein: 18 g;

Carbs: 44 g;

Fiber: 9 g;

Sugar: 9 g

45. Minestrone with Turkey

Preparation time: 5 minutes

Cooking time: 18 minutes

Servings: 6

Ingredients:

- 2/3 cup frozen corn, thawed
- 1/2 cup elbow macaroni, uncooked
- 1 cup cubed turkey, cooked
- 1 medium white onion, peeled, chopped
- 2/3 cup frozen peas, thawed
- 1 small zucchini, 1/4-inch thick sliced
- 1 medium carrot, peeled, sliced
- 14.5 ounces diced tomatoes
- 1 celery rib, sliced
- ½ teaspoon minced garlic
- 4 cups turkey stock
- 2/3 cup frozen cut green beans, thawed
- 1 teaspoon salt
- 1/4 teaspoon dried basil
- 1/4 teaspoon ground black pepper
- 1/4 teaspoon dried oregano
- 1 tablespoon olive oil
- 1 bay leaf
- 1/4 cup grated Parmesan cheese

Directions:

1. Take a 4-quart Dutch oven, place it over medium-high heat, add oil and when hot, add celery, onion, and carrot and cook for 5 minutes until tender.
2. Add garlic, continue cooking for 1 minute until fragrant, add remaining vegetables and seasoning, then add macaroni, stir and bring the mixture to boil.
3. Switch to medium-low level and then simmer the soup for 5 minutes, uncovering the pan.
4. Add zucchini and turkey, cook for 3 minutes until zucchini is tender-crisp, and then discard bay leaf.
5. Sprinkle with cheese and serve.

Nutrition: Per Serving:

Calories: 172;

Total Fat: 5 g;

Saturated Fat: 1 g;

Protein: 12 g;

Carbs: 20 g;

Fiber: 4 g;

Sugar: 7 g

46. Orzo Shrimp Stew

Preparation time: 5 minutes

Cooking time: 15 minutes

Servings: 4

Ingredients:

- 1 cup orzo pasta, uncooked
- 1 pound medium shrimp, peeled, deveined
- 5 cups fresh broccoli florets
- 14.5 ounces diced tomatoes
- 1/4 teaspoon ground black pepper
- 1/4 teaspoon salt
- 2 teaspoons dried basil
- 2 tablespoons unsalted butter
- 2 1/2 cups chicken broth

Directions:

1. Take a 4-quart Dutch oven, place it over medium-high heat, add broth and bring it to boil.
2. Then add pasta and vegetables, stir and cook for 5 minutes, uncovering the pan.
3. Add shrimps, season stew with salt and black pepper, and cook for 5 minutes until shrimps turn pink and pasta is tender.
4. Add butter and basil, stir until mixed and serve.

Nutrition: Per Serving:

Calories: 387;

Total Fat: 8 g;

Saturated Fat: 4 g;

Protein: 30 g;

Carbs: 48 g;

Fiber: 5 g;

Sugar: 7 g

47. Spicy Chicken Stew

Preparation time: 5 minutes

Cooking time: 25 minutes

Servings: 6

Ingredients:

- 15 ounces cooked chickpeas
- 2 pounds boneless chicken thighs, 1/2-inch cubed
- 14.5 ounces diced tomatoes with onions
- 2 teaspoons minced garlic
- 1 teaspoon ground cumin
- 2 tablespoons olive oil
- 1 cup lime and garlic salsa
- 1/3 cup minced cilantro

Directions:

1. Take a 4-quart Dutch oven, place it over medium-high heat, add oil and when hot, add chicken and cook for 5 minutes until golden browned.
2. Add remaining ingredients except for cilantro, stir and simmer for 15 minutes until chicken is cooked.
3. When done, stir in cilantro and then serve.

Nutrition: Per Serving: Calories: 359; Total Fat: 17 g; Saturated Fat: 4 g; Protein: 31 g; Carbs: 18 g; Fiber: 4 g; Sugar: 5 g

48. Kale and White-Bean Stew

Preparation time: 5 minutes

Cooking time: 15 minutes

Servings: 4

Ingredients:

- 4 cups cooked cannellini beans
- 1/4 pound hot sausages, casings removed
- 1 pound kale, shredded
- 2 medium white onions, peeled, chopped
- 3 1/3 cups diced tomatoes with their juice
- 1 ½ teaspoon minced garlic
- 1 1/4 teaspoons salt
- 1/2 teaspoon ground black pepper
- 2 tablespoons olive oil

Directions:

1. Take a 4-quart Dutch oven, place it over medium-high heat, add 1 tablespoon oil and when hot, add sausage, crumble it and cook for 2 minutes until no longer pink.
2. Add remaining oil, then add onion and continue cooking for 3 minutes.
3. Add kale leaves and garlic, cook for 2 minutes until leaves have wilted, then add remaining ingredients except for

beans and bring the mixture to simmer.

4. Switch heat to medium-low level, add beans, stir and cook for 5 minutes until thoroughly heated.

5. Mash the bean, stir and then serve.

Nutrition: Per Serving:

Calories: 113.2;

Total Fat: 3 g;

Saturated Fat: 0.7 g;

Protein: 6.1 g;

Carbs: 17.3 g;

Fiber: 4.2 g;

Sugar: 2.5 g

49. Chicken Mushroom Soup

Preparation time: 10 minutes

Cooking time: 30 minutes

Servings: 8

Ingredients:

- 2 tablespoons olive oil
- 2 cups fresh mushrooms, sliced
- 2 medium carrots, chopped
- 2 celery ribs, chopped
- 1 small onion, chopped
- 1-quart chicken broth
- 1/3 cup all-purpose flour
- 2 cups cooked chicken, cubed
- 1 (8¾-ounce) package precooked chicken-flavored rice
- 2 cups Fat-free half-and-half
- ½ teaspoon pepper

Directions

1. Add the oil to the Dutch oven and heat it over medium-high heat.
2. Add the vegetables and stir-cook until the carrots become soft, crisp, and tender.
3. Add the broth and flour to a mixing bowl. Mix well.

4. Pour the broth into the Dutch oven and bring to a boil, stirring occasionally.
5. Stir-cook for 5–6 minutes until thickened.
6. Add the other ingredients and cook over medium-low heat until cooked to satisfaction.
7. Serve warm.

Nutrition:

Calories 224,

Fat 7 g,

carbs 23 g,

Protein 15 g,

sodium 741 mg

50. Creme Potato Chicken Soup

Preparation time: 10 minutes

Cooking time: 10 minutes

Servings: 8

Ingredients:

- 3½ cups water
- 4 cups shredded cooked chicken breast
- 2 (10¾-ounce) cans condensed cream of chicken soup, undiluted
- 1 pound frozen mixed vegetables, thawed
- 1 (14½-ounce) can potatoes, drained and diced
- 1 pound Velveeta, cubed
- Minced chives (optional)

Directions

1. Add the water, chicken breast, chicken soup, vegetables, and potatoes to the Dutch oven. Bring to a boil.
2. Reduce heat to low, cover, and simmer for 8–10 minutes until the veggies are tender, stirring occasionally.
3. Mix in the cheese.
4. Serve warm with minced chives on top.

Nutrition:

Calories 429,

Fat 22 g,

carbs 23 g,

Protein 33 g,

sodium 1464 mg

51. Beef and Cabbage Soup

Preparation time: 15 minutes

Cooking time: 2 hours

Servings: 8

Ingredients:

- 1 pound beef stew meat, cut into ¾-inch pieces
- Salt and pepper
- 2 tablespoons olive oil
- 6 cups beef stock, divided
- 1 medium-sized green cabbage, shredded
- 6 tomatoes, crushed
- 1 large onion, diced
- 3 cups of water
- 2 cloves garlic, minced
- 1 ½ teaspoon Italian seasoning

Directions

1. Pat the beef dry with paper towels and season with salt and pepper.
2. Add oil to a large Dutch oven and sear the meat over medium heat on all sides until well browned. Do not overcrowd the oven, work in batches if needed. Place the browned beef on a plate.

3. Add about half of the beef stock and bring to a boil. Stir and scrape the brown bits. Return the beef to the Dutch oven.

4. Add the cabbage, tomatoes, onion, remaining beef stock, water, garlic, Italian seasoning.

5. Bring to a boil over medium-high heat.

6. Decrease the heat to medium-low and let cook for 2 hours until the beef is tender and cabbage soft, taking care of stirring a few times.

7. Taste and adjust seasoning with salt and pepper.

Nutrition:

Calories 176,

Fat 3 g,

carbs 15 g

Protein 13 g,

Sodium:816mg

52. Quinoa Chickpea Corn Soup

Preparation time: 10 minutes

Cooking time: 25 minutes

Servings: 6

Ingredients:
- 1 tablespoon olive oil
- 1 medium red onion, chopped
- 1–2 jalapeño peppers, seeded and chopped (optional)
- 4 cloves garlic, minced
- ¼ teaspoon pepper
- 1 cup red quinoa, rinsed
- 2 quarts vegetable broth
- 3 medium tomatoes, chopped
- 1 cup fresh or frozen corn
- 2 (15-ounce) cans unsalted chickpeas or garbanzo beans, rinsed and drained
- Chopped fresh cilantro (optional)

Directions

1. Add the oil to the Dutch oven and heat it over medium-high heat.

2. Add the onion, jalapeño, and garlic. Stir-cook for 3–5 minutes until softened and tender.

3. Mix in the quinoa and broth.

4. Bring to a boil.

5. Reduce heat to low and simmer for about 10 minutes until the quinoa is tender, stirring occasionally.

6. Mix in the tomatoes, corn, chickpeas, and continue cooking until warm through, about 10 minutes.

7. Serve warm with chopped cilantro on top if desired.

Nutrition:

Calories 289,

Fat 5 g,

carbs 48 g,

Protein 13 g,

sodium 702 mg

53. Sweet Potato Soup

Preparation time: 20 minutes

Cooking time: 60 minutes

Servings: 8

Ingredients:

- 4 sweet potatoes, peeled and diced
- 1 onion, minced
- 2 (14-ounce) can of light coconut milk
- 2 cup vegetable broth
- 4 cloves garlic, minced
- 2 teaspoon dried basil
- Salt and pepper

Directions:

1. Place all the ingredients in the Dutch oven and stir.
2. Cover and cook for 1 hour 30 minutes, or until the sweet potatoes are tender.
3. Puree with an immersion blender until the soup is smooth.

Nutrition:

Calories 127,

Fat 5 g,

carbs 20 g

Protein 1 g,

sodium 159 mg

54. Pork and Bean Soup

Preparation time: 15 minutes

Cooking time: 55 minutes

Servings: 8

Ingredients:

- 1-quart water
- 3 cups pork roast, cooked and cubed
- 1 (15-ounce) can navy beans, rinsed and drained
- 2 medium potatoes, peeled and chopped
- 1 large onion, chopped
- 1 (14½-ounce) can Italian diced tomatoes with juices
- ½ cup unsweetened apple juice
- ½ teaspoon salt
- ½ teaspoon pepper
- Minced fresh basil (optional)

Directions

1. Add the water, pork roast, beans, potatoes, and remaining ingredients to the Dutch oven.
2. Bring to a boil.
3. Reduce heat to low, cover, and simmer, stirring occasionally, for 40–45 minutes until the roast is cooked to perfection and veggies are tender and crisp.
4. Serve warm with minced basil on top.

Nutrition:

Calories 206,

Fat 5 g,

carbs 23 g,

Protein 18 g,

sodium 435 mg

55. Tomato Cream Soup with Basil

Preparation time: 15 minutes

Cooking time: 2 hours

Servings: 8

Ingredients:

- 3 large carrots, peeled
- 2 celery stalks
- 2 medium onions
- 4 whole cloves garlic, peeled
- 4 (28-ounce) cans whole peeled tomatoes
- 1-quart chicken broth, low sodium
- ½ cup fresh basil leaves, roughly chopped, more for serving
- Salt and pepper to taste
- 1/3 Cup heavy cream

Directions:

1. Dice the carrots, celery, and onions.
2. Combine the carrots, celery, onions, garlic, tomatoes, chicken broth, and basil in the Dutch oven.
3. Bring to a boil, cover, reduce heat to low, and cook for 2 hours or until the vegetables are soft and tender. The tomatoes should be soft and easy to puree.
4. Use an immersion blender to puree.
5. Add the cream and blend it in. Season to taste with salt and pepper.
6. Serve garnished with more basil leaves, if desired.

Nutrition:

Calories 180,

Fat 5 g,

carbs 31 g

Protein 5 g,

sodium 470 mg

56. Chicken Bean Barley Soup

Preparation time: 15 minutes

Cooking time: 3 hours

Servings: 8

Ingredients:

- 2 strips thick-cut bacon
- 1 large onion, diced
- 2 cloves garlic, minced
- 1 cup dried barley, soaked overnight, rinsed, and drained
- 1 ½ cups dried navy beans, soaked overnight, rinsed and drained
- 6 cups low sodium chicken broth
- 4 cups of water
- 1 pound spinach, washed and roughly chopped
- 1 small rotisserie chicken, skin removed, and meat shredded
- Salt and pepper to taste

Directions:

1. Brown the bacon in the Dutch oven over medium heat. When crisp, drain and transfer to a plate lined with paper towels. Set aside.
2. Drain off the drippings, leaving about 1 tablespoon. Sauté the onion and garlic until tender.
3. Place the barley and beans in the Dutch oven.
4. Pour in the broth and water, and stir.
5. Bring to a boil over medium-high heat. Cover, reduce heat to medium-low, and cook 60-75 minutes until beans and barley are tender. Check a few times and add more water if needed.
6. Add the spinach and chicken continue cooking for another 20 minutes.
7. Crumble the reserved bacon. Serve warm with some of the bacon on top.

Nutrition:

Calories 149,

Fat 3 g,

carbs 15g

Protein 16 g,

Sodium 392 mg

57. Collard Green White Bean Soup with Sausages

Preparation time: 10 minutes

Cooking time: 2 hours 30 minutes

Servings: 8

Ingredients:

- 1 pound dried white beans, soaked overnight, rinsed, and drained
- Water
- Salt and pepper
- ½ pound Cajun Andouille sausages, sliced
- 1/2 large onion, chopped
- 2 stalks celery, chopped
- 4 sprigs fresh thyme
- 8 cups chicken broth, low-sodium
- 8 cups collard greens, leaves only, cut into 1-inch pieces
- 1 tablespoon red wine vinegar

Directions:

1. Place the beans in a Dutch oven and cover with water. Season with salt and pepper.
2. Bring to a boil over high heat. Reduce heat to medium-low, cover, and cook for 45-50 hours or until the beans are tender. Remove from heat and drain the water.
3. Add the sausages, onion, celery, thyme, and chicken broth. Bring a boil over high heat, reduce heat to low, cover and cook for 30 minutes over medium-low heat.
4. Remove the thyme stems and drop in the collard greens. Cover and cook 15-20 minutes longer or until the greens are tender.
5. Add the vinegar, and season with salt and pepper to taste.

Nutrition:

Calories 393,

Fat 8 g,

carbs 51 g

Protein 30 g,

sodium 670 mg

58. Bacon and Potato Soup

Preparation time: 15 minutes

Cooking time: 60 minutes

Servings: 8

Ingredients:

- 8 strips bacon
- 2 teaspoons bacon drippings or olive oil
- 1 large onion, chopped
- 3 pounds potatoes, peeled, cut into ¼-inch slices
- 1 cup of water
- 2 (14 ½-ounce) cans chicken broth, Fat-free, lower-sodium
- ½ teaspoon salt
- ½ teaspoon freshly ground black pepper
- 2 cups low-Fat milk
- ¾ cup cheddar cheese, shredded, more for serving

For serving

- ½ cup light sour cream (optional)
- 4 teaspoons fresh chives, chopped (optional)

Directions

1. Fry the bacon strips in the Dutch oven until crispy over medium heat, about 4-5 minutes. Remove the bacon and place on a plate lined with paper towels.
2. Keep about 2 tablespoons of the bacon drippings (or oil) in the Dutch oven. Add olive oil if necessary. Warm the drippings over medium heat, and stir-fry the onions until tender. Remove from heat.
3. Place the potato slices in the Dutch oven. Stir in the water, broth, salt, and pepper and stir.
4. Cover and cook for 40-45 minutes over medium-low heat or until the potatoes are tender.
5. Mash potatoes with a potato masher or blender stick. Stir in milk and cheese. Stir to combine.
6. Let simmer over low heat for about 20-25 minutes or until heated through and smooth.
7. Serve with sour cream, sprinkled with bacon, chives, more cheese, if desired.

Nutrition:

Calories 259, Fat 6 g, carbs 38 g

Protein 13 g, Sodium 683 mg

59. Tomato Bisque with Shrimp

Preparation time: 10 minutes

Cooking time: 20 minutes

Servings: 6

Ingredients:

- 3 tablespoons olive oil
- 1 yellow onion, roughly chopped
- 2 celery stalks, roughly chopped
- 2 teaspoons sea salt
- 1 teaspoon freshly ground black pepper
- 1 garlic clove, minced
- 1 teaspoon paprika
- 1 (28-ounce) can whole peeled tomatoes
- 1 (14-ounce) can full-fat coconut milk
- 8 ounces fresh shrimp, peeled and deveined

Directions:

1. Sweat the vegetables. Heat the olive oil in a Dutch oven over medium heat. Add the onion, celery, salt, and pepper. Sauté for about 4 minutes or until tender, stirring occasionally. Add the garlic. Cook for 1 minute, stirring frequently. Add the paprika. Cook the onion mixture with the paprika for 1 minute, until fragrant.
2. Add the liquids. Add the tomatoes with their juices and the coconut milk. Cover the pot and simmer for 5 minutes. Turn off the heat.
3. Blend the soup and poach the shrimp. Using an immersion blender, blend the soup until smooth.
4. Alternatively, working in batches, carefully transfer the soup to a regular blender and blend on high speed until very smooth. Return the soup to the pot. While the soup is still piping hot, add the shrimp and stir.
5. Cook the shrimp in the hot soup for 2 to 3 minutes or until it is pink and white and fully cooked. Ladle the soup into bowls. Refrigerate leftover soup for up to 3 days.

Nutrition:

Carbohydrates: 61.8 g

Fat: 6.8 g

Protein: 4.5 g

Calories: 326

60. Creamy Broccoli Soup

Preparation time: 10 minutes

Cooking time: 25 minutes

Servings: 6

Ingredients:

- ¼ cup olive oil
- ½ white onion, chopped
- 2 celery stalks, chopped
- 2 carrots, chopped
- 2½ teaspoons salt
- 1 small russet potato, chopped
- 2 garlic cloves, minced
- 4 cups vegetable stock
- 1 large head broccoli, chopped (5 cups florets)
- ½ cup shredded cheddar cheese (optional)

Directions:

1. Sweat the vegetables. Heat a Dutch oven over medium heat. Add the olive oil, onion, celery, carrots, and salt. Sauté for 3 minutes, stirring occasionally to prevent browning.
2. Cook the potato. Add the potato and garlic. Sauté for about 7 minutes or until the potato softens and cooks through, stirring occasionally.
3. Simmer and blend with the broccoli. Add the vegetable stock, increase the heat to medium-high, and bring the soup to a simmer.
4. Cook for 8 minutes. Turn off the heat and use a slotted spoon to transfer the cooked vegetables to a blender.
5. Scoop out about 2 cups of liquid from the pot and add it to the blender. Add the broccoli florets to the blender and blend on high speed until the mixture is very smooth and creamy.
6. Return the creamy soup to the pot and serve. Pour the blended soup back into the Dutch oven and bring it to a simmer.
7. Stir well, then turn off the heat to preserve the broccoli's color. You can add cheddar cheese (if using) to the soup in the Dutch oven, or you can serve the soup and garnish with the cheese. Refrigerate leftovers in the Dutch oven for easy reheating for up to 3 days.

Nutrition:

Carbohydrates: 21.8 g

Fat: 6.8 g

Protein: 4.5 g

Calories: 326

61. Vegetable and Lentil Soup

Preparation time: 10 minutes

Cooking time: 25 minutes

Servings: 6

Ingredients:

- 3 tablespoons olive oil
- 1 onion, chopped
- 2 carrots, chopped
- 2 celery stalks, chopped
- 1 tablespoon garam masala, plus more for seasoning
- 1 tablespoon salt, plus more for seasoning
- 2 teaspoons curry powder, plus more for seasoning
- 1 teaspoon freshly ground black pepper, plus more for seasoning
- 6 cups filtered water
- 2 cups red or yellow lentils

Directions:

1. Sweat the vegetables. In a Dutch oven over medium heat, warm the olive oil. Add the onion, carrots, and celery. Sweat the vegetables for 7 minutes, stirring occasionally. Stir in the garam masala, salt, curry powder, and pepper. Cook for about 2 minutes, until aromatic.

2. Simmer the lentils. Pour the water over the vegetables and add the lentils. Stir, then cover the pot and simmer, stirring occasionally, for about 15 minutes, until the lentils are tender and cooked through.

3. Adjust the seasoning and serve. Taste the soup and add more salt or spices as desired. Ladle the soup into bowls and top as desired. Refrigerate leftovers for up to 3 days.

Nutrition:

Carbohydrates: 61.8 g

Fat: 6.8 g

Protein: 4.5 g

Calories: 326

62. Cauliflower-Leek Potage

Preparation time: 10 minutes

Cooking time: 45 minutes

Servings: 6

Ingredients:

- 1 head cauliflower, cut into florets
- 1 tablespoon sea salt, plus more as needed
- Juice of 1 lemon, divided
- 2 leeks
- 2 tablespoons olive oil
- 4 cups vegetable stock
- Freshly ground black pepper
- 4 tablespoons (½ stick) unsalted butter
- ¼ cup slivered almonds
- Freshly grated nutmeg, for seasoning

Directions:

1. Boil and drain the cauliflower. Fill a Dutch oven about halfway with water and add the cauliflower, salt, and the juice of ½ a lemon. Bring to a boil and cook for 15 minutes. Place a colander in the sink and drain the cauliflower.
2. Sweat the leeks and simmer with stock. Remove the leeks' tough outer green portions. Cut lengthwise down the center of the white stalks but keep the root ends intact. Fan the leeks under running water to wash away any sand.
3. Thinly slice the leeks and discard the roots. In a Dutch oven over medium heat, heat the olive oil. Add the leeks with a pinch of salt.
4. Cook for 15 minutes until very tender, stirring occasionally to prevent browning. Add the cooked cauliflower and vegetable stock and bring to a simmer.
5. Blend. Using a slotted spoon, carefully transfer the leeks and cauliflower to a blender. Using a liquid measuring cup, transfer 1 cup of cooking liquid to the blender. Blend on high speed until very smooth.
6. Return the puree to the Dutch oven. Taste and season with salt and pepper. Spritz with the juice of the remaining ½ lemon.
7. Brown the butter with the almonds. In a small skillet over medium-low heat, combine the butter and almonds.
8. Cook for about 5 minutes, stirring occasionally, until the nuts turn lightly golden and the butter is browned. Pour the browned butter into the soup, reserving the almonds for garnish. Swirl the butter into the soup.

9. Ladle into bowls and garnish with almonds for crunch and a dash of nutmeg, preferably freshly grated. Refrigerate leftovers for up to 4 days, or let the soup cool and then freeze it in freezer-safe plastic bags for up to 2 months.

Nutrition:

Carbohydrates: 11.8 g

Fat: 3.8 g

Protein: 4.5 g

Calories: 226

63. Pork Green Chili

Preparation time: 10 minutes

Cooking time: 1 hour 40 minutes

Servings: 6

Ingredients:

- 2 tablespoons olive oil
- 2 pounds boneless pork shoulder
- 2 teaspoons salt
- 1 teaspoon dried oregano
- 1 teaspoon ground cumin
- 1 teaspoon onion powder
- 1 teaspoon ground coriander
- 1 cup salsa verde
- ½ cup sour cream
- 1 (4-ounce) can diced green chiles
- 1 cup filtered water
- 1 (15-ounce) can black beans, drained and rinsed

Directions:

1. Cook the pork. Cut the pork shoulder into cubes, roughly 1 inch thick. In a Dutch oven over medium heat, warm the olive oil.

2. Add the pork and season with the salt. Sear for 3 minutes to brown the meat on all sides, turning it with a spatula.

3. Add the spices and other ingredients, then simmer. Stir in the oregano, cumin, onion powder, and coriander.

4. Cook for 30 seconds, until aromatic. Pour in the salsa verde, sour cream, green chiles, and water. Stir to combine, scraping along the bottom of the pot with a wooden spoon or spatula to release any browned bits.

5. Cover the pot and reduce the heat to medium-low. Simmer the soup for 1½ hours or until the pork is tender and shreds easily with a fork.

6. Add the black beans, adjust seasonings, and serve. Add the black beans and bring the soup back to a simmer.

7. Taste and adjust the seasoning as desired. Ladle into bowls and garnish with cilantro (if using) and cheese (if using). Refrigerate leftovers for up to 4 days.

Nutrition:

Carbohydrates: 61.8 g

Fat: 6.8 g

Protein: 4.5 g

Calories: 326

64. Black Bean Soup with Citrus

Preparation time: 10 minutes

Cooking time: 20 minutes

Servings: 4

Ingredients:

- 3 tablespoons olive oil
- 1 white or yellow onion, chopped
- 1 red bell pepper, chopped
- 2 celery stalks, chopped
- 6 garlic cloves, chopped
- 2 teaspoons ground cumin
- 1 teaspoon chili powder
- 1 teaspoon salt
- 2 (15-ounce) cans black beans, drained and rinsed
- 2 cups water
- Grated zest and juice of 1 orange
- Juice of 2 limes
- Chopped fresh cilantro, for garnish (optional)

Directions:

1. Sauté the vegetables. Heat a Dutch oven over medium heat. Add the olive oil, onion, bell pepper, and celery.

2. Cook for about 7 minutes, stirring occasionally. Add the garlic, cumin,

chili powder, and salt. Stir to coat the vegetables and turn off the heat to avoid burning.

3. Simmer the beans. Add the black beans and water. Using a spatula, stir to combine, scraping along the bottom of the pot to release any browned bits.

4. Bring the soup to a simmer over medium heat and cook for 8 minutes.

5. Season and serve. Stir in the orange zest, orange juice, and lime juice to taste. (Salt and acid lift the savory flavors of this soup.)

6. Garnish with cilantro (if using). Refrigerate leftovers for up to 2 days.

Nutrition:

Carbohydrates: 21.8 g

Fat: 6.8 g

Protein: 4.5 g

Calories: 314

65. Turmeric Vegetable Soup

Preparation time: 10 minutes

Cooking time: 20 minutes

Servings: 6

Ingredients:

- 2 tablespoons olive oil
- 1 sweet potato, peeled and diced
- 1 teaspoon salt, plus more for seasoning
- 5 garlic cloves, minced
- 1 poblano chile, seeded and chopped
- 2 cups frozen corn
- 1 tablespoon chili powder
- 1 teaspoon ground cumin
- 1 teaspoon ground turmeric
- ½ cup dry white wine
- 4 cups water
- 1 (14-ounce) can coconut milk

Directions:

1. Sauté the vegetables. In a Dutch oven over medium heat, warm the olive oil. Add the sweet potato and salt.

2. Stir to combine and cook for 7 minutes or until the potato begins to brown. Stir in the garlic, poblano, and corn. Cook for 3 minutes more.

3. Deglaze and simmer. Add the chili powder, cumin, and turmeric, and toss to coat the vegetables. Cook for 1 minute.

4. Stir in the white wine and deglaze the pot, scraping along the bottom of the pot to release any browned bits.

5. Add the water and increase the heat to medium-high. Bring the soup to a simmer and cook for about 5 minutes, until heated through.

6. Season and serve. Turn off the heat and stir in the coconut milk. Taste and, if the soup is bland, season with salt. Refrigerate leftovers for up to 3 days.

SERVING TIP: Since turmeric gives this soup such an earthy flavor, I recommend serving it with a floral garnish such as chopped fresh cilantro. Add delicate herbs at the last moment to maximize their aromatic properties.

Nutrition:

Carbohydrates: 61.8 g

Fat: 6.8 g

Protein: 4.5 g

Calories: 326

Chapter 5. Vegetables and Vegetarian

66. Beans with Chard

Preparation time: 15 minutes

Cooking time: 26 minutes

Servings: 2

Ingredients:

- 1 bunch red or rainbow chard
- 2 to 3 tablespoons olive oil
- ½ small onion, chopped
- 2 garlic cloves, chopped
- Kosher salt, to taste
- ¼ cup dry white wine
- 1 medium tomato, seeded and diced
- 2 tablespoons diced or puréed sun-dried tomatoes
- ¼ teaspoon red pepper flakes
- 1 (14-ounce / 397-g) can cannellini beans, drained and rinsed

Directions:

1. Rinse the chard and cut the leaves from the stems. Dice enough of the stems to make ½ cup; reserve the rest for another use or discard. Stack the leaves up and cut into ½-inch ribbons.
2. Place the Dutch oven over medium heat and add the olive oil. Heat until the oil shimmers and then add the onion, garlic, and chard stems. Season with salt and cook, stirring, for 5 to 6 minutes, or until the onion pieces have separated and the chard has softened.
3. Add the wine and bring to a simmer. Add the diced tomato, sun-dried tomatoes, and red pepper flakes.
4. Add the chard leaves by big handfuls, stirring to wilt. When all the chard is added, bring to a simmer and cover the Dutch oven. Cook for about 15 minutes, or until the chard is very soft. Taste and adjust the seasoning, adding more salt or red pepper flakes if necessary. Add the beans and cook for another 5 minutes, or until the beans are heated through.

Nutrition:

Carbohydrates: 14 g

Fat: 9 g

Protein: 4 g

Calories: 226

67. Savory Beans Rice

Preparation time: 15 minutes

Cooking time: 21 minutes

Servings: 2

Ingredients:

- 2 to 3 tablespoons olive oil
- ½ small onion, chopped (about 1/3 cup)
- 1 large garlic clove, minced
- 1 small jalapeño pepper, seeded and chopped (about 1 tablespoon)
- ½ cup long-grain white rice
- 3 tablespoons red salsa
- 2 tablespoons tomato sauce
- ¾ cup vegetable stock
- ¼ teaspoon ground cumin
- ½ teaspoon kosher salt
- 1 (14-ounce / 397-g) can pinto beans, drained and rinsed
- 1 tablespoon chopped fresh parsley

Directions:

1. Preheat the oven to 350°F (180°C).
2. Place the Dutch oven over medium heat. Add enough oil to coat the bottom of the pot and heat until the oil shimmers. Add the onion, garlic, and jalapeño and cook, stirring, for 4 to 5 minutes, or until the onion pieces have separated and the vegetables have softened. Add the rice and stir to coat. Cook for about 1 minute.
3. Add the salsa, tomato sauce, vegetable stock, cumin, salt, and beans and stir to combine. Bring the liquid to a strong simmer and cover the Dutch oven.
4. Place the pot in the oven and cook for 18 minutes. Remove from the oven and let sit, covered, for 15 minutes. Remove the lid and add the parsley. Gently toss the rice with two large forks to fluff the rice and mix in the parsley.

Nutrition:

Carbohydrates: 16 g

Fat: 6 g

Protein: 4 g

Calories: 267

68. Corn and Bean Succotash

Preparation time: 15 minutes

Cooking time: 40 minutes

Servings: 2

Ingredients:

- 2 to 3 tablespoons olive oil
- 1 garlic clove, minced
- ½ medium green bell pepper, seeded and diced (about ½ cup)
- ½ small onion, chopped
- 1/3 cup long-grain rice
- 2/3 cup frozen lima beans, thawed
- 2/3 cup fresh or frozen (thawed) corn kernels
- 1 bay leaf
- ¼ teaspoon cayenne pepper
- ½ teaspoon Old Bay seasoning
- 2/3 cup low-sodium vegetable stock
- ¼ teaspoon kosher salt
- 1 large tomato, seeded and chopped
- ¼ cup chopped fresh parsley or basil, or a combination

Directions:

1. Preheat the oven to 350°F (180°C).
2. Place the Dutch oven over medium heat. Add enough oil to coat the bottom of the pot and heat until the oil shimmers. Add the garlic, bell pepper, and onion and cook, stirring, for 4 to 5 minutes, or until the onion pieces have separated and softened. Add the rice and stir to coat with oil. Cook for about 1 minute. Stir in the lima beans, corn, bay leaf, cayenne, and Old Bay seasoning.
3. Add the vegetable stock and salt and stir to combine. Bring the liquid to a strong simmer and cover the Dutch oven. Place the pot in the oven and cook for 18 minutes.
4. Remove the pot from the oven and rest, covered, for 15 minutes. Taste the rice to make sure it's done. Fluff the rice mixture and stir in the tomatoes and parsley or basil. Rest for a few more minutes to warm the tomatoes through.

Nutrition:

Carbohydrates: 12 g

Fat: 6 g

Protein: 4 g

Calories: 316

69. Panko Eggplant

Preparation time: 15 minutes

Cooking time: 40 minutes

Servings: 6

Ingredients:

Eggplant:

- 1 medium eggplant (about 1 pound / 454 g), sliced about ½-inch thick
- Kosher salt, to taste
- 1/3 cup all-purpose flour
- 1 egg, whisked with 1 tablespoon water or milk
- 2/3 cup Panko bread crumbs
- ½ teaspoon dried Italian herbs (or a mix of thyme, basil, and oregano)
- ½ cup grated Parmigiano-Reggiano or similar cheese, divided
- Vegetable oil, for frying
- ¼ cup shredded whole milk Mozzarella cheese (or more)

Sauce:

- 2 tablespoons olive oil
- ½ small onion, chopped
- 1 large garlic clove, minced
- 1 (14-ounce / 397-g) can diced tomatoes, with their juice
- 2 tablespoons diced sun-dried tomatoes (optional)
- ¼ teaspoon dried Italian herbs
- ¼ teaspoon kosher salt

Directions:

1. Place the eggplant slices on a rack set over a sheet pan. Season heavily with salt. Carefully turn the slices over and salt the other side. Set aside for 15 minutes while you prepare the breading.
2. In a shallow bowl, place the flour; in another shallow bowl, place the egg. In a third bowl, stir together the Panko, Italian herbs, and ¼ cup of grated Parmigiano-Reggiano.
3. Place the Dutch oven over medium-high heat. Add enough oil to form a ½-inch layer in the bottom of the pot and heat until the oil reaches about 360°F (182°C).
4. While the oil heats, rinse off the eggplant slices with water and blot dry on both sides with paper towels. Working with a few slices at a time, dredge both sides of the eggplant slices in the flour, then coat with the egg. Place slices in the Panko mixture and coat both sides.
5. When the oil is hot, carefully place the slices in the oil and fry for 2 to 3 minutes or until golden brown. Turn the slices over and cook for 2 minutes or until the second side is browned. Work in batches until all slices are

browned. As the slices finish frying, move them to a rack placed over a sheet pan.

6. Preheat the oven to 375°F (190°C).

7. Pour the frying oil out of the Dutch oven (no need to wipe it out).

8. For the sauce, place the pot over medium heat and add the olive oil. Heat until the oil shimmers, and then add the onion and garlic. Cook, stirring, for 4 to 6 minutes, or until the onion pieces have separated and softened and the garlic is very fragrant.

9. Add the canned tomatoes with their juice, the sun-dried tomatoes (if using), and Italian herbs; bring to a simmer. Add the salt (slightly more if you're not using the sun-dried tomatoes) and stir.

10. Bring to a simmer and cook for about 10 minutes. Using a potato masher or the back of a spoon, crush the tomatoes to form a smooth sauce. Taste and adjust the seasoning. Remove about ½ cup of the sauce.

11. Remove from the heat and use tongs to place the eggplant slices on top of the tomato sauce. Depending on the size of your Dutch oven and the number of slices, you may need to overlap them slightly.

12. Drizzle the reserved sauce over the eggplant slices and sprinkle with the Mozzarella and the remaining ¼ cup of Parmigiano-Reggiano.

13. Place the pot in the oven, uncovered, and bake for 12 to 18 minutes, or until the sauce is bubbling and the cheese is melted.

Nutrition:

Carbohydrates: 19 g

Fat: 6 g

Protein: 4 g

Calories: 286

70. Navy Beans and Zucchini

Preparation time: 20 minutes

Cooking time: 30 minutes

Servings: 2

Ingredients:

- Kosher salt, to taste
- 1 medium zucchini, sliced ½-inch thick
- 2 to 3 tablespoons olive oil
- ½ small onion, sliced (about 2/3 cup)
- 2 garlic cloves, minced or pressed
- ½ small green bell pepper, seeded and cut into ½-inch chunks (about ½ cup)
- ½ small red bell pepper, seeded and cut into ½-inch chunks (about ½ cup)
- 2 small tomatoes, seeded and diced
- 1 cup canned navy beans, drained and rinsed
- ½ teaspoon dried oregano
- ¼ teaspoon freshly ground black pepper
- 2 tablespoons minced fresh basil

Directions:

1. Very liberally salt one side of the zucchini slices. Place the slices salted-side down on a rack placed over a baking sheet. Salt the other side.
2. Let the slices sit for 15 to 20 minutes, or until they start to exude water (you'll see it beading up on the surface of the slices and dripping down into the sheet pan). Rinse the slices and blot them dry. Cut the zucchini slices in half.
3. Place the Dutch oven over medium heat. Add enough oil to coat the bottom of the pot and heat until the oil shimmers.
4. Add the zucchini slices in a single layer and cook without moving for 3 to 5 minutes, or until browned. Turn and brown the other sides, about 3 minutes. Remove to the rack or a plate.
5. Add the onion and garlic to the Dutch oven and season with a pinch of salt. Cook, stirring, until the onions just begin to brown, about 3 minutes.
6. Add the bell peppers and cook for about 3 minutes, or until they just start to brown. Add the zucchini, tomatoes, beans, oregano, and black pepper.
7. Bring to a simmer and cover. Reduce the heat to medium-low and simmer for 15 to 20 minutes, or until the vegetables are soft. If there is too much liquid in the pot, simmer uncovered for a few minutes until it is reduced.
8. Garnish with the basil and serve.

Nutrition:

Carbohydrates: 23 g, Fat: 6 g, Protein: 4 g

Calories: 326

71. Butternut Squash Risotto

Preparation time: 15 minutes

Cooking time: 1 hour

Servings: 2

Ingredients:

- 1 (8-ounce / 227-g) container butternut squash, peeled and diced
- 3 to 4 tablespoons olive oil
- Kosher salt, to taste
- 1 large shallot, finely chopped
- ¾ cup Arborio or Carnaroli rice
- ¼ cup dry white wine
- Pinch dried sage
- 2½ cups water
- 1 cup vegetable stock, divided
- ¼ teaspoon freshly ground black pepper
- 2 tablespoons unsalted butter
- ¼ cup grated Parmigiano-Reggiano or similar cheese, plus more for garnish

Directions:

1. Preheat the oven to 400°F (205°C).
2. Add the butternut squash cubes to the Dutch oven and drizzle with enough olive oil to coat the squash completely. Season with salt. Place the pot in the oven, uncovered, and roast the squash for about 15 minutes, then gently stir.
3. Return the pot to the oven for another 15 minutes and stir again. Return to the oven and roast until tender with some crisp edges, probably another 10 to 15 minutes. Remove the squash from the Dutch oven and set aside.
4. Place the Dutch oven over medium heat. Add enough oil to coat the bottom of the pot and heat until the oil shimmers.
5. Add the shallot and cook, stirring, for 3 to 4 minutes, until softened. Add the rice and stir to coat with the oil. Cook for about a minute; move the rice and shallots to the perimeter of the Dutch oven.
6. Add 3 or 4 cubes of the squash to the center of the pot and smash with a potato masher or the back of a spoon until they form a coarse paste.
7. Add the wine and the sage and stir the rice into the squash. Bring to a simmer and cook until the wine is mostly absorbed.
8. While the wine is reducing, mix the water and stock and heat in a saucepan or a heat-proof bowl in the microwave.
9. Pour ½ of the water-stock mixture into the Dutch oven and stir vigorously. Bring to a simmer and cover the Dutch oven.
10. Place the pot in the oven and bake for 15 minutes. Uncover and stir vigorously once more.

The rice should be fairly soupy; if it seems at all dry, pour in another ½ cup of the water-stock mixture.

11. Cover the pot and return to the oven. Bake for another 10 to 15 minutes, or until most of the liquid is absorbed and the rice is barely tender.
12. Place the Dutch oven over low heat on the stovetop and add ¼ cup of the water-stock mixture. Stir the risotto for 3 to 5 minutes, or until the liquid is mostly absorbed, then stir in the pepper, butter, and half the cheese.
13. Gently stir in as much of the reserved roasted squash as you like and let the risotto sit for a few minutes to warm the squash through.
14. Spoon into bowls and top with the remaining cheese and additional pepper, if desired.

Nutrition:

Carbohydrates: 9 g

Fat: 6 g

Protein: 4 g

Calories: 326

72. Cheese Mushrooms Bake

Preparation time: 20 minutes

Cooking time: 30 minutes

Servings: 2

Ingredients:

- 4 portobello mushrooms, about 3 inches across
- 4 tablespoons sherry vinegar
- 4 teaspoons minced fresh oregano or 2 teaspoons dried
- 4 garlic cloves, minced or pressed, divided
- 1 teaspoon Dijon mustard
- ½ teaspoon kosher salt, plus more for seasoning
- ½ cup plus 2 to 3 tablespoons extra-virgin olive oil, divided
- 2/3 cup julienned green bell pepper (about ½ a small pepper)
- 2/3 cup julienned red, yellow or orange bell pepper (about ½ a small pepper)
- 1 small onion, sliced thin
- ¼ teaspoon red pepper flakes
- 2 ounces (57 g) Gruyère or Emmenthal cheese (about ½ cup), shredded

Directions:

1. Prepare the mushrooms by removing the stem and scraping out the gills with a small spoon.
2. In a small bowl, whisk together the vinegar, oregano, half the garlic, mustard, and salt. Slowly whisk in ½ cup of olive oil. Pour the marinade into a sealable plastic bag and add the mushrooms, turning the bag over to coat all the mushrooms. Let them marinate for 1 to 2 hours at room temperature, turning the bag every 15 minutes or so.
3. Preheat the oven to 375°F (190°C).
4. While the mushrooms are marinating, place the Dutch oven over medium heat. Add enough of the remaining oil to coat the bottom of the pot and heat until the oil shimmers. Add the bell pepper slices and stir to coat with the oil. Cook without stirring for 2 to 3 minutes, or until the slices just start to brown.
5. Add the onion and remaining garlic, and cook, stirring, until the onion slices start to brown, 2 to 3 minutes. Add the red pepper flakes and salt. Transfer the sofrito mixture to a small bowl.
6. Add another coat of oil to the Dutch oven and let it heat until shimmering. While the oil heats, remove the mushrooms from the marinade and pat dry.
7. Add to the pot, under-side down and cook for 1 to 2 minutes, or until slightly browned. Depending on the size of your Dutch oven, you may need to do this in batches.
8. Turn the mushrooms over, under-side up. Divide the sofrito stuffing evenly among the mushrooms and top with the cheese.
9. Place the mushrooms back in the pot. Place in the oven and bake for 10 minutes or until the cheese has melted and the mushrooms are cooked through.

Nutrition:

Carbohydrates: 13 g

Fat: 6 g

Protein: 4 g

Calories: 276

73. Cream Mushroom Pasta Bake

Preparation time: 15 minutes

Cooking time: 45 minutes

Servings: 2

Ingredients:

- Kosher salt, to taste
- 6 ounces penne, farfalle, or other short pasta
- ½ pound (227g) cremini or white button mushrooms
- 3 tablespoons extra-virgin olive oil
- 1 large garlic clove, minced
- ¾ cup heavy cream
- ½ cup fresh Ricotta
- 5 ounces (142 g) Fontina cheese, grated (1¼ cups)
- ¼ teaspoon freshly ground black pepper
- 2 ounces (57 g) aged Parmigiano-Reggiano or similar cheese, grated (½ cup)

Directions:

1. Add 8 cups of water to the Dutch oven and place over high heat. Add about 2 teaspoons kosher salt and bring the water to a boil. Add the pasta and cook according to the package directions. (If you prefer, you can use a separate pot to cook the pasta while you prepare the mushrooms.) Drain, reserving at least a cup of the hot pasta water. Cover the reserved water with a lid or plate to keep warm, and set both the water and the pasta aside.
2. While the water heats and the pasta cooks, wash the mushrooms and trim the stems. Quarter the mushrooms if small to medium; cut into eighths if they are large. Set aside.
3. Preheat the oven to 375°F (190°C).
4. When the pasta is done cooking, add the mushrooms to the Dutch oven and cover with enough water to make the mushrooms float.
5. Pour in the oil and season generously with salt. Place the pot over high heat and bring to a boil. Continue boiling until the water has evaporated and you can hear the mushrooms begin to sizzle.
6. Add the garlic and cook, stirring the mushrooms occasionally, until brown on all sides, about 5 minutes.
7. Pour the cream into the Dutch oven. Cook for about 3 minutes, or until the cream has reduced by about one-third.
8. Pour the reserved hot pasta water over the cooked pasta to loosen it up, then add the pasta to the cream and mushrooms in the pot. Stir in the Ricotta, fontina, and pepper and toss gently to coat.

9. Sprinkle the Parmigiano-Reggiano cheese over the top of the pasta and place the pot in the oven. Bake for 10 minutes, or until the top is browned and the pasta is bubbling.

Nutrition:

Carbohydrates: 8 g

Fat: 6 g

Protein: 14 g

Calories: 326

74. Tomato and Peas Korma

Preparation time: 20 minutes

Cooking time: 20 minutes

Servings: 2

Ingredients:

- 2/3 cup canned diced tomatoes, drained (about half a 14-ounce / 397-g can)
- ½ small onion, cut into chunks
- 1 small jalapeño pepper, seeded and cut into chunks
- 1 teaspoon grated fresh ginger
- 2 medium garlic cloves, smashed
- 1 teaspoon ground coriander
- ½ teaspoon ground cardamom
- ½ teaspoon ground cinnamon
- ¼ teaspoon ground turmeric
- 1 1teaspoon kosher salt
- ¼ teaspoon freshly ground black pepper
- 2 to 3 tablespoons vegetable oil
- 2 cups mixed frozen "stir-fry" vegetables, thawed
- ½ cup frozen peas, thawed
- ¼ teaspoon red pepper flakes (optional)

- ¼ cup whole-milk yogurt

Directions:

1. Place the tomatoes, onion, jalapeño, ginger, garlic, coriander, cardamom, cinnamon, turmeric, salt, and pepper in a blender or small food processor and blend to a smooth paste (or use an immersion blender and a deep sturdy cup to blend).
2. Place the Dutch oven over medium heat. Add enough oil to coat the bottom of the pot and heat until the oil shimmers. Add the puréed tomato mixture and bring to a simmer. Cook for about 15 minutes, or until the sauce has thickened slightly and is very fragrant.
3. Add the thawed mixed vegetables and peas and bring back to a simmer. Cook for about 5 minutes, or until the vegetables are heated through. Taste and add the red pepper flakes if you want a spicier sauce. Stir in the yogurt and bring back to just a simmer. Serve over steamed basmati rice.

Nutrition:

Carbohydrates: 11 g

Fat: 6 g

Protein: 4 g

Calories: 326

75. Rice with Kale and Lentils

Preparation time: 15 minutes

Cooking time: 25 minutes

Servings: 6

Ingredients:

- ½ cup brown lentils
- 2 to 3 tablespoons olive oil
- ½ medium onion, chopped
- 2 garlic cloves, minced
- Kosher salt, to taste
- 1/3 cup long-grain rice
- 1 teaspoon ground cumin
- ½ teaspoon ground coriander
- ¼ teaspoon cayenne pepper
- 1/8 teaspoon ground cinnamon
- 3 cups low-sodium vegetable stock
- 2 cups chopped kale or other sturdy greens
- 2 tablespoons chopped toasted pistachios

Directions:

1. Rinse the lentils and then place them in a small bowl. Cover with water and let them soak while you chop and cook the onion and garlic.
2. Place the Dutch oven over medium-high heat. Add enough

oil to coat the bottom of the pot and heat until the oil shimmers. Add the onion and cook, stirring, for 6 to 8 minutes, or until browned. Add the garlic and season with salt. Cook for a minute or so, or until the garlic is fragrant.

3. Add the rice and stir to coat with the oil. Cook, stirring, for 2 to 3 minutes, or until the rice smells nutty. Add the cumin, coriander, cayenne, and cinnamon and stir to coat the rice with the spices.

4. Cook for a minute, then add the stock and ¼ teaspoon of salt.

5. Drain the lentils and add to the Dutch oven. Stir to combine. Bring the liquid to a simmer and stir again.

6. Cover and reduce the heat to low. After cooking for 15 minutes, stir gently. Taste the rice and lentils; they should be a bit firm in the center but almost done. Add the kale and press into the rice and lentil mixture.

7. Cover and cook for an additional 8 to 10 minutes, or until the kale, rice, and lentils are all tender.

8. Ladle into bowls and top with the pistachios.

Nutrition:

Carbohydrates: 8 g

Fat: 6 g

Protein: 10 g

Calories: 206

76. Lentils and Tomato over Rice

Preparation time: 25 minutes

Cooking time: 35 minutes

Servings: 2

Ingredients:

- 1 medium onion
- 4 garlic cloves
- 2 to 4 tablespoons vegetable oil
- 1 jalapeño pepper or serrano chile, seeded and diced
- 1 cup dried red lentils, rinsed
- 3½ cups water
- ½ teaspoon ground turmeric
- ¼ teaspoon ground cumin
- 1 bay leaf
- 1 teaspoon kosher salt
- 1 cup canned diced tomatoes, drained
- 2 tablespoons coarsely chopped fresh cilantro

Directions:

1. Slice half the onion, and dice the other half. Slice two cloves of garlic and mince or press the other two. Set aside the diced onion and the minced garlic.

2. Place the Dutch oven over medium heat. Add enough oil to coat the bottom of the pot and heat until the oil shimmers.

3. Add the sliced onion and garlic. Stir to coat the onion and garlic slices with the oil, then let them sit in a single layer until browned, about 4 minutes. Don't stir until you can see them browning.
4. Stir them to expose the other side to the heat and repeat. The onion and garlic should be browned, but still slightly firm. Remove the mixture from the pan and set aside.
5. Add more oil if necessary to coat the bottom of the Dutch oven. When it's hot, add the chopped onions, minced garlic, and jalapeño; cook, stirring, for 2 minutes, or until softened slightly and fragrant.
6. Add the lentils, water, turmeric, cumin, bay leaf, and salt, and bring to a simmer. Cover and cook for 15 minutes, stirring once or twice.
7. Add the tomatoes. Simmer, uncovered, for another 5 to 8 minutes, or until the lentils are tender.
8. When the lentils are done, stir in the reserved onion-garlic mixture and simmer for another minute or two, or until the onions are warmed through. Garnish with the cilantro and serve plain or over rice.

Nutrition:

Carbohydrates: 11 g

Fat: 6 g

Protein: 4 g

Calories: 326

77. Tofu with Cashews and Spinach

Preparation time: 12 minutes

Cooking time: 23 minutes

Servings: 2

Ingredients:

Tofu:

- ½ pound (227g) extra-firm tofu
- Vegetable oil for frying
- 5 to 6 ounces fresh baby spinach
- ½ cup cornstarch
- 1 tablespoon minced garlic (about 3 cloves)
- 2 teaspoons minced ginger
- 3 scallions, minced
- ¼ cup roasted unsalted cashews

Sauce:

- 1 tablespoon soy sauce
- 2 tablespoons rice vinegar
- ¼ cup water or vegetable stock
- 2 teaspoons Asian chile-garlic sauce, like Sriracha (or more)
- ¼ teaspoon freshly ground black pepper
- 1 teaspoon cornstarch
- 1 teaspoon granulated sugar

- 2 teaspoons sesame oil

Directions:

1. Slice the tofu into ½-inch-thick slices. Place on a layer of paper towels and cover with another layer. Press lightly to dry the slices. Uncover and let air-dry for 15 minutes while you prepare the sauce and aromatics, and cook the spinach.
2. For the sauce, whisk all the ingredients together in a small bowl. Keep the whisk handy, as you'll need to whisk the sauce again right before using.
3. Place the Dutch oven over medium heat. Add enough oil to coat the bottom of the pot and heat until the oil shimmers. Add the spinach and toss just to wilt. Remove from the Dutch oven and wipe the pot dry.
4. To make the tofu, increase the heat to high, and pour in enough oil to form a layer about 1-inch deep. Heat to 365°F (185°C). While the oil is heating, cut the tofu slices into bite-size pieces, about 1 inch by 1½ inches. Pour the cornstarch into a small bowl and toss the tofu pieces in the cornstarch until they are coated heavily.
5. Use a slotted spoon or spider to remove about half the tofu from the cornstarch and add to the hot oil.
6. Cook for 4 to 5 minutes or until golden brown and crisp. Use the spoon or spider to remove the pieces to a rack placed over a sheet pan, and let the oil heat back up to 365°F (185°C).
7. Repeat with the remaining tofu. (Depending on the size of your Dutch oven, you may have to cook three batches; don't crowd the pan).
8. Pour off all but a light coating of the oil. Return the pot to medium-high heat and add the garlic, ginger, and scallions.
9. Cook, stirring, for a minute or two, or until fragrant and just slightly browned. Whisk the sauce to combine, and add to the Dutch oven. Bring to a simmer and let cook for 2 to 3 minutes, or until thickened.
10. Add the tofu, spinach, and cashews, and toss gently to coat with the sauce. Serve with or without steamed rice.

Nutrition:

Carbohydrates: 12 g

Fat: 6 g

Protein: 4 g

Calories: 198

78. Kidney Bean and Tomato Pasta Soup

Preparation time: 5 minutes

Cooking time: 40 minutes

Servings: 6

Ingredients:

- 1 tablespoon extra-virgin olive oil
- 1 small yellow onion, chopped
- 1 (14-ounce / 397-g) can diced fire-roasted tomatoes
- 8 cups vegetable broth
- 2 cups uncooked small elbow pasta
- 1 pound (454 g) frozen soup vegetables
- 1 (15-ounce / 425-g) can red kidney beans, drained and rinsed
- Salt and freshly ground black pepper, to taste

Directions:

1. In a Dutch oven over medium-high heat, heat the olive oil. Add the onion and sauté for 5 minutes or until translucent. Add the tomatoes and vegetable broth and cook over medium heat for 5 to 10 minutes, until the liquid comes to a boil.
2. Add the pasta, soup vegetables, and beans. Bring to a boil, reduce the heat to low, cover, and simmer for 20 to 25 minutes, until the pasta is tender. Season with salt and pepper before serving.

Nutrition:

Carbohydrates: 61 g

Fat: 6 g

Protein: 4 g

Calories: 326

79. Peas and Carrot Fried Rice

Preparation time: 25 minutes

Cooking time: 15 minutes

Servings: 4

Ingredients:

- 3 tablespoons butter, divided
- 1 (10-ounce / 283-g) package frozen peas and carrots
- 3 cups leftover cooked rice, cold
- 3 tablespoons low-sodium soy sauce (gluten-free if needed), plus more for serving
- 2 eggs, beaten
- Freshly ground black pepper, to taste

Directions:

1. In a Dutch oven over medium-high heat, heat 1 tablespoon of the butter. Add the frozen peas and carrots. Sauté for about 5 minutes, until the peas and carrots are soft.
2. Increase the heat to high, add the remaining 2 tablespoons of butter, and stir until melted. Immediately add the rice and soy sauce, and stir until combined. Continue cooking, stirring constantly, for 3 more minutes to fry the rice.
3. Push the fried rice to one side of the pot, and add the eggs to the other side. Stir well so the eggs are scrambled while cooking. Mix the cooked eggs into the rice.
4. Remove from the heat. Season with pepper and more soy sauce before serving.

Nutrition:

Carbohydrates: 13 g

Fat: 6 g

Protein: 4 g

Calories: 226

80. Cabbage Noodles

Preparation time: 10 minutes

Cooking time: 35 minutes

Servings: 6

Ingredients:

- 1 (16-ounce / 454-g) package egg noodles
- 1 tablespoon extra-virgin olive oil
- 3 tablespoons butter
- 1 medium onion, peeled and chopped
- 6 cups shredded cabbage (about half a head)
- 3 garlic cloves, crushed
- Salt and freshly ground black pepper, to taste

Directions:

1. Fill a Dutch oven with water, and bring to a boil over medium-high heat. Cook the egg noodles for 8 minutes or according to the package directions. (Different thicknesses of egg noodles will have different cooking times.) Drain and set aside.
2. In the pot over medium heat, heat the olive oil. Add the butter and cook for a minute or two, until melted. Add the onion and cook until softened, about 5 minutes. Add the cabbage and garlic. Cook until tender, 10 to 15 minutes, and give it a few good stirs.
3. Stir in the noodles, and season with salt and pepper. Cook, stirring often, for another 3 minutes or until the pasta is heated through.

Nutrition:

Carbohydrates: 8 g

Fat: 6 g

Protein: 4 g

Calories: 326

81. Asparagus Peas Risotto with Cheese

Preparation time: 15 minutes

Cooking time: 55 minutes

Servings: 6

Ingredients:

- 5 cups vegetable broth, divided, plus more if needed
- 1 cup frozen peas
- ½ pound (227g) asparagus, trimmed and cut into bite-size pieces
- 1½ cups arborio rice
- 1 cup freshly grated Parmesan cheese
- 3 tablespoons salted butter, cut into pieces
- Salt and freshly ground black pepper, to taste

Directions:

1. Preheat the oven to 350°F (180°C).
2. Pour 4 cups of the vegetable broth into a Dutch oven. Turn the heat to medium-high and cook until the broth comes to a boil, 5 to 10 minutes. Stir in the peas, asparagus, and rice, and mix well.
3. Cover the pot, transfer it to the oven, and bake for 40 minutes or until most of the liquid is absorbed and the rice is tender.
4. Remove the risotto from the oven. Microwave the remaining cup of vegetable broth for 2 minutes. Stir the heated broth, Parmesan cheese, and butter into the pot.
5. Continue to stir vigorously for 2 to 3 minutes, until the rice is very creamy. (You can add extra warm broth to thin the risotto if necessary.) Season with salt and pepper before serving.

Nutrition:

Carbohydrates: 10 g

Fat: 6 g

Protein: 4 g

Calories: 216

82. Cheesy Spinach Ziti Bake

Preparation time: 5 minutes

Cooking time: 45 minutes

Servings: 6

Ingredients:

- 1 (16-ounce / 454-g) box ziti pasta
- 3 cups marinara sauce
- 1 (10-ounce / 283-g) package frozen chopped spinach, thawed
- Salt and freshly ground black pepper, to taste
- 2 cups Ricotta cheese
- 3 cups shredded Mozzarella cheese, divided

Directions:

1. Preheat the oven to 350°F (180°C).
2. Fill a Dutch oven with water, and bring to a boil over high heat. Add the ziti and cook until al dente, according to the package instructions. Drain the pasta and keep warm.
3. In the Dutch oven over medium-high heat, heat the marinara sauce. Add the spinach and cook for 10 minutes or until the mixture comes to a simmer. Season with salt and pepper, then remove the pot from the heat.
4. Add the drained pasta to the pot, and mix in the Ricotta cheese and 2 cups of the Mozzarella cheese. Make sure everything is well mixed. Sprinkle the remaining cup of Mozzarella cheese on top.
5. Cover the pot, transfer it to the oven, and bake for about 20 minutes, until the pasta is bubbling. Remove the lid and bake for 5 more minutes, until the cheese melts and starts to turn golden. Remove the pot from the oven, and let it cool slightly before serving.

Nutrition:

Carbohydrates: 12 g

Fat: 6 g

Protein: 12 g

Calories: 326

83. Chickpeas Pasta with Cheese

Preparation time: 10 minutes

Cooking time: 30 minutes

Servings: 6

Ingredients:

- 1 (16-ounce / 454-g) box penne pasta
- 2 tablespoons extra-virgin olive oil
- 1 (15-ounce / 425-g) can chickpeas, drained and rinsed
- 10 to 12 ounces (283 to 340 g) baby greens, such as spinach
- 2 cups marinara sauce
- 1/3 cup grated Parmesan cheese, plus more for serving
- Salt and freshly ground black pepper, to taste

Directions:

1. Fill a large Dutch oven with water, and bring to a boil over medium-high heat. Add the pasta and cook for 10 to 12 minutes (or per package directions), until al dente. Drain in a colander, reserving ½ cup of pasta water, and keep warm.
2. In the pot over medium heat, heat the olive oil. Add the chickpeas and greens. Cook for about 5 minutes or until the greens are wilted.
3. Add the cooked pasta, marinara sauce, and reserved pasta water. Reduce the heat to low and cook for another 5 to 10 minutes, until the sauce is thickened and bubbly.
4. Transfer the pasta mixture to a large bowl, and mix in the Parmesan cheese. Season with salt and pepper. Serve with extra Parmesan cheese on top.

Nutrition:

Carbohydrates: 9 g

Fat: 6 g

Protein: 4 g

Calories: 226

84. Cheesy Butter Pasta

Preparation time: 10 minutes

Cooking time: 25 minutes

Servings: 6

Ingredients:

- 1 (16-ounce / 454-g) box medium pasta shells
- 3 tablespoons butter
- 1/3 cup all-purpose flour
- 4 cups low-fat milk
- 1 teaspoon salt
- 8 ounces (227 g) mild Cheddar cheese, shredded
- 8 ounces (227 g) smoked Gouda cheese, shredded

Directions:

1. Fill a Dutch oven with water, and bring to a boil over medium-high heat. Add the pasta shells and cook according to package instructions for al dente (about 6 to 8 minutes). Drain well and keep warm.
2. Add the butter to the pot, and melt it over medium heat. Stir in the flour, and keep stirring to form a thick paste. Mix with a wire whisk, and slowly add the milk and salt.
3. Cook over medium heat for about 10 minutes, until the sauce is thickened and simmering. Make sure to stir to remove any lumps in the sauce constantly.
4. Add both cheeses, a handful at a time, and mix well until the sauce is smooth and thick.
5. Stir in the cooked pasta, and combine well until the pasta is well coated with the cheese sauce.
6. Cook for another 5 minutes, until the pasta is heated through and the sauce has thickened. Serve warm in bowls.

Nutrition:

Carbohydrates: 9 g

Fat: 6 g

Protein: 4 g

Calories: 316

85. Spaghetti with Cheese

Preparation time: 10 minutes

Cooking time: 20 minutes

Servings: 6

Ingredients:

- Salt, to taste
- 1 (16-ounce / 454-g) box thick spaghetti
- 1 teaspoon freshly ground black pepper
- 4 tablespoons butter
- ½ cup freshly grated Parmesan cheese, plus more for serving
- 2 tablespoons extra-virgin olive oil
- Small handful chopped fresh basil or parsley

Directions:

1. Fill a Dutch oven with salted water, and bring to a boil over high heat. Add the spaghetti and cook for 9 minutes or until al dente. Reserve 1 cup of pasta water, then drain the pasta.
2. Add the pepper to the Dutch oven, and toast it over medium heat for 30 seconds. Add the butter and cook for 1 to 2 minutes, until melted.
3. Add the reserved pasta water and the Parmesan cheese. Mix well, so the cheese melts into the pasta water. Add the pasta and toss vigorously, until it is well coated with the cheese sauce. Mix in the olive oil, and season with salt.
4. Sprinkle and toss with the fresh herbs right before serving. Serve with additional Parmesan cheese, if desired.

Nutrition:

Carbohydrates: 11 g

Fat: 6 g

Protein: 4 g

Calories: 326

86. White Bean and Tomato Chili

Preparation time: 10 minutes

Cooking time: 35 minutes

Servings: 4

Ingredients:

- 2 tablespoons extra-virgin olive oil
- 1 medium onion, chopped
- 3 medium sweet potatoes, peeled and cubed
- 1 to 2 tablespoons chili powder (depending how much spice you like)
- 1 (28-ounce / 794-g) can diced tomatoes with chiles
- 2 cups vegetable broth
- 2 (15-ounce / 425-g) cans white cannellini beans, drained and rinsed
- Salt and freshly ground black pepper, to taste

Optional Toppings:

- Shredded Cheddar cheese
- Sour cream
- Chopped scallions, white and green parts
- Sliced avocado
- Chopped fresh cilantro

Directions:

1. In a Dutch oven over medium-high heat, heat the olive oil. Add the onion and cook for 5 minutes or until translucent.
2. Add the sweet potatoes, chili powder, tomatoes, and broth. Cook, stirring constantly, for 5 minutes, then let the mixture come to a boil. Reduce the heat to low, cover, and simmer for 10 minutes, until the sweet potatoes are tender.
3. Stir in the beans and cover the pot. Cook for 10 to 15 minutes more, until the beans are tender and the chili is to your desired thickness. If it gets too thick, add a little water to thin it out.
4. Season with salt and pepper. Serve hot, with optional toppings as desired.

Nutrition:

Carbohydrates: 12 g

Fat: 6 g

Protein: 9 g

Calories: 254

87. Baked Cheese Pizza

Preparation time: 15 minutes

Cooking time: 40 minutes

Servings: 4

Ingredients:

- 1 pound (454 g) pizza dough
- 1 tablespoon extra-virgin olive oil
- 1 cup marinara sauce
- 2 cups shredded Mozzarella cheese, divided

Directions:

1. Preheat the oven to 450°F (235°C). Place your Dutch oven (uncovered) on the lowest rack in your oven so it also preheats.
2. Roll half the pizza dough out to a 10- to 12-inch disk (about the size of the bottom of your Dutch oven). Transfer the dough to a piece of parchment paper, and let it rest for about 10 minutes. If it starts to shrink, roll it out a bit more.
3. When the dough is ready, brush it with the olive oil, then spread ½ cup of the sauce on top of the dough. Top with 1 cup of the cheese.
4. Slide the pizza, paper and all, onto a cutting board or pizza paddle to bring it to the oven. Carefully place the pizza in the Dutch oven by holding onto the edges of the parchment paper and gently dropping it into the pot. The parchment paper will still be under the pizza.
5. Bake for about 15 to 20 minutes, until the crust is golden brown and the cheese is melted. Remove the Dutch oven from the oven, and use the parchment paper to lift the pizza out and onto a board. Cool for 5 minutes before slicing.
6. While you're eating the first pizza, repeat everything for the second pizza.

Nutrition:

Carbohydrates: 10 g

Fat: 6 g

Protein: 4 g

Calories: 196

88. Rice and Quinoa Stuffed Pepper

Preparation time: 10 minutes

Cooking time: 35 minutes

Servings: 4

Ingredients:

- 2 tablespoons olive oil, divided
- 4 medium bell peppers, red, green, or yellow, tops removed and cored
- 1 medium onion, peeled and chopped
- 1 clove garlic, peeled and minced
- 1 (14½-ounce / 411-g) can diced tomatoes, drained
- ¼ teaspoon cumin
- ¼ teaspoon salt
- ¼ teaspoon freshly cracked black pepper
- 1 cup cooked brown rice
- 1 cup cooked quinoa

Directions:

1. Heat oven to 375°F (190°C).
2. Lightly brush bell peppers inside and out with 1 tablespoon olive oil. Place peppers into a Dutch oven and roast 8 to 10 minutes, or until peppers are just starting to become tender. Remove from oven and set aside.
3. Heat the Dutch oven over medium heat add remaining olive oil. Once oil shimmers add onion and cook until tender, about 5 minutes.
4. Add garlic, tomato, cumin, salt, and pepper and cook until tomatoes are heated and the garlic is fragrant, about 3 minutes. Fold in rice and quinoa, then turn off heat.
5. Divide rice mixture evenly among peppers and clean out the Dutch oven, then return the peppers to the Dutch oven and bake, uncovered, for 10 to 15 minutes or until peppers are very tender and filling is hot.

Nutrition:

Carbohydrates: 13 g

Fat: 6 g

Protein: 4 g

Calories: 326

89. Barley Butternut Squash Risotto

Preparation time: 10 minutes

Cooking time: 1 hour

Servings: 6

Ingredients:

- 1 butternut squash, peeled and cut into ½-inch cubes
- 3 tablespoons olive oil, divided
- 1 teaspoon salt, divided
- 1 teaspoon freshly cracked black pepper, divided
- 6 cups vegetable broth
- 1 medium onion, peeled and finely chopped
- 1 clove garlic, peeled and minced
- 1½ cups pearl barley
- ½ cup white wine
- 2 tablespoons finely chopped fresh parsley

Directions:

1. Heat oven to 400°F (205°C).
2. In a large bowl combine butternut squash, 1 tablespoon olive oil, ¼ teaspoon salt, and ¼ teaspoon pepper. Toss to coat squash thoroughly, then transfer to a baking sheet and roast until squash is tender, about 25 to 30 minutes. Remove from the oven and set aside to cool.
3. In a medium saucepan bring vegetable broth to a simmer.
4. In a Dutch oven over medium heat add remaining olive oil. Once it shimmers add onion and cook, stirring often, until tender, about 5 minutes. Add garlic and remaining salt and pepper, and cook until the garlic is fragrant, about 30 seconds.
5. Add barley and cook, stirring frequently, until barley is coated in oil and is lightly toasted, about 5 minutes. Add white wine and cook, stirring constantly, until wine is absorbed, about 2 minutes.
6. Begin ladling in vegetable broth ½ cup at a time, stirring frequently, allowing broth to be absorbed by barley after each addition, about 45 to 50 minutes.
7. Once all the broth is absorbed fold in roasted squash and chopped parsley. Serve immediately.

Nutrition:

Carbohydrates: 6 g

Fat: 6 g

Protein: 4 g

Calories: 316

90. Barley and Mushroom Casserole

Preparation time: 10 minutes

Cooking time: 1 hour

Servings: 6

Ingredients:

- 2 tablespoons unsalted butter
- 1 medium onion, peeled and chopped
- 3 cloves garlic, peeled and minced
- 2 cups sliced cremini mushrooms
- 1 cup sliced button mushrooms
- 1½ cups pearl barley
- ½ cup chopped celery
- 1 teaspoon salt
- ¼ teaspoon pepper
- 1 teaspoon dried thyme leaves
- 3½ cups vegetable broth
- ¼ cup chopped flat-leaf parsley
- ½ cup grated Parmesan cheese

Directions:

1. Heat oven to 350°F (180°C).
2. In a Dutch oven melt butter over medium heat. Add onion and garlic, and cook until just softened, about 3 minutes. Add mushrooms and cook 4 minutes longer.
3. Add barley and cook 5 to 6 minutes, stirring often, until barley is lightly browned. Add celery, salt, pepper, thyme, and broth and bring to a simmer.
4. Bake 50 to 65 minutes, or until barley is tender. Mix in chopped parsley and cheese and serve.

Nutrition:

Carbohydrates: 16 g

Fat: 3 g

Protein: 9 g

Calories: 226

91. Corn and Black Bean Couscous

Preparation time: 10 minutes

Cooking time: 25 minutes

Servings: 8

Ingredients:

- 2 tablespoons olive oil
- 1 (10-ounce / 283-g) bag frozen whole kernel corn
- 1 medium onion, peeled and finely chopped
- 1 medium red bell pepper, seeded and finely chopped
- 2 cloves garlic, peeled and minced
- ¼ teaspoon chili powder
- ¼ teaspoon salt
- ¼ teaspoon freshly cracked black pepper
- 1 cup pearl or Israeli couscous
- 1½ cups vegetable broth
- 1 (14½-ounce / 411-g) can low-sodium black beans, rinsed and drained
- 2 Roma tomatoes, seeded and chopped

Directions:

1. In a Dutch oven over medium heat add olive oil. Once oil starts to shimmer add corn. Cook, stirring often, until corn starts to brown, about 10 minutes.
2. Add onion and bell pepper and cook until they soften slightly, about 5 minutes. Add garlic, chili powder, salt, and pepper and cook until fragrant, about 1 minute.
3. Add couscous and stir well to mix with the vegetables. Add vegetable broth, bring to a boil, then reduce heat to low and cover with the lid. Cook until couscous has absorbed all the liquid, about 10 to 15 minutes.
4. Once couscous has absorbed the liquid remove the lid and fluff with a spoon. Fold in black beans and tomatoes. Serve warm or at room temperature.

Nutrition:

Carbohydrates: 10 g

Fat: 6 g

Protein: 4 g

Calories: 178

92. Roast Chickpeas and Zucchini

Preparation time: 10 minutes

Cooking time: 20 minutes

Servings: 6

Ingredients:

- 4 medium zucchini, cut into ½-inch-thick slices
- 1 (15-ounce / 425-g) can chickpeas, drained and rinsed
- 1 medium onion, peeled and roughly chopped
- 3 tablespoons olive oil
- 1 tablespoon fresh lemon juice
- ½ teaspoon curry powder
- ¼ teaspoon salt
- ¼ teaspoon freshly cracked black pepper
- 2 tablespoons chopped fresh parsley

Directions:

1. Heat oven to 400°F (205°C).
2. In a Dutch oven combine all ingredients expect chopped parsley. Toss until everything is evenly coated.
3. Roast 20 minutes, stirring halfway through the cooking time, or until zucchini and onion are tender. Garnish with chopped parsley. Serve immediately.

Nutrition:

Carbohydrates: 11 g

Fat: 6 g

Protein: 4 g

Calories: 186

93. Lentils with Carrot and Turnip

Preparation time: 10 minutes

Cooking time: 1 hour

Servings: 8

Ingredients:

- 2 medium carrots, peeled and cut into ½-inch pieces
- 1 medium turnip, scrubbed and cut into ½-inch cubes
- 1 medium beet, peeled and cut into ½-inch cubes
- 1 medium sweet potato, peeled and cut into ½-inch pieces
- 2 tablespoons olive oil, divided
- 1 tablespoon honey
- ½ teaspoon salt
- ½ teaspoon freshly cracked black pepper
- 2 cups green lentils
- 4 cups water
- 1 clove garlic, peeled and smashed
- 2 sprigs fresh thyme
- 1 bay leaf
- 2 tablespoons fresh chopped parsley

Directions:

1. In a large bowl add carrot, turnip, beet, sweet potato, 1 tablespoon olive oil, honey, salt, and pepper. Toss to coat, then let stand at room temperature 30 minutes.
2. Heat oven to 425°F (220°C).
3. Spread vegetables out on a baking sheet in a single layer. Roast until vegetables are tender, about 25 to 30 minutes. Remove from oven and let cool.
4. In a Dutch oven combine lentils, water, garlic, thyme, and bay leaf. Bring mixture to a simmer over medium heat, then reduce the heat to medium-low and cook lentils at a bare simmer until they are tender, adding additional water if needed to keep them covered, about 30 minutes.
5. Drain lentils, discard garlic, thyme, and bay leaf, and return lentils to the Dutch oven.
6. Add remaining olive oil and roasted vegetables to lentils and toss to combine. Garnish with chopped parsley. Serve warm or room temperature.

Nutrition:

Carbohydrates: 13 g

Fat: 6 g

Protein: 10 g

Calories: 226

94. Cauliflower with Chickpeas

Preparation time: 10 minutes

Cooking time: 15 minutes

Servings: 6

Ingredients:

- 1 medium white onion, peeled and chopped
- 1 tablespoon olive oil
- 5 tablespoons yellow or black mustard seeds
- 1 head cauliflower, divided into florets
- Pinch salt
- 1 (15-ounce / 425-g) can chickpeas, drained and rinsed
- ¼ cup white wine

Directions:

1. Place a Dutch oven over medium heat. Once the Dutch oven is heated add onion, olive oil, and mustard seeds. Stir frequently and let onion cook until it starts to turn brown, about 8 minutes.
2. Add the cauliflower florets to the Dutch oven with a sprinkle of salt.
3. Stir to combine and cook 4 minutes. Add chickpeas to the Dutch oven with white wine. Stir to combine.
4. Cover the Dutch oven and cook 3 to 4 minutes. Remove the lid and let liquid evaporate. Serve when cauliflower is fork tender.

Nutrition:

Carbohydrates: 19 g

Fat: 6 g

Protein: 4 g

Calories: 209

95. Spinach and Mushroom Curry

Preparation time: 10 minutes

Cooking time: 30 minutes

Servings: 6

Ingredients:

- ¼ cup jarred green curry paste
- 2 cups vegetable broth
- 1 large sweet potato, peeled and cut into ½-inch cubes
- ¼ pound (113 g) green beans, stems removed
- 8 ounces (227 g) sliced button mushrooms
- 8 ounces (227 g) fresh spinach leaves
- Juice from 1 medium lime
- 1 (14-ounce / 397-g) can coconut milk

Directions:

1. Place a Dutch oven over medium heat. Once it is heated, add curry paste and vegetable broth and stir to combine.
2. Stir in sweet potato cubes, cover, and cook 15 to 20 minutes or until you can pierce them with a fork. Stir the contents occasionally to keep them from sticking.
3. Turn heat to medium-high and remove the lid. Add remaining vegetables and cook 5 to 7 minutes, stirring frequently.
4. Once liquid has reduced, lower the heat to medium-low and add lime juice and coconut milk. Keep coconut milk from boiling and cook 2 to 3 minutes. Serve.

Nutrition:

Carbohydrates: 17 g

Fat: 6 g

Protein: 4 g

Calories: 324

96. Okra Corn and Tomato Stew

Preparation time: 15 minutes

Cooking time: 30 minutes

Servings: 4

Ingredients:

- 3 tablespoons oil or unsalted butter
- 1 medium onion, peeled and finely diced
- 1 small green bell pepper, seeded and finely diced
- 1 stalk celery, finely diced
- 2 cloves garlic, peeled and minced
- 2 cups sliced okra
- 2 cups diced ripe tomatoes
- 2 cups fresh corn kernels
- 1 cup water or vegetable broth
- ¼ teaspoon cayenne
- 1 green onion, sliced
- 2 tablespoons minced fresh parsley
- ½ teaspoon salt
- ¼ teaspoon freshly cracked black pepper

Directions:

1. In a Dutch oven, heat oil or butter over medium-high heat. Add onion, green pepper, celery, and garlic, and cook until tender, about 5 minutes.
2. Add okra and cook, stirring constantly, 3 minutes or until okra begins to release thick liquid.
3. Add tomatoes, corn, and water or broth. Bring to a boil then reduce heat to medium-low and simmer, stirring often and adding more liquid if needed, 20 minutes, or until corn is tender.
4. Stir in cayenne, green onion, parsley, salt, and pepper. Remove the Dutch oven from heat. Serve.

Nutrition:

Carbohydrates: 13 g

Fat: 6 g

Protein: 14 g

Calories: 326

97. Ratatouille with Tomato

Preparation time: 15 minutes

Cooking time: 25 minutes

Servings: 6

Ingredients:

- 1 medium eggplant, diced
- 2 teaspoons salt, divided
- 2 tablespoons olive oil
- 1 small onion, peeled and diced
- 1 large green bell pepper, seeded and diced
- 3 cloves garlic, peeled and minced
- 1 large zucchini, diced
- 2 medium yellow squash, diced
- 4 ounces (113 g) white mushrooms, quartered
- 1 (28-ounce / 794-g) can crushed tomatoes
- 1 teaspoon dried Italian seasoning mix
- ¼ teaspoon freshly cracked black pepper
- ¼ cup chopped fresh basil leaves

Diirections:

1. Sprinkle eggplant with 1½ teaspoons salt and leave in a colander 1 hour.
2. Rinse eggplant well and pat dry with paper towels.
3. In a Dutch oven heat olive oil over medium-high heat. Once oil shimmers add onion, bell pepper, and garlic. Cook until just tender, about 3 minutes.
4. Add eggplant, zucchini, squash, and mushrooms to the Dutch oven. Pour in crushed tomatoes and Italian seasoning, then reduce heat to medium and simmer 10 to 15 minutes or until eggplant is tender.
5. Season with remaining salt and pepper and then stir in fresh basil. Remove the Dutch oven from the heat and allow to stand 5 minutes before serving.

Nutrition:

Carbohydrates: 20 g

Fat: 6 g

Protein: 4 g

Calories: 287

Chapter 6. Side and Appetizer Dishes

98. Korean Fried Chicken

Preparation time: 10 minutes

Cooking time: 20 minutes

Servings: 4

Ingredients:

- 2 pounds of chicken wings
- 1/4 cup and 2 tablespoons sugar
- 1 ½ teaspoon salt
- ¾ teaspoon ground black pepper
- 1/2 cup soy sauce
- 2 cups olive oil

Directions:

1. Take a 4-quart Dutch oven, place it over medium-high heat, add oil, and bring it to 300 degrees F.
2. Meanwhile, prepare chicken wings, and for this, season them with salt and black pepper.
3. Add chicken wings into the hot oil in a single layer and cook for 3 minutes per side until browned.
4. Take a small saucepan, place it over medium-high heat, pour in soy sauce, and bring it to boil.
5. Then switch heat to the low level, simmer the sauce for 3 minutes and then pour into a large bowl.
6. Add chicken wings into soy sauce, toss until well coated, and then serve.

Nutrition: Per Serving:

Calories: 146;

Total Fat: 8.1 g;

Saturated Fat: 1.4 g;

Protein: 5.4 g;

Carbs: 13 g;

Fiber: 0.5 g;

Sugar: 6 g

99. Scallion Baked Beans

Preparation time: 15 minutes

Cooking time: 4 hours

Servings: 12

Ingredients:

- 1 pound dried white beans, soaked overnight
- 2 medium yellow squash, sliced, divided
- 2 medium white onions, peeled, sliced
- 1 bunch of scallions, trimmed
- 3 cloves of garlic, peeled, sliced
- ¾ teaspoon salt
- 2 sprigs of thyme
- 1/3 teaspoon ground black pepper
- 1 tablespoon honey
- 2 tablespoons Dijon mustard
- 1 tablespoon apple cider vinegar
- 1/4 cup olive oil, divided
- 4 cup chicken stock
- 1 cup of water

Directions:

1. Switch on the oven, then set it to 300 degrees F and let it preheat.
2. Take a 4-quart Dutch oven, place it over medium-high heat, add 2 tablespoons oil and when hot, add onions, season with salt and black pepper and cook for 10 minutes until golden brown.
3. Add slices of 1 squash along with thyme and garlic, cook for 10 minutes, then stir in honey and mustard, add beans, pour in stock and water, and stir until mixed and bake for 2 hours until beans are almost tender, covering the pan.
4. Meanwhile, place remaining oil in a bowl, add remaining slices of squash along with scallion, season with salt and black pepper to taste and toss until mixed.
5. Top beans with scallion mixture, stir in vinegar and continue baking for 1 hour and 30 minutes until beans are tender, uncovering the pan.
6. Then switch on the broiler, bake for 6 minutes until squash pieces are slightly charred, and when done, let cool for 10 minutes.
7. Serve straight away.

Nutrition:

Per Serving: Calories: 150; Total Fat: 1 g; Saturated Fat: 0 g; Protein: 7 g; Carbs: 30 g; Fiber: 5 g; Sugar: 12 g

100. Old Bay French Fries

Preparation time: 10 minutes

Cooking time: 30 minutes

Servings: 6

Ingredients:

- 3 pounds russet potatoes, cut into ½-inch sticks
- ½ teaspoon ground black pepper
- 1 teaspoon salt
- 2 teaspoons Old Bay seasoning
- 3 quarts peanut oil

Directions:

1. Cut potatoes into sticks, place them in a large bowl, pour in enough cold water to cover the potatoes and let them stand for 1 hour.
2. Then take a 4-quart Dutch oven, place it over medium-high heat, add oil and bring it to 325 degrees F.
3. Drain the potatoes, pat dry with paper towels and cook them into heated oil in four batches for 7 to 10 minutes until golden browned.
4. Transfer fries to a plate lined with paper towels, then season fries with Old Bay seasoning, black pepper, and salt, toss until mixed and serve.

Nutrition: Per Serving:

Calories: 179;

Total Fat: 8.5 g;

Saturated Fat: 1.3 g;

Protein: 2 g;

Carbs: 24 g;

Fiber: 2.2 g;

Sugar: 0.2 g

101. Crab Hush Puppies

Preparation time: 10 minutes

Cooking time: 20 minutes

Servings: 8

Ingredients:

- 8 ounces crabmeat
- 1/2 cup all-purpose flour
- 2 scallions, chopped
- 1 cup ground cornmeal
- 1 tablespoon chopped fresh chives
- ¾ teaspoon salt
- 1/4 teaspoon baking soda
- 1/2 teaspoon cayenne pepper
- 3/4 cup baking powder
- 1 cup buttermilk
- 1 cup grated Gruyere cheese
- 1 egg
- 6 cups canola oil

Directions:

1. Take a 4-quart Dutch oven, place it over medium-high heat, add oil, and bring it to 350 degrees F.
2. Meanwhile, place flour in a bowl, add remaining ingredients and whisk well until incorporated.
3. Drop the crab mixture into the hot oil, don't over-crowd the pan, and cook for 5 minutes until fried.
4. When done, transfer hush puppies onto a plate lined with paper towels and then serve.

Nutrition: Per Serving:

Calories: 580;

Total Fat: 32 g;

Saturated Fat: 6 g;

Protein: 9 g;

Carbs: 65 g;

Fiber: 3 g;

Sugar: 13 g

102. Chicken Pesto with Pasta

Preparation time: 10 minutes

Cooking time: 50 minutes

Servings: 8

Ingredients:

- 2 cups cubed chicken, rotisserie
- 1/4 cup toasted pine nuts
- 2 medium tomatoes, chopped
- 7 ounces basil pesto
- 16 ounces cellentani pasta, cooked

Directions:

1. Take a 4-quart Dutch oven, place it over medium-high heat, pour in salted water to cook pasta, bring it to boil, then add pasta and cook for 10 minutes until tender.
2. Drain the pasta, return pan over medium heat, add chicken tomatoes and pesto, return pasta in the pan and stir until mixed.
3. Cook for 5 minutes until thoroughly heated, then sprinkle with nuts and serve.

Nutrition:

Per Serving: Calories: 404; Total Fat: 16 g; Saturated Fat: 3 g; Protein: 20 g; Carbs: 46 g; Fiber: 3 g; Sugar: 4 g

103. Peas with Collard Greens

Preparation time: 10 minutes

Cooking time: 20 minutes

Servings: 4

Ingredients:

- 31 ounce cooked black-eyed peas
- 8 cups chopped collard greens
- 4 tomatoes, deseeded, chopped
- 1/4 teaspoon cayenne pepper
- ½ teaspoon minced garlic
- 1/2 teaspoon salt
- 2 tablespoons olive oil
- 1/4 cup lemon juice
- 2 tablespoons grated Parmesan cheese

Directions:

1. Take a 4-quart Dutch oven, place it over medium-high heat, add oil and when hot, add garlic and cook for 1 minute.
2. Then add greens, season with cayenne pepper and salt, cook for 8 minutes until greens are softened, then add remaining ingredients, except for cheese and stir until mixed.
3. Cook for 5 minutes until thoroughly heated, then stir in cheese and serve.

104. Creamed Corn

Preparation time: 5 minutes

Cooking time: 15 minutes

Servings: 8

Ingredients:

- 1/3 cup all-purpose flour
- 40 ounces frozen corn, thawed
- 2 tablespoons sugar
- 1/2 teaspoon ground black pepper
- 2 teaspoons salt
- 1/4 cup unsalted butter, cubed
- 1/2 cup shredded cheddar cheese
- 2 cups milk, unsweetened
- 1 cup half-and-half cream
- 2 tablespoons minced parsley

Directions:

1. Take a 4-quart Dutch oven, place it over medium heat and when hot, add corn, cream, and butter, season with black pepper, salt, and sugar, stir until mixed and cook for 10 minutes until thoroughly heated.

2. Whisk together flour and milk until combined, pour into the pan, bring the mixture to boil, and continue cooking for 2 minutes until thickened.

Nutrition: Per Serving:

Calories: 177;

Total Fat: 5 g;

Saturated Fat: 1 g;

Protein: 9 g;

Carbs: 24 g;

Fiber: 6 g;

Sugar: 3 g

3. Stir in cheese, cook for 2 minutes until it has melted, then top with parsley and serve.

Nutrition: Per Serving:

Calories: 234;

Total Fat: 9 g;

Saturated Fat: 6 g;

Protein: 8 g;

Carbs: 33 g;

Fiber: 3 g;

Sugar: 8 g

105. Buffalo Sloppy Joes

Preparation time: 10 minutes

Cooking time: 15 minutes

Servings: 8

Ingredients:

- 1 medium white onion, peeled, chopped
- 2 pounds ground turkey
- 2 celery ribs, chopped
- 1 ½ teaspoon minced garlic
- 1 medium carrot, grated
- 1/4 teaspoon ground black pepper
- 2 tablespoons brown sugar
- 8 ounces tomato sauce
- 1 tablespoon Worcestershire sauce
- 1/4 cup hot sauce
- 2 tablespoons red wine vinegar
- 1/2 cup chicken broth
- 8 hamburger buns, split

Directions:

1. Take a 4-quart Dutch oven, place it over medium heat, add turkey, onion, celery, carrot, and garlic, stir well and cook for 10 minutes until no longer pink.

2. Then add remaining ingredients, except for buns, stir until mixed and cook for 5 minutes until thoroughly heated.

3. Serve mixture on buns.

Nutrition: Per Serving:

Calories: 279;

Total Fat: 3 g;

Saturated Fat: 0 g;

Protein: 33 g;

Carbs: 30 g;

Fiber: 2 g;

Sugar: 9 g

106. Garlic Mashed Potatoes

Preparation time: 5 minutes

Cooking time: 18 minutes

Servings: 6

Ingredients:

- 2 1/2 pounds red potatoes, peeled, 1 inch cubed
- 1 teaspoon ground black pepper
- 1 ½ teaspoon salt
- 10 cloves garlic, peeled
- 4 tablespoons unsalted butter
- 1/2 cup buttermilk

Directions:

1. Take a 4-quart Dutch oven, place it over medium-high heat, add potatoes and garlic, then pour in enough water to cover vegetables by 1 inch, stir in salt and bring to boil.

2. Then switch heat to medium-low level and simmer potatoes for 10 minutes until very tender.

3. Meanwhile, take a small saucepan, place it over low heat, add butter and when it melts, whisk in milk and cook for 1 minute until hot, remove the pan from heat.

4. Drain the cooked potatoes and garlic, return them into the pan, mash well,

and then stir in milk mixture until incorporated.

5. Season mashed potatoes with salt and black pepper and then serve.

Nutrition: Per Serving:

Calories: 252;

Total Fat: 9.6 g;

Saturated Fat: 5.6 g;

Protein: 8.6 g;

Carbs: 34 g;

Fiber: 2.7 g;

Sugar: 3.2 g

107. Almond and Herb Couscous

Preparation time: 5 minutes

Cooking time: 10 minutes

Servings: 8

Ingredients:

- 2 cups couscous, uncooked
- 2/3 cup sliced almonds
- 2/3 cup chopped parsley
- 2 teaspoons minced garlic
- 1 teaspoon smoked paprika
- 3/4 teaspoon salt
- 2 tablespoons olive oil
- 2 1/4 cups water

Directions:

1. Take a 4-quart Dutch oven, place it over medium heat, add oil and when hot, add garlic and almonds and cook for 2 minutes until fragrant.

2. Then stir in paprika, cook for 10 seconds, pour in water, stir and bring it to a boil.

3. Remove pan from heat, stir in salt and couscous and let it stand for 5 minutes until all the liquid is absorbed by couscous, covering the pan.

4. Fluff couscous with a fork, stir in parsley and then serve.

Nutrition: Per Serving:

Calories: 242;

Total Fat: 7.6 g;

Saturated Fat: 0.8 g;

Protein: 7.4 g;

Carbs: 36.1 g;

Fiber: 3.4 g;

Sugar: 0.4 g

108. Golden Onion Rings

Preparation time: 10 minutes

Cooking time: 10 minutes

Servings: 4

Ingredients:

- 3 large Walla Walla (or Vidalia) sweet onions, peeled and cut into ½-inch-thick slices
- 1 egg, separated
- 1 cup milk
- 8 cups plus 1 tablespoon vegetable oil for deep-frying, divided
- ¾ cup plus 2 tablespoons all-purpose flour
- 2 teaspoons kosher salt
- 1½ teaspoons baking powder
- Sea salt, for sprinkling

Directions:

1. Separate the onions into rings. Cover with cold water for 30 minutes. Drain well on paper towels. In a large bowl, mix together the egg yolk, milk, and 1 tablespoon of the oil. In a medium bowl, mix together the flour, salt, and baking powder and add to the liquid mixture, blending into a smooth batter.

2. Heat the remaining 8 cups oil in a Dutch oven over medium heat to 360°F (182°C). Meanwhile, beat

the egg white until stiff and fold into the batter.

3. Dip the onion slices into the batter and fry in the hot oil until golden, turning once. Drain on paper towels and sprinkle with sea salt. Serve right away!

Nutrition:

Carbohydrates: 16 g

Fat: 6 g

Protein: 4 g

Calories: 326

109. Tomato and Cauliflower Antipasto

Preparation time: 10 minutes

Cooking time: 40 minutes

Servings: 4

Ingredients:

- ¼ cup extra-virgin olive oil
- 1 cup diced celery
- 1½ cups peeled and diced carrots
- 2½ cups diced yellow onion
- 6 cloves garlic, minced
- 4 cups sliced cauliflower florets
- 2 cups diced firm zucchini (the smaller dice the better)
- 2 (6-ounce / 170-g) cans tomato sauce
- ¼ cup tomato paste
- ¼ cup small capers
- 2 (8-ounce / 227-g) jars pearl onions, drained
- ½ cup chopped sweet pickles
- ½ cup chopped Kalamata olives
- 1 cup sliced pimento-stuffed green olives
- 2 (2-ounce / 57-g) jars quartered olive oil-marinated artichoke hearts, undrained

- ½ cup red wine vinegar
- ¼ cup sugar
- 1 small tin anchovy fillets, drained and chopped
- 1 cup chopped fresh basil
- ½ cup chopped fresh parsley

Directions:

1. Pour the oil into an enameled Dutch oven over medium heat. Add the celery, carrots, onions, garlic, and cauliflower, and braise in the oil, covered, for 5 minutes. Add the zucchini, and steam, covered, for 3 minutes more. Mix in the tomato sauce, tomato paste, capers, pearl onions, sweet pickle, kalamata and green olives, artichoke hearts, vinegar, sugar, and anchovy fillets. Cook, uncovered, for 5 minutes.
2. Refrigerate for several days before serving to let the flavors mingle together. Add the basil and parsley just before serving.

Nutrition:

Carbohydrates: 21 g

Fat: 6 g

Protein: 14 g

Calories: 336

110. Egg and Butter Spaetzle

Preparation time: 5 minutes

Cooking time: 10 minutes

Servings: 4

Ingredients:

- 2 cups all-purpose flour
- 3 large eggs
- ½ cup whole milk
- 1 teaspoon kosher salt, plus more for seasoning
- 4 tablespoons butter (½ stick), melted
- Freshly ground black pepper, to taste

Directions:

1. Fill a Dutch oven with water and bring it to a boil over medium-high heat. In a medium bowl mix together with a fork the flour, eggs, milk, and salt.
2. Put ½ cup of the noodle dough into the spaetzle maker or a potato ricer (using the large hole disk). Firmly squeeze the squiggly noodles into the boiling water. Use a knife to cut away any remaining noodles.
3. Cook for 2 minutes. Remove the noodles from the water with a large slotted spoon and put them in a colander to drain. Continue this process until all of the dough is gone.

4. Transfer the spaetzle to a medium glass baking dish and mix with the butter. Season with salt and pepper. When ready to serve, reheat in the microwave or in a 10- or 12-inch skillet over low heat.

Nutrition:

Carbohydrates: 21 g

Fat: 6 g

Protein: 4 g

Calories: 226

111. Buffalo Style Cauliflower

Preparation time: 15 minutes

Cooking time: 25 minutes

Servings: 4

Ingredients:

- 2 Tbsp olive oil
- 1 head cauliflower
- Salt and pepper, to taste
- 2 Tbsp unsalted butter
- ¼ cup Frank's red hot sauce
- 1 Tbsp fresh lime juice
- Chopped parsley or cilantro

Directions:

1. Preheat oven to 375°F.
2. Chop off tough flower part at the base of the cauliflower. Break into small to medium sized florets.
3. In a microwave-safe bowl, melt butter.
4. Add hot sauce and lime juice to butter and stir.
5. Heat Dutch oven to medium-low heat.

6. Add oil and cauliflower florets. Saute until nicely browned, 4-5 minutes.
7. Pour in hot sauce mixture and stir to coat evenly.
8. Place in oven for 15-20 minutes, until cauliflower is softened.
9. Remove from oven and sprinkle with parsley or cilantro.

Nutrition:

Carbohydrates – 4.7 g

Fat – 12.9 g

Protein – 1.5 g

Calories – 132

112. Crispy Asian Green Beans

Preparation time: 5 minutes

Cooking time: 5 minutes

Servings: 4

Ingredients:

- 1 tsp peanut oil
- 1 pound green beans, ends trimmed
- 2 cloves garlics, minced
- Coarse sea salt, to taste
- ½ tsp toasted sesame oil

Directions:

1. Heat Dutch oven on medium heat and add peanut oil until it shimmers.
2. Add garlic and cook about 30 seconds.
3. Add green beans and salt to the pan and roast until golden brown. I
4. At the last minute of cooking, drizzle on toasted sesame oil.

Nutrition:

Carbohydrates – 8.6 g

Fat – 1.9 g

Protein – 2.2 g   Calories – 52

113. Riederalp Swiss Fondue

Preparation time: 15 minutes

Cooking time: 15 minutes

Servings: 6

Ingredients:

- 2 cups grated Emmenthaler cheese
- 2 cups grated Gruyère cheese
- 2 Tbsp cornstarch
- 1 cup dry white wine
- 1 Tbsp Kirschwasser
- Sliced apples and cubed bread, for serving

Directions:

1. In a bowl, mix the two cheeses and the cornstarch with a wooden spoon.
2. Pour the wine and kirschwasser into a 2-quart Dutch oven and bring to a gentle simmer over medium-low heat.
3. Add the cheese mixture to the liquid, a handful at a time, and stir until all the cheese is melted.
4. Serve fondue in a bowl over the fire. With a fondue fork, stab a slice of apple or a cube of bread and dip into the melted cheese.

Nutrition:

Carbohydrates – 9.6 g

Fat – 3.9 g

Protein – 7.5 g

Calories – 302

114. Crunchy Parmesan and Garlic Zucchini

Directions:
1. Preheat oven to 450°F.
2. Heat oil in a large Dutch oven on medium-low heat.
3. Add zucchini and let brown on one side for 3 minutes and flip over pieces. Cook for another 3 minutes.
4. Sprinkle with salt and pepper.
5. Add sliced garlic and saute for 1 minute.
6. Sprinkle panko crumbs and grated cheese on top.
7. Transfer to oven until brown and bubbly, about 5-10 minutes.

Nutrition:

Carbohydrates – 12.2 g

Fat – 8.3 g

Protein – 3.6 g

Calories – 135

Preparation time: 15 minutes

Cooking time: 20 minutes

Servings: 4

Ingredients:
- 3 Tbsp olive oil
- 4-6 small green zucchini, sliced into spears by cutting into ½ lengthwise and then into thirds
- Coarse salt and pepper, to taste
- 4 garlic cloves, sliced thin
- 1 cup panko crumbs, seasoned with salt, pepper and paprika
- 1 cup freshly grated parmesan

115. Garlicky-Lemon Zucchini

Preparation time: 5 minutes

Cooking time: 5 minutes

Servings: 2

Ingredients:

- 4 small green zucchini, any color, sliced about ¼-inch thick
- 1½ Tbsp extra virgin olive oil
- 1 Tbsp garlic, minced
- Coarse salt and black pepper, to taste
- ½ tsp thyme, minced
- ½ lemon

Directions:

1. Heat Dutch oven over medium-low heat. Add oil and let heat for 1 minute.
2. Sprinkle zucchini with salt and pepper.
3. Add to the pan in a single layer. When zucchini is nicely browned, flip and brown on other side.
4. Add garlic and saute for 1 minute.
5. Sprinkle thyme and additional salt if necessary.
6. Remove from pan and squeeze lemon juice on zucchini.

Nutrition:

Carbohydrates – 7 g

Fat – 7 g

Protein – 1.6 g

Calories – 93

116. Ginger-Infused Kabocha Squash

Preparation time: 15 minutes

Cooking time: 10 minutes

Servings: 4

Ingredients:

- 2 Tbsp canola oil
- 1 piece ginger, peeled, cut into thin strips
- Kosher salt and pepper, to taste
- 1-2 tsp maple syrup
- 1 kabocha squash, peeled, seeded and cut into 1½ inch pieces

Directions:

1. Preheat oven to 400°F.
2. Heat Dutch oven over medium heat and add oil.
3. Cook ginger in oil until fragrant, 1-2 minutes.
4. Toss squash in a bowl with salt, pepper and maple syrup.
5. Add squash to the pot and sear for 2 minutes on each side or until browned.
6. Cover Dutch oven and place in oven until squash cooks through, for 5-7 minutes.

Nutrition:

Carbohydrates – 4.9 g

Fat – 7.1 g

Protein – 0.4 g

Calories – 82

117. Glazed Carrots

Preparation time: 3 minutes

Cooking time: 10 minutes

Servings: 4

Ingredients:

- 6 carrots, peeled and cut into thirds crosswise, then cut into halves for spears
- 3 Tbsp butter
- 2 tsp honey
- Coarse salt and pepper, to taste
- ¼-½ cup water
- ½ tsp chopped thyme
- Bunch flat leaf parsley, chopped

Directions:

1. Heat Dutch oven over medium heat.
2. Melt butter and place carrots in the pot, cut side down. Carrots will brown quickly, about 3 minutes.
3. Add honey, salt, pepper, water and thyme and stir constantly until carrots are cooked and coated with honey, about 4-5 minutes.
4. Sprinkle fresh parsley on top.

Nutrition:

Carbohydrates – 12.2 g

Fat – 8.3 g

Protein – 3.6 g

Calories – 135

118. Herbed Focaccia Bread

Nutrition:

Carbohydrates – 2.8 g

Fat – 10.8 g

Protein – 3.3 g

Calories – 118

Preparation time: 15 minutes

Cooking time: 30 minutes

Servings: 6

Ingredients:

- 1 package pizza dough, defrosted if necessary
- Flour for dusting
- 3 Tbsp extra virgin olive oil
- 1 Tbsp prepared minced garlic
- 2 tsp chopped fresh rosemary
- Salt and pepper, to taste
- 2 Tbsp grated Romano cheese

Directions:

1. Preheat your Dutch oven to 400°F.
2. Roll out pizza dough on floured surface. Stretch out to a 12-inch circle.
3. Remove the pot from oven and coat with 1 Tbsp olive oil.
4. Add dough to Dutch oven and carefully stretch up the sides.
5. Sprinkle with remaining olive oil, garlic, rosemary, salt, pepper and cheese.
6. Bake until golden brown, about 30 minutes.
7. Slice into wedges.

119. Pancetta and Asparagus with Fried Egg

Preparation time: 15 minutes

Cooking time: 10 minutes

Servings: 4

Ingredients:

- 1 Tbsp olive oil
- ¼ pound pancetta
- 3 small shallots, sliced thin
- ½ lb asparagus, tough ends broken off
- Salt and pepper, to taste
- 2 eggs

Directions:

1. Heat olive oil in Dutch oven.
2. Fry the pancetta, stirring frequently. Transfer to a plate.
3. Add shallots and cook for 2 minutes.
4. Add asparagus pieces and saute for several minutes.
5. Sprinkle with salt and pepper and continue to watch closely that asparagus is browned and cooked through.
6. Add pancetta back to the pan and stir together. Transfer to a plate.
7. Add a little oil if necessary and fry an egg in pan.
8. Top asparagus pancetta mixture with fried egg and season with salt and pepper.

Nutrition:

Carbohydrates – 3.4 g

Fat – 17.6 g

Protein – 14.6 g

Calories – 229

120. Laqua Family Slow-Cooked Beans

Preparation time: 15 minutes

Cooking time: 2 hours 10 minutes

Servings: 8

Ingredients:

- 2 cups Great Northern beans
- 8 cups water, divided
- 4 celery stalks, cut in half
- 2 chicken bouillon cubes
- 2 bay leaves
- 1 clove garlic, minced
- 1 tsp ground cloves
- ¼ tsp ground ginger
- 2 Tbsp brown sugar
- 2 cups chopped yellow onion
- 2 Tbsp Dijon mustard
- 1 cup diced canned tomatoes, drained
- ¾ cup tomato sauce
- 3 Tbsp tomato paste
- 1½ lbs smoked ham hock (cut into 4 pieces)

Directions:

1. Soak the beans overnight in water in a 5½-quart Dutch oven. Drain the next day.
2. Add 6 cups of the water to the pot.
3. In a small saucepan, boil the celery stalks in the remaining 2 cups water until tender. Discard the celery stalks.
4. Pour 1 cup of the celery liquid into a small bowl. Add the bouillon cubes, bay leaves, garlic, cloves, ginger, sugar, onions, and mustard.
5. Pour this mixture into the pot with the beans. Cook for 40 minutes over medium-low heat.
6. Meanwhile, preheat the oven to 325 F.
7. Add the tomatoes, tomato sauce, tomato paste, and ham hock to Dutch oven and transfer to the oven. Bake until tender for 1½ hours. Serve warm.

Nutrition:

Carbohydrates – 9.8 g

Fat – 7.6 g

Protein – 4.4 g

Calories – 207

121. Golden Hash Brown Cake

Preparation time: 2 minutes

Cooking time: 20 minutes

Servings: 6

Ingredients:

- 6 russet potatoes, peeled and coarsely grated
- 2 tsp kosher salt
- ¼ tsp fresh black pepper
- 6 Tbsp vegetable oil

Directions:

1. Rinse potatoes in a colander and squeeze out excess moisture. Transfer to a bowl and season with salt and pepper.
2. Heat Dutch oven over medium heat. Add the oil and allow to smoke.
3. Add potatoes and press down firmly with a spatula. Cook until sides and bottom are golden brown, about 15 minutes.
4. Once cooled, flip Dutch oven onto a plate and invert hash browns. Place back in the Dutch oven with a drop of oil and cook until reverse side browns nicely. Top with additional sea salt.

Nutrition:

Carbohydrates – 25.2 g

Fat – 10.4 g

Protein – 2.7 g

Calories – 201

Chapter 7. Pasta, Pizza and Rice

122. Ginger-Scented Rice

Preparation time: 10 minutes

Cooking time: 1 hour 15 minutes

Servings: 2

Ingredients:

- 1 cup brown basmati rice
- 2 teaspoons unrefined coconut oil
- 2¼ cups boiling water
- ½ teaspoon salt
- 1 (1-inch) piece fresh ginger, halved

Directions:

1. Preheat the oven. Preheat the oven to 375°F.
2. Rinse the rice. Place the rice in a medium bowl, then fill the bowl with water. Swirl the rice with your hands. Drain.
3. Dry the rice and add the oil. In a Dutch oven over medium heat, cook the rice, stirring, for about 3 minutes or until the grains are dry. Add the coconut oil and stir to coat the rice.
4. Add the water and cook the rice. Add the boiling water, salt, and ginger. Cover the pot and bake for about 1 hour, until all the water is absorbed.
5. Steam and fluff the rice. Remove the pot and let the rice steam, covered, for 10 minutes. Using a spatula, fluff the rice. Remove and discard the ginger before serving.

VARIATION TIP: Instead of coconut oil, add 1 tablespoon of unsalted butter for a richer flavor.

Nutrition:

Carbohydrates: 6 g

Fat: 6 g

Protein: 4 g

Calories: 126

123. Lemony Quinoa and Kale Salad

Preparation time: 15 minutes

Cooking time: 35 minutes

Servings: 4

Ingredients:

- ¼ cup olive oil, plus more for seasoning
- 2 tablespoons pine nuts
- 2 garlic cloves, minced
- ¼ teaspoon red pepper flakes
- 1 cup white quinoa
- 1 teaspoon salt, divided
- 1¾ cups boiling water
- Juice of 3 lemons, plus more for seasoning
- 1 (2.25-ounce) can sliced black olives, drained
- 1 bunch curly kale, ribbed and roughly chopped
- 1 bunch fresh parsley, finely chopped
- 4 Roma tomatoes, seeded and chopped

Directions:

1. Infuse the oil and make the sauce. In a Dutch oven over medium heat, combine the olive oil, pine nuts, garlic, and red pepper flakes.
2. Warm for about 2 minutes, just until the pine nuts begin to lightly brown, then transfer the mixture to a large bowl and set aside.
3. Rinse and cook the quinoa. Place the quinoa in a fine-mesh sieve, and rinse it well. Transfer the quinoa to the Dutch oven; add ½ teaspoon of salt and the boiling water.
4. Place the pot over high heat and bring the water back to a boil. Reduce the heat to low, cover the pot, and simmer for 15 minutes. Remove from the heat and let the quinoa steam, covered, for 10 minutes.
5. Make the kale salad. Add the lemon juice and the remaining ½ teaspoon of salt to the bowl with the olive oil and pine nuts.
6. Stir well, then add the black olives, kale, parsley, and tomatoes, tossing to coat. Using a fork, fluff the quinoa, then, a bit at a time, mix it into the kale salad.
7. Taste and adjust the seasoning, adding extra lemon juice, olive oil, or salt as desired. Serve cold or at room temperature. Refrigerate leftovers, which keep very well, for up to 4 days.

Nutrition:

Carbohydrates: 12 g

Fat: 6 g

Protein: 4 g

Calories: 226

124. Spanakorizo

Preparation time: 10 minutes

Cooking time: 1 hour

Servings: 6

Ingredients:

- ½ cup olive oil
- 1 yellow or white onion, chopped
- 6 scallions, thinly sliced
- 1 cup medium-grain brown rice
- ¼ cup freshly squeezed lemon juice
- 1 tablespoon finely chopped fresh dill
- 1 teaspoon salt
- 2½ cups water
- 1 pound fresh baby spinach

Directions:

1. Sweat the onions. In a Dutch oven over medium heat, heat the olive oil. Add the onion and scallions and sweat for about 8 minutes until soft, stirring occasionally.
2. Cook the rice. Stir in the rice, lemon juice, dill, salt, and water. Bring to a boil over high heat. Cover the pot, reduce the heat to medium-low, and simmer for 40 minutes, or until most of the water is absorbed.
3. Stir in the spinach. Turn off the heat and stir in the spinach. Re-cover the

pot and let steam for 10 minutes. Transfer the pilaf to a serving platter. Refrigerate leftovers for up to 4 days.

Nutrition:

Carbohydrates: 11 g

Fat: 6 g

Protein: 4 g

Calories: 186

125. Salmon Congee with Sesame

Preparation time: 10 minutes

Cooking time: 45 minutes

Servings: 6

Ingredients:

- ¼ cup sesame seeds
- 4½ cups water
- ½ cup white basmati rice
- 1½ teaspoons salt
- 8 ounces fresh salmon fillet, skin removed, cut into 1-inch pieces
- 1 tablespoon unsalted butter
- 1 tablespoon toasted sesame oil
- ½ cup thinly sliced fresh chives

Directions

1. Toast the sesame seeds. If your seeds are toasted, skip this step. Warm a Dutch oven over medium heat. Add the sesame seeds and cook for about 4 minutes, stirring occasionally, until they have a nutty smell and crunchy texture. Remove the seeds from the pot and set them aside.

2. Cook the rice. Combine the water, rice, and salt in the Dutch oven over high heat. Bring to a boil. Turn the heat to medium to maintain a simmer and cook, stirring frequently, for

about 30 minutes or until the liquid is creamy and the rice is tender.

3. Add the salmon. Stir in the salmon, butter, and sesame oil. Cover the pot and cook for 5 minutes, until the salmon is pink and opaque.

4. Season and serve. Stir in the chives, then ladle the congee into bowls. Garnish with a generous pinch of the toasted sesame seeds. Refrigerate leftovers for up to 3 days.

INGREDIENT TIP: If you buy sesame seeds in a labeled container, look for the words "toasted" or "roasted." Raw seeds are flat and chewy; toasted seeds are incredibly crunchy and have an intense, nutty flavor.

Nutrition:

Carbohydrates: 17 g

Fat: 6 g

Protein: 4 g

Calories: 326

126. Rigatoni with Pumpkin Seed Pesto

Preparation time: 2 minutes

Cooking time: 20 minutes

Servings: 6

Ingredients:

- 1 teaspoon salt, plus more for seasoning
- 1 pound rigatoni pasta
- 1 cup raw pumpkin seeds
- 5 ounces fresh baby spinach and kale mix
- 3 garlic cloves, roughly chopped
- 1 ounce Pecorino Romano cheese, roughly chopped
- ½ cup olive oil
- ½ cup red wine vinegar
- 1 teaspoon red pepper flakes
- Freshly ground black pepper

Directions:

1. Cook the pasta. Fill a Dutch oven three-fourths full with water, and place it over high heat. When the water comes to a boil, add several large pinches of salt and the rigatoni.

2. Cook for 10 to 14 minutes, until the pasta is al dente. Place a colander in the sink, and drain the pasta.

3. Meanwhile, make the pesto. In a blender or food processor, combine the pumpkin seeds, spinach and kale mix, garlic, Pecorino Romano, olive oil, vinegar, red pepper flakes, and salt. Blend on high speed until the mixture is mostly creamy with a bit of texture.

4. Sauce the noodles. Transfer the noodles to a large serving bowl. Add the pesto. Toss to coat. Taste and season with salt and pepper as desired. Refrigerate leftovers for up to 2 days.

VARIATION TIP: Pesto is highly adaptable—as long as you maintain the same ratio of ½ cup olive oil to ½ cup vinegar, mix and match different leafy greens, nuts, and seeds. Try walnut with arugula and a handful of fresh basil.

Nutrition:

Carbohydrates: 12 g

Fat: 6 g

Protein: 4 g

Calories: 346

127. Parmesan Polenta with Thyme-Roasted Mushrooms

Preparation time: 15 minutes

Cooking time: 30 minutes

Servings: 4

Ingredients:

- 2½ cups vegetable stock
- 1 teaspoon balsamic vinegar
- ½ teaspoon salt, plus more for seasoning
- ¾ cup polenta corn grits
- ½ cup finely grated Parmesan cheese
- 8 ounces cremini mushrooms, thinly sliced
- 8 ounces shiitake mushrooms, thinly sliced
- Leaves from 4 thyme sprigs, or 1 teaspoon dried thyme
- 2 tablespoons olive oil
- Pinch red pepper flakes, for seasoning (optional)

Directions:

1. Preheat the oven. Preheat the oven to 450°F.

2. Cook the polenta. In a Dutch oven over high heat, combine the vegetable stock, vinegar, and salt. Bring to a boil.

3. Add the polenta and stir well. Lower the heat to maintain a simmer and cook for 10 minutes, stirring often, until creamy and tender.

4. Remove from the heat and stir in the Parmesan. Smooth the top of the polenta and set aside to firm.

5. Roast the polenta with the mushrooms. In a medium bowl, stir together the cremini and shiitake mushrooms, thyme, olive oil, and a large pinch of salt.

6. Spread the mushroom mixture over the polenta. Roast for about 15 minutes, until the mushrooms are tender. Using a spatula, cut the polenta into portions and serve with the mushrooms and the red pepper flakes (if using). Refrigerate leftovers for up to 3 days.

INGREDIENT TIP: When shopping for polenta, look for coarsely ground yellow corn grits—these bags are often labeled "polenta." To clarify, there is a breakfast cereal called "grits" that is not the same as polenta; it is made from a finer grind of white corn.

Nutrition:

Carbohydrates: 6 g

Fat: 6 g

Protein: 4 g

Calories: 156

128. Italian Beef and Tomato Goulash

Preparation time: 10 minutes

Cooking time: 40 minutes

Servings: 6

Ingredients:

- 2 pounds lean ground beef
- 2 garlic cloves, minced
- 2 tablespoons Italian seasoning
- 1 teaspoon salt
- ½ teaspoon freshly ground black pepper
- 1 (14.5-ounce) can diced tomatoes
- 1 (26-ounce) jar pasta sauce
- 3 cups water
- 3 tablespoons tamari
- 2 cups dried elbow macaroni
- 1 cup shredded cheddar cheese

Directions:

1. Cook the beef. In a Dutch oven over medium heat, cook the ground beef for 5 minutes, crumbling it with a spatula or wooden spoon, until mostly cooked through. Stir in the garlic, Italian seasoning, salt, and pepper. Cook for 2 minutes.

2. Add the liquids. Add the tomatoes and their juices, pasta sauce, water, and tamari. Stir, cover the pot, and simmer for 10 minutes.

3. Cook the pasta in the sauce. Stir in the macaroni. Cover the pot and simmer for about 20 minutes, until the pasta is just cooked, stirring every few minutes to prevent the noodles from sticking and burning.

4. Add the cheese and serve. Stir in the cheddar cheese and serve. The goulash reheats well. Refrigerate leftovers for up to 4 days.

VARIATION TIP: Shoyu and soy sauce are both good substitutes for tamari.

Nutrition:

Carbohydrates: 11 g

Fat: 6 g

Protein: 14 g

Calories: 326

129. Beef Stroganoff

Preparation time: 15 minutes

Cooking time: 15 minutes

Servings: 6

Ingredients:

- Salt
- 4 tablespoons (½ stick) unsalted butter, divided
- 2 pounds lean ground beef
- Freshly ground black pepper
- 1 pound egg noodles
- 1 yellow onion, finely chopped
- 4 garlic cloves, minced
- 1 pound cremini mushrooms, sliced
- ½ cup dry white wine
- 1 tablespoon Worcestershire sauce
- ½ cup sour cream
- Finely chopped fresh parsley, for garnish (optional)

Directions:

1. Boil the water. Bring a large pot of salted water to a boil over high heat.

2. Cook the beef. Meanwhile, in a Dutch oven over medium heat, melt 2 tablespoons of butter. Add the ground beef and season well with salt and pepper.

3. Cook for 4 minutes, crumbling the beef with a spatula or wooden spoon, until brown. Transfer the beef with its juices to a large bowl; set aside.

4. Cook the pasta. Add the egg noodles to the boiling water and cook for 8 to 10 minutes, until al dente. Place a colander in the sink, and drain the pasta; do not rinse the noodles.

5. While the pasta cooks, sauté the vegetables. In a Dutch oven over medium heat, melt the remaining 2 tablespoons of butter.

6. Add the onion and sauté for about 3 minutes. Stir in the garlic and mushrooms. Sauté for about 5 minutes, until the onion and mushrooms are soft and beginning to brown.

7. Pour the wine over the vegetables and stir well, scraping along the bottom of the pot to release any browned bits.

8. Mix the beef with the vegetables and serve. Return the beef with its juices to the pot and stir in the Worcestershire sauce and sour cream.

9. Immediately serve the warm beef sauce over the just-cooked noodles and garnish with parsley (if using).

10. Taste and adjust the seasoning with salt and pepper as desired. Refrigerate leftovers for up to 3 days. When reheating, add a splash of water to thin the sauce.

TECHNICAL TIP: For a thicker sauce, make a quick roux by adding 2 tablespoons of all-purpose flour after sautéing the vegetables. Cook, stirring, for at least 3 minutes to toast the flour, then proceed with the wine and other liquids. Once the sauce comes to a simmer, it will thicken into a gravy.

Nutrition:

Carbohydrates: 13 g

Fat: 6 g

Protein: 4 g

Calories: 286

130. Sesame-Ginger Soba Noodle Salad

Preparation time: 10 minutes

Cooking time: 20 minutes

Servings: 4

Ingredients:

- Salt
- 8 ounces gluten-free soba noodles
- ¼ cup sesame oil
- 8 ounces shiitake mushrooms, thinly sliced
- 2 heads bok choy, cut into ½-inch-thick slices
- 2 teaspoons peeled and minced fresh ginger
- 1 teaspoon red pepper flakes
- ¼ cup tamari
- ¼ cup rice vinegar
- 2 tablespoons brown rice syrup
- 2 tablespoons mirin

Directions:

1. Cook the pasta. Bring a Dutch oven filled with salted water to a boil over high heat. Add the soba noodles and cook according to the package instructions.
2. Place a colander in the sink, drain the noodles, and rinse them under cold water. Set aside.
3. Cook the vegetables and make the sauce. Combine the sesame oil and shiitake mushrooms in the Dutch oven over medium-low heat.
4. Cook, undisturbed, for 3 minutes. Stir in the bok choy, ginger, and red pepper flakes. Sauté for 1 minute, then add the tamari, vinegar, brown rice syrup, and mirin.
5. Stir to form a smooth sauce, then add the noodles, just tossing to coat. Serve warm or cool.

TECHNICAL TIP: You can tell when the soba noodles are fully cooked by breaking a noodle in half. If you see any white starch, continue to cook the noodles until that starch is no longer visible.

Nutrition:

Carbohydrates: 19 g

Fat: 6 g

Protein: 4 g

Calories: 190

131. Gouda-Cheddar Mac and Cheese

Preparation time: 15 minutes

Cooking time: 40 minutes

Servings: 6

Ingredients:

- 5 ounces Gouda cheese
- 5 ounces sharp cheddar cheese
- Salt
- 1 pound large dried elbow macaroni
- 1 tablespoon olive oil
- 5 tablespoons unsalted butter
- 1/3 cup all-purpose flour
- 2½ cups whole milk
- 2 teaspoons paprika (optional)

Directions:

1. Preheat the oven and prepare the cheeses. Preheat the oven to 375°F. Shred the Gouda and cheddar cheeses and mix them together in a large bowl. Set aside.
2. Cook the pasta. Fill a Dutch oven three-fourths full with salted water and bring it to a boil over high heat.
3. Add the pasta and cook for 1 minute shy of al dente, according to the package instructions. Place a colander in the sink and drain the pasta. Add the olive oil and toss the pasta to prevent sticking.
4. Make a roux and simmer the milk. Place the butter in the Dutch oven and set the pot over medium-low heat.
5. When the butter has melted, add the flour and cook, stirring frequently, for 2 minutes or until the mixture is golden and bubbly.
6. Slowly stir in the milk, bring the mixture to a simmer (it will thicken), and then turn off the heat.
7. Mix in the cheese and pasta. Add the cheese and pasta to the milk mixture, folding well to coat the pasta evenly.
8. Sprinkle the top with the paprika (if using). Bake for about 15 minutes, until golden and bubbly. Serve immediately. Refrigerate leftovers for up to 3 days.

Nutrition:

Carbohydrates: 20 g

Fat: 6 g

Protein: 4 g

Calories: 326

132. Meat Overload Pizza

Preparation Time: 25 minutes

Cooking Time: 25 minutes

Serves: 8

Ingredients

- 1 thin pizza crust, or crust of choice
- 1/2-3/4 cups marinara sauce
- 2 Tablespoons olive oil
- 1 1/2-2 pounds assorted meat like ground beef, pepperoni, Italian sausage, breakfast sausage, ham (chopped) and bacon
- Salt and pepper, to taste
- 2 cups mozzarella cheese

Directions

1. Heat oven to 425 degrees F.
2. Cook bacon until crisp. Cool slightly and then crumble.
3. Cook sausages in a little oil over medium heat to brown. Drain over paper towels.
4. Season ground beef with salt and pepper and sauté until browned. Drain.
5. Spread sauce over dough.
6. Sprinkle with about 1/2 cup mozzarella followed by half of the meat ingredients.
7. Continue layering with cheese and meat.
8. Bake until golden brown and bubbly (about 25 minutes).
9. Let set for 3-5 minutes before slicing.

Nutrition:

Calories 542

Carbs 24 g

Fat 4 g

Protein 32 g

Sodium 1685 mg

133. Classic Pepperoni

Preparation Time: 15 minutes

Cooking Time: 12-15 minutes

Serves: 8

Ingredients

- 1 thin crust pizza dough, or any dough of choice
- 1/2-3/4 basic pizza or marinara sauce
- 2 cups mozzarella, freshly shredded
- 6 ounces pepperoni

Directions

1. Preheat oven to 500 degrees F.
2. Spread sauce over crust.
3. Sprinkle with cheese.
4. Top with mozzarella.
5. Bake until golden and bubbly (about 12-15 minutes).

Nutrition:

Calories 276

Carbs 25 g

Fat 14 g

Protein 12 g

Sodium 656 mg

134. Meat with Bell Pepper & Mushrooms

Preparation Time: 15 minutes

Cooking Time: 30 minutes

Serves: 8

Ingredients

- 1 pizza crust of choice
- 1/2-3/4 cup marinara sauce
- 2 cups mozzarella, freshly shredded
- 1 1/2-2 pounds seasoned beef or pork
- 16-24 pieces pepperoni
- 1 cup mushrooms, sliced thinly
- 1 medium green bell pepper, sliced thinly
- 1 red onion, sliced

Seasoned Meat Topping:

- 2 pounds ground lean beef or pork (or combination)
- 1 teaspoon ground black pepper
- 1 teaspoon dried parsley
- 1 teaspoon oregano
- 1 teaspoon dried basil
- 1/2 teaspoon garlic powder
- 1/2 teaspoon onion powder
- 1/8 teaspoon chilli flakes

- 1/2 teaspoon paprika
- 2 teaspoons salt

Directions

1. Preheat oven to 425 degrees F.
2. Prepare the meat topping. Mix all the ingredients together well and sauté over medium heat until well-browned (about 10 minutes). Remove from heat and let cool.
3. Spread sauce over crust. and sprinkle with cheese.
4. Top with seasoned meat, pepperoni, mushrooms, bell pepper and onion.
5. Bake until golden brown (about 20 minutes).

Nutrition:

Calories 496

Carbs 27 g

Fat 30 g

Protein 27 g

Sodium 1096 mg

135. Barbecue Pizza

Preparation Time: 15 minutes

Cooking Time: 15 minutes

Serves: 8

Ingredients

- 1 pizza crust of choice
- 1/2-3/4 cup barbecue sauce plus more for drizzling
- 2 cups mozzarella, freshly shredded, divided
- 1/4 cup cheddar, freshly grated
- 1 1/2-2 pounds combination of cooked smoked bacon, cooked ham and seasoned meat

Directions

1. Preheat oven to 500 degrees F.
2. Spread sauce over crust.
3. Sprinkle with 1 cup shredded mozzarella.
4. Add meat and top with cheddar cheese and remaining mozzarella.
5. Bake until cheese is melted and crust is golden (about 15 minutes).
6. Drizzle with barbecue sauce and let cool for 3-5 minutes to set.
7. Serve.

136. Meat with Mushrooms, Bell Pepper & Olives

Preparation Time: 20 minutes

Cooking Time: 20-30 minutes

Serves: 8

Ingredients

- 1 pizza crust of choice
- 1/2 cup marinara sauce
- 2 cups mozzarella, freshly shredded
- 2 pounds combination of seasoned meat (pork and/or beef), Italian sausage, pepperoni, and ham
- 1/2 cup mushrooms, sliced thinly
- 1 medium green bell pepper, sliced into rings
- 1 red onion, sliced
- 1/4 cup black olives, pitted and sliced

Directions

1. Preheat oven to 425 degrees F.
2. Brown the meat and sausage in a little oil over medium heat until browned.
3. Slice the ham.
4. Spread sauce over crust. and sprinkle with cheese.

Nutrition:

Calories 508

Carbs 40 g

Fat 27 g

Protein 26 g

Sodium 1012 mg

5. Top with seasoned meat, sausage, ham, pepperoni, mushrooms, bell pepper, onion and olives.

6. Bake until golden brown (about 20 minutes).

Nutrition:

Calories 470

Carbs 27 g

Fat 28 g

Protein 25 g

Sodium 827 mg

137. Meatball Pizza

Preparation Time: 20 minutes

Cooking Time: 30 minutes

Serves: 8

Ingredients

- 1 pizza crust of choice
- 1/2-3/4 cup marinara sauce
- 1 cup diced tomato
- 1 1/2 cups mozzarella, freshly shredded
- 1 red onion, sliced
- Meatballs (recipe below)
- Fresh basil, chopped, for garnish

Classic Meatballs:

- 2 pounds lean ground beef
- 2 eggs
- 3/4 cup dry breadcrumbs
- 1/4 cup fresh parsley, chopped
- 1 garlic clove, minced
- 1/2 teaspoon salt or to taste
- 1/4 cup Parmesan cheese

Directions

1. Preheat oven to 425 degrees F. Line or grease a baking sheet.

2. Let diced tomatoes drain in a colander.

3. Prepare meatballs by mixing ingredients together well. Scoop out heaping Tablespoonfuls and shape into balls (about 18 meatballs). Arrange on baking sheet and bake until browned (about 10-15 minutes). Remove from oven and let cool.

4. Spread sauce over crust.

5. Add drained tomatoes and sprinkle with cheese.

6. Top with onion and meatballs.

7. Bake until crust and meatballs are golden brown (about 20-25 minutes).

8. Garnish with basil.

Nutrition:

Calories 247

Carbs 27 g

Fat 11 g

Protein 11 g

Sodium 452 mg

138. Spicy Italian Sausage Pizza

Preparation Time: 10 minutes

Cooking Time: 25-30 minutes

Serves: 8

Ingredients

- 1 pizza crust of choice
- 1/2-3/4 cup basic pizza or marinara sauce
- 1 1/2 cups shredded mozzarella cheese
- 1/4 cup grated Parmigiano-Reggiano cheese
- 4 ounces spicy Italian turkey sausage
- 1 cup onion, thinly sliced
- 1 8-ounce package pre-sliced mushrooms
- 1 cup red or green bell pepper, seeded and diced (optional)

Directions

1. Preheat oven to 450 degrees.

2. Prepare toppings. Remove sausage from casing and cook in non stick skillet until it crumbles (about 3 minutes). Add mushrooms and onions and sauté until tender (about 4 minutes). Add bell pepper and sauté until

fragrant (about 3 minutes). Remove mixture from heat and let cool.

3. Pour pizza sauce over center of dough and spread to the sides, leaving about 1/2-inch from edge without sauce.
4. Top with toppings.
5. Sprinkle with mozzarella and Parmigiano-Reggiano.
6. Bake until cheese is golden brown and bubbly (about 15-20 minutes).

Nutrition:

Calories 305

Carbs 45 g

Fat 8 g

Protein 17 g

Sodium 1318 mg

139. Brussels Sprouts & Pancetta Pizza

Preparation Time: 10 minutes

Cooking Time: 12-15 minutes

Serves: 8

Ingredients

- 1 pizza crust of choice
- 4 Brussels sprouts, cored, with leaves separated
- 1 1/2 cup shredded mozzarella cheese, torn into 10-12 pieces
- 1 garlic clove, sliced into slivers
- 2 ounces pancetta, chopped
- 1/4 cup grated Parmigiano-Reggiano cheese
- 2 Tablespoons olive oil
- kosher or sea salt, to taste

Directions

1. Preheat oven to 550 degrees F.
2. Distribute torn mozzarella evenly over crust.
3. Sprinkle with Brussels sprout leaves, garlic, pancetta and grated Parniggiano-Reggiano.
4. Drizzle with olive oil and sprinkle with salt.

5. Bake on lowest rack until evenly browned (about 12-15 minutes).

Nutrition:

Calories 233

Carbs 24 g

Fat 11 g

Protein 10 g

Sodium:455mg

140. Hawaiian Pizza

Preparation Time: 10 minutes

Cooking Time: 21 minutes

Serves: 6-8

Ingredients

- 1 pizza crust of choice
- 1/2 cup basic pizza sauce
- 2 cups shredded mozzarella cheese, divided
- 1/2 cup shredded Romano cheese
- 1 cup ham, chopped
- 1 cup pineapple tidbits, drained
- 24 slices pepperoni

Directions

1. Preheat oven to 425 degrees.
2. Spread sauce, beginning from the center of the crust going outward in a circular motion, leaving 1/2-inch space around the edge.
3. Sprinkle with 1 cup mozzarella and the Romano.
4. Arrange ham, pineapple and pepperoni slices on top and sprinkle with remaining mozzarella.

5. Bake until cheese is melted and crust is golden brown (about 15 minutes).

Nutrition:

Calories 411

Carbs 46 g

Fat 16 g

Protein 23 g

Sodium:1799mg

141. Breakfast Sausage Pizza

Preparation Time: 15 minutes

Cooking Time: 23-25 minutes

Serves: 6-8

Ingredients

- 1 pizza crust of choice
- 8 ounces breakfast sausage
- 2 teaspoons butter
- 4 ounces processed cheese (like Velveeta), sliced
- 4 eggs, scrambled
- 1 cup mozzarella cheese, freshly shredded
- 3/4 cup cooked bacon, chopped (optional)

Directions

1. Preheat oven to 400 degrees F.
2. Cook the breakfast sausage in a skillet over high heat, breaking apart with a spatula until lightly browned (about 8-10 minutes).
3. If you've par-baked the crust, brush with butter while still hot. Or simply brush with softened butter.
4. Place cheese slices over the buttered crust.

5. Distribute scrambles eggs and sausage on top.
6. Sprinkle with shredded mozzarella and bacon bits (optional).
7. Bake until crust is lightly golden and cheese is melted (about 15 minutes).

Nutrition:

Calories 330

Carbs 24 g

Fat 20 g

Protein 15 g

Sodium:668mg

142. Philly Cheesesteak Pizza

Preparation Time: 15 minutes

Cooking Time: 20-22 minutes

Serves: 6-8

Ingredients

- 1 pizza crust of choice
- 1/2-3/4 cup basic or marinara sauce
- 2 ounces cream cheese
- 2 cups provolone cheese, shredded and divided
- 1 cup precooked roast beef, cut into thin strips
- 1/3 cup pickled pepper rings
- 1/4 cup grated Parmesan cheese
- 1/2 teaspoon dried oregano

For pepper mixture:

- 1 Tablespoon olive oil
- 2 small bell peppers (green, red or combination), sliced into thin strips
- 1 1/2 cups sliced fresh mushrooms
- 1 small onion, chopped

Directions

1. Preheat oven to 450 degrees F.

2. Par bake crust until set (about 5 minutes). Remove from oven and let cool.

3. Prepare pepper mixture. Heat oil in a skillet over medium heat and add peppers, mushrooms and onion. Sauté until tender. Remove from heat and let cool.

4. Spread sauce over crust.

5. Scoop cream cheese evenly on top and sprinkle with 1 cup provolone.

6. Add beef, pepper mixture and pepper rings.

7. Sprinkle with remaining provolone, parmesan and oregano.

8. Bake until crust is golden and cheese is melted (about 10-12 minutes).

Nutrition:

Calories 439

Carbs 36 g

Fat 20 g

Protein 29 g

Sodium 826 mg

143. Veggie Pizza

Preparation Time: 15 minutes

Cooking Time: 20 minutes

Serves: 6-8

Ingredients

- 1 thin pizza crust dough, or dough of choice
- 1/2 cup marinara sauce
- 3 roma tomatoes, sliced
- 1 cup mushrooms, sliced thinly
- 1 red onion, sliced thinly
- 1 large green bell pepper, seeded and sliced into strips
- 1/4 cup black olives, pitted and sliced
- 2 cups mozzarella cheese, shredded

Directions

1. Preheat oven to 450 degrees F.
2. Spreads sauce over crust dough.
3. Arrange the tomatoes, mushrooms, onion, pepper and olives on top as desired.
4. Sprinkle with shredded mozzarella.
5. Bake until golden and bubbly (about 20 minutes).
6. Let set for 3 minutes before slicing.

Nutrition:

Calories 227

Carbs 27g

Fat 9 g

Protein 10 g

Sodium 235 mg

144. Neopolitan Apollonia Pizza

Preparation Time: 15 minutes

Cooking Time: 3-5 minutes

Serves: 6-8

Ingredients

- 1 thin crust or any dough of choice
- 1 cup mozzarella di bufala
- 2 cloves garlic, sliced very thinly
- 1 cup Italian salami or cured meat like coppa, pancetta or mortadella, chopped
- 2 eggs, beaten
- Coarse sea salt and freshly-ground black pepper, to taste
- Fresh basil leaves
- 1 Tablespoon extra-virgin olive oil
- 1/4 cup parmigianoreggiano, grated

Directions

1. Preheat oven to hottest temperature (500-550 degrees F for most home ovens), with rack positioned closest to grill. When well-heated, turn on grill.

2. Place the crust in a heated skillet or non-stick pan and cook until dough begins to puff up and

bottom begins to brown (about 60-90 seconds).

3. Transfer to pan or pizza peel.
4. Tear mozzarella di bufala and scatter over dough.
5. Sprinkle with garlic and chopped salami.
6. Drizzle with beaten eggs and season with salt and pepper.
7. Top with basil leaves and drizzle with olive oil.
8. Place under grill and bake until eggs are just set and crust is browned (about 2-5 minutes).
9. Sprinkle with parmigianoreggiano.
10. Serve hot.

Nutrition:

Calories 254

Carbs 23 g

Fat 8 g

Protein 11 g

Sodium:658mg

145. Chicago-Style Deep-Dish Pizza

Preparation Time: 20 minutes

Cook Time: 40-50 minutes

Serves: 8

Ingredients

- 1 deep dish pizza crust, par-baked to set
- 1-2 Tablespoons butter (optional)
- 2 cups shredded mozzarella (Stella, Frigo or Sorrento), preferably whole-milk, divided
- 1-2 cups filling of choice
- Options for filling (combination of 2 or more, as desired):
- Italian sausage, cooked and crumbled
- pancetta, cooked and crumbled
- pepperoni, sliced thinly
- green pepper, sliced thinly
- yellow onion, sliced
- mushrooms, sliced
- black olives, sliced
- 1 cup basic pizza sauce
- 1/4 cup grated parmesan cheese

- 1-2 Tablespoons olive oil

Directions

1. Preheat oven to 375 degrees F.
2. Par-bake crust just to set (about 5-10 minutes).
3. Brush hot crust with butter, if using.
4. Spread 1/2 cup mozzarella over crust.
5. Mix 1 cup mozzarella with filling and add to crust.
6. Top with remaining mozzarella.
7. Cover with sauce.
8. Sprinkle with parmesan and drizzle with olive oil.
9. Bake until crust is golden brown and top is bubbly (40-50 minutes). Cover loosely with foil if crust browns too quickly.
10. Let set for 15 minutes before slicing.

Nutrition:

Calories 515 , Carbs 45 g

Fat 31 g, Protein 18 g

Sodium 1396 mg

146. Sicilian Pizza

Preparation Time: 15 minutes

Cooking Time: 10 minutes

Serves: 8-12

Ingredients

- 1 rectangular pan pizza crust
- 1/2 cup marinara sauce
- 1 pound mozzarella cheese, sliced thinly
- 12 ounces pepperoni, sliced thinly
- 4 ounces ground Pecorino Romano cheese, divided
- Fresh basil leaves (optional)

Directions

1. Preheat oven to 550 degrees F.
2. Arrange the mozzarella slices so that dough is covered evenly.
3. Spread marinara sauce over cheese.
4. Cover with pepperoni slices and sprinkle with half of the ground cheese.
5. Bake until crust is browned and pepperoni look crisp (about 10 minutes). Lift slightly to check bottom of crust (It should be golden brown).

6. Sprinkle with remaining cheese and serve immediately.

Nutrition:

Calories 337

Carbs 6 g

Fat 24 g

Protein 18 g

Sodium 1177 mg

Chapter 8. Chicken

147. Chicken Cacciatore with Tomato

Preparation time: 15 minutes

Cooking time: 1 hour

Servings: 4

Ingredients:

- 2 tablespoons extra-virgin olive oil
- 3½ to 4 pounds (1.59 to 1.8 kg) chicken thighs
- 1 onion, sliced
- 1 red bell pepper, seeded and sliced
- 8 ounces (227 g) button mushrooms, sliced
- 2 garlic cloves, sliced
- 1/3 cup white wine
- 1 (28-ounce / 794-g) can plum tomatoes
- 2 teaspoons chopped fresh thyme
- 2 teaspoons chopped fresh oregano
- Salt and freshly ground black pepper, to taste

Directions:

1. In a Dutch oven over medium heat, heat the olive oil. Working in batches, cook the chicken pieces, skin-side down, until evenly browned, about 5 minutes. Turn over and repeat. Transfer to a platter and continue with the next batch.
2. Drain off all but 2 tablespoons of fat. Add the onion, pepper, and mushrooms to the pot. Increase the heat to medium-high. Cook about 10 minutes, stirring frequently, or until the onions are translucent. Add the garlic and cook for 1 minute. Add the wine and scrape up any browned bits at the bottom of the pot. Simmer until the wine is reduced by half.
3. Add the tomatoes. Stir in the thyme and oregano, and season with salt and pepper. Simmer, uncovered, for 5 minutes. Place the chicken pieces on top of the tomato sauce. Lower the heat and cover with the lid slightly ajar.
4. Cook on a low simmer, turning and basting from time to time, for 30 to 40 minutes, or until the chicken is tender.

Nutrition:

Carbohydrates: 61 g

Fat: 6 g

Protein: 4 g

Calories: 326

148. Carrot Chicken With Pea

Preparation time: 10 minutes

Cooking time: 70 minutes

Servings: 4

Ingredients:

- 2 tablespoons extra virgin olive oil
- 1 whole chicken, cut into individual pieces
- Sea salt and freshly cracked black pepper, to taste
- 1 onion, finely chopped
- ¼ cup finely chopped garlic scapes
- 3 tablespoons flour
- 1 cup dry white wine
- 2 cups chicken broth
- 10 baby carrots
- 2 cups pearl onions
- 2 cups peas
- 2 tablespoons chopped fresh thyme
- ¼ cup chopped fresh parsley

Directions:

1. Preheat the oven to 350°F (180°C). Season the chicken pieces liberally with salt and pepper.
2. In a large Dutch oven, heat the olive oil over medium-high heat until it shimmers.
3. Working in batches without overcrowding the pot, brown the chicken pieces on all sides, about 5 minutes per side.
4. Set the chicken aside on a platter, tented with foil.
5. Add the onions to the oil in the pot and cook, stirring occasionally, until they are soft, about 5 minutes.
6. Add the garlic scapes and cook, stirring constantly, for 1 minute.
7. Add the flour to the pot and cook, stirring constantly, for 1 minute.
8. Add the white wine to the pot. Use a spoon to scrape any browned bits from the bottom of the pan.
9. Add the chicken stock, baby carrots, pearl onions, peas, and thyme to the pot.
10. Return the chicken to the pot, adding any juices that have collected on the platter. Stir together, and bring the mixture to a simmer.
11. Cover the Dutch oven, put it in the oven, and bake until the chicken is cooked through, about 40 minutes.
12. Remove the pot from the oven and stir in the chopped parsley. Serve immediately.

Nutrition: Carbohydrates: 21 g, Fat: 6 g, Protein: 4 g, Calories: 326

149. Rice With Chicken & Sausage

Preparation time: 15 minutes

Cooking time: 1 hour 20 minutes

Servings: 6

Ingredients:

- 8 skinless, boneless chicken thighs (or breasts, if you prefer)
- Salt and freshly ground black pepper, to taste
- 2½ tablespoons extra-virgin olive oil
- 1 onion, chopped
- 3 cloves garlic, minced
- 2 cups long-grain rice
- 2 teaspoons ground cumin
- 2 teaspoons crushed dried oregano leaves
- 5 cups low-sodium chicken broth or stock
- 1 green bell pepper, seeded and diced
- 1¾ cups thick and chunky salsa (mild, medium, or hot)
- ¾ pound (340 g) spicy chorizo chicken sausage, diced
- 6 to 8 sprigs of cilantro leaves, for garnish
- ¼ cup chopped scallions, for garnish
- 6 to 8 lime wedges, for garnish

Directions:

1. Preheat the oven to 350°F (180°C).
2. Trim any visible fat from the chicken, and season with salt and pepper.
3. In a Dutch oven over medium heat, heat the olive oil. Add half of the chicken pieces, and cook for about 3 minutes. Turn over and cook for 3 minutes, or until the chicken is lightly browned on both sides. Transfer the chicken to a platter, as they cook and repeat with the remaining pieces.
4. Add more oil to the pot, if needed, and add the onion. Cook until softened. Add the garlic and cook for 2 minutes, or until softened.
5. Add the rice, cumin, oregano, and some salt, and cook for 2 to 3 minutes, stirring until the rice is coated with oil. Stir in the broth. Add the green pepper and the salsa. Bring to a boil.
6. Cover, place in the preheated oven, and bake for 30 minutes, or until the liquid is almost completely absorbed.
7. Stir in the chorizo. Tuck the chicken pieces into the rice mixture, and pour in any juices that have collected on the platter. Cover, return to the oven, and bake for 20 minutes, or until the chicken is cooked through and the rice is tender.

8. Garnish with the cilantro leaves, chopped scallions, and lime wedges.

Nutrition:

Carbohydrates: 12 g

Fat: 6 g

Protein: 4 g

Calories: 226

150. Chicken Pot with Tomato Sauce

Preparation time: 15 minutes

Cooking time: 1 hour 30 minutes

Servings: 6

Ingredients:

- 1 tablespoon vegetable oil
- 4 cups tomato sauce
- 3 garlic cloves, minced
- 1 large onion, chopped
- 2 bay leaves
- 2 teaspoons crumbled dried oregano
- 1 teaspoon ground chili powder
- 1 tablespoon red or white wine vinegar
- Salt and freshly ground black pepper, to taste
- 4 to 5 pounds (1.8 to 2.3 kg) chicken thighs (or a combination of thighs and legs), skinned but left on the bone

Directions:

1. Preheat the oven to 350°F (180°C).
2. Combine in a Dutch oven the vegetable oil, tomato sauce, garlic, onion, bay leaves, oregano, chili powder, and vinegar. Season with salt and pepper, and stir to blend. Add the chicken to the pot, and

stir to cover each piece with the sauce.

3. Cover, place in the heated oven, and bake for 1½ hours.

Nutrition:

Carbohydrates: 16 g

Fat: 6 g

Protein: 14 g

Calories: 326

151. Bamboo Shoot Chicken

Preparation time: 15 minutes

Cooking time: 15 minutes

Servings: 4

Ingredients:

- 4 boneless, skinless chicken breasts, sliced
- 2 tablespoons soy sauce
- 2 tablespoons rice wine or dry sherry
- 2 garlic cloves, crushed
- 1 (1-inch) piece fresh ginger root, finely chopped
- 2 tablespoons peanut oil, divided
- 4 scallions, thinly sliced
- 4 ounces (113 g) snow peas
- 4 ounces (113 g) bok choy, chopped into bite-size pieces
- 1 (8-ounce / 227-g) can bamboo shoots, drained
- 2 tablespoons hoisin sauce
- Freshly ground black pepper, to taste

Directions:

1. In a medium bowl, combine the chicken, soy sauce, rice wine, garlic, and ginger, and marinate while preparing the vegetables.
2. Heat 1 tablespoon of peanut oil in a Dutch oven over medium

heat. Add the scallions and sauté for 1 minute. Remove the chicken from the marinade. Add to the pot and stir-fry briskly for 4 to 5 minutes, until cooked through and browned on all sides. Use a slotted spoon to remove the chicken from the pot.

3. Heat the remaining 1 tablespoon of peanut oil. Add the snow peas and bok choy. Stir-fry for 1 to 2 minutes. Add the bamboo shoots, and cook for 1 to 2 minutes.

4. Return the chicken to the pot. Add the hoisin sauce and stir. Season with a little black pepper.

Nutrition:

Carbohydrates: 23 g

Fat: 6 g

Protein: 4 g

Calories: 298

152. Lemony Chicken with Tomato

Preparation time: 15 minutes

Cooking time: 1 hour 20 minutes

Servings: 6

Ingredients:

- 2 tablespoons extra-virgin olive oil
- 6 boneless, skinless chicken breasts
- 8 ounces (227 g) pearl onions
- 2 garlic cloves, crushed
- 1 pound (454 g) tomatoes, peeled and chopped
- 1 bay leaf
- 1 tablespoon roughly chopped fresh thyme leaves
- 2 tablespoons chopped fresh parsley
- Pinch saffron
- 2 tablespoons dry white wine
- Salt and freshly ground black pepper, to taste
- Juice of 1 lemon

Directions:

1. In a Dutch oven over medium heat, heat the olive oil. Add the chicken and cook until each breast is a pale golden brown. Transfer the chicken to a platter.

2. Add the onions and garlic to the pot. Cook over a low heat, stirring occasionally, until the onions begin to brown.
3. Stir in the chopped tomatoes, bay leaf, thyme, parsley, saffron, wine, salt, and pepper. Bring to a boil.
4. Return the chicken breasts to the Dutch oven. Cover and cook over low heat for 1 hour.
5. Stir in the lemon juice. Season with salt and pepper. Remove the bay leaf before serving.

Nutrition:

Carbohydrates: 18 g

Fat: 6 g

Protein: 19 g

Calories: 256

153. Cheese Lemon Chicken Pasta Bake

Preparation time: 10 minutes

Cooking time: 45 minutes

Servings: 4

Ingredients:

- ½ pound (227g) penne pasta
- 3 tablespoons extra-virgin olive oil, divided
- 1 onion, chopped
- 3 cloves garlic, minced
- 3 bunches kale, shredded
- Salt and freshly ground black pepper, to taste
- 1½ cups cooked shredded chicken
- 1 cup grated Gruyère cheese
- Juice of 1 lemon
- ¼ cup grated Parmesan cheese
- ¼ cup Panko crumbs

Directions:

1. Preheat the oven to 375°F (190°C).
2. Bring a pot of salted water to a boil in a Dutch oven, and cook the pasta according to the directions on the package. Drain and set aside.

3. In a Dutch oven over medium heat, heat 2 tablespoons of olive oil. Cook the onion until translucent, or about 5 minutes. Add the garlic and sauté for 30 seconds.
4. Add the kale to the pot, and season with salt and pepper. Stir a few times to wilt the greens. Cover, reduce heat to medium-low, and cook until the greens are tender, for about 10 minutes.
5. Add the pasta, chicken, Gruyère, and lemon juice to the greens, and season with salt and pepper.
6. In a small bowl, combine the Parmesan, Panko crumbs, and the remaining 1 tablespoon olive oil. Sprinkle the mixture over the top of the pasta, and place in the heated oven, uncovered, for 30 minutes, or until the top is golden.

Nutrition:

Carbohydrates: 13 g

Fat: 6 g

Protein: 4 g

Calories: 326

154. Lemony Chicken with Parsnip

Preparation time: 15 minutes

Cooking time: 1 hour

Servings: 4

Ingredients:

- 4 lemons, cut in half, divided
- 1 medium (3½- to 4-pound / 1.59- to 1.8-kg) chicken, rinsed and patted dry, giblets removed
- 1 sprig rosemary
- 1 sprig thyme
- 1 sprig oregano
- 1 sprig parsley
- Pinch salt
- Pinch freshly ground black pepper
- 6 tablespoons extra-virgin olive oil, divided
- 1 tablespoon herbes de Provence
- 8 shallots, peeled
- 16 baby parsnips, peeled

Directions:

1. Preheat the oven to 450°F (235°C).
2. Squeeze the juice from 2 lemon halves into the chicken cavity, and place the 2 halves inside. Add

rosemary, thyme, oregano, parsley, salt, and pepper.

3. Loosely tie the legs together with kitchen twine. Rub 3 tablespoons olive oil over the chicken. Sprinkle with the herbes de Provence and another pinch of salt and pepper.

4. Coat the bottom of the Dutch oven with the remaining 3 tablespoons of olive oil. Place the chicken in the pot, and surround it with the shallots, parsnips, and the remaining 6 lemon halves.

5. Roast in the oven for 15 minutes. Lower the heat to 350°F (180°C), and roast for 45 minutes, or until the chicken juices run clear when the leg is pierced with a fork. Serve on a platter surrounded with the vegetables and lemons.

Nutrition:

Carbohydrates: 12 g

Fat: 6 g

Protein: 8 g

Calories: 206

155. Cheese–Stuffed Chicken Breasts

Preparation time: 15 minutes

Cooking time: 30 minutes

Servings: 6

Ingredients:

The Filling:

- 4 tablespoons Goat cheese
- 2 teaspoons chopped fresh thyme
- Salt and freshly ground black pepper, to taste

The Chicken:

- 4 boneless, skinless chicken breasts
- 2 tablespoons extra-virgin olive oil, divided
- 12 ounces (340 g) baby Yukon Gold or fingerling potatoes, halved
- 6 stalks asparagus, quartered
- 2 shallots, thinly sliced
- Salt and freshly ground black pepper, to taste

Directions:

1. Preheat the oven to 375°F (190°C). In a small bowl, combine the Goat cheese and thyme, and season with salt and pepper. Set aside.

2. Cut a deep pocket inside each chicken breast, using a sharp

paring knife. Using your fingers, pack each pouch with a quarter of the Goat cheese mixture. Gently press the opening closed. Season the chicken with salt and pepper.

3. In a Dutch oven over medium heat, heat 1 tablespoon of olive oil. Add 2 of the chicken breasts, and cook for 2 to 3 minutes per side, or until golden brown. Transfer to a platter. Repeat with the next batch.

4. Heat the remaining 1 tablespoon olive oil in the Dutch oven over a medium heat. Add the potatoes, asparagus, and shallots. Stir together, seasoning with salt and pepper.

5. Arrange the chicken breasts on top of the vegetables. Place in the oven, uncovered, and bake for 20 minutes, or until the potatoes are tender and the chicken is cooked through.

Nutrition:

Carbohydrates: 14 g

Fat: 6 g

Protein: 4 g

Calories: 126

156. Chicken and Potato Broccoli Casserole

Preparation time: 10 minutes

Cooking time: 2 hours

Servings: 4

Ingredients:

- Cooking spray, for frying
- 1 (15-ounce / 425-g) can condensed cream of broccoli soup
- 1 cup sour cream
- 1½ cups shredded Swiss cheese
- ½ cup milk
- 6 cups cubed new potatoes
- 3 cups chopped cooked chicken
- 1 teaspoon Italian seasoning
- Salt and freshly ground black pepper, to taste
- 2 cups broccoli florets
- ¼ cup chopped fresh basil leaves

Directions:

1. Preheat the oven to 350°F (180°C).
2. Lightly coat a Dutch oven with the cooking spray. Combine the soup and the sour cream. Stir in the cheese, milk, potatoes, chicken, and seasoning. Season with salt and pepper.

3. Cover, place in the heated oven, and bake for 1 to 1½ hours.
4. Stir in the broccoli. Return to the oven and bake, uncovered, for 10 minutes. Stir in the basil and serve.

Nutrition:

Carbohydrates: 20 g

Fat: 6 g

Protein: 4 g

Calories: 298

157. Chicken Fricassee with Onion

Preparation time: 10 minutes

Cooking time: 1 hour 40 minutes

Servings: 4

Ingredients:

- 1 teaspoon salt
- ½ teaspoon freshly ground black pepper
- ½ teaspoon cayenne pepper
- ½ teaspoon garlic powder
- 1 (4-pound / 1.8-kg) chicken, cut into 8 pieces
- ½ cup vegetable oil
- 2/3 cup all-purpose flour
- 1 large onion, peeled and diced, divided
- 6 cups chicken broth
- 1 large green bell pepper, seeded and diced
- Pinch thyme
- 3 green onions, minced

Directions:

1. Combine salt, pepper, cayenne, and garlic powder in a small bowl. Sprinkle the seasonings over the chicken.

2. Heat a Dutch oven over medium-high heat. Add oil and once it shimmers add chicken and brown well on both sides, about 5 minutes per side. Remove chicken to a plate to rest.
3. Add flour into hot oil and cook, stirring constantly, until flour turns dark brown, about 8 to 10 minutes. Add ½ of onion and cook until fragrant, about 1 minute.
4. Carefully add the broth, stirring constantly, until flour mixture is dissolved in broth. Return chicken to pot along with remaining onion, bell pepper, and thyme.
5. Reduce heat to medium and cook, stirring occasionally, for 1½ hours, or until chicken is tender and sauce is thick. Stir in green onions.

Nutrition:

Carbohydrates: 16 g

Fat: 6 g

Protein: 4 g

Calories: 326

158. Broccoli Chicken with Almond

Preparation time: 10 minutes

Cooking time: 45 minutes

Servings: 6

Ingredients:

- ¼ cup unsalted butter
- ¼ cup all-purpose flour
- 1 cup chicken broth
- 1 cup milk
- ½ teaspoon salt
- ½ teaspoon freshly cracked black pepper
- 1/8 teaspoon ground nutmeg
- ½ cup freshly grated Parmigiano-Reggiano
- 3 tablespoons dry sherry
- 3 cups cooked chicken, cut into bite-sized pieces
- 1 (1-pound / 454-g) bag broccoli florets, thawed
- 1 cup slivered almonds, divided
- ½ cup heavy cream

Directions:

1. Heat oven to 350°F (180°C).
2. Melt butter over medium heat in an ovenproof 2-quart or larger

Dutch oven. Add flour and cook, stirring constantly, 1 minute.

3. Gradually whisk in broth and milk; cook 3 minutes, or until it begins to thicken. Stir in salt, pepper, nutmeg, ¼ cup cheese, and sherry; cook until cheese melts.

4. Remove from heat and stir in the chicken, broccoli, half of almonds, and cream. Sprinkle remaining almonds and cheese over the top. Bake uncovered 35 minutes, or until bubbly and golden brown.

Nutrition:

Carbohydrates: 12 g

Fat: 8 g

Protein: 4 g

Calories: 312

159. Golden Fried Chicken Tenders

Preparation time: 15 minutes

Cooking time: 15 minutes

Servings: 4

Ingredients:

- 1 cup all-purpose flour
- 1 teaspoon salt
- 1 teaspoon freshly cracked black pepper
- 2 large eggs, beaten
- 1 cup buttermilk
- 1 teaspoon hot sauce, optional
- 2 pounds (907 g) chicken tenders
- Oil, for frying

Directions:

1. In a large zip-top bag add flour, salt, and pepper. Shake well to coat.

2. In a shallow dish or pie pan add eggs and buttermilk. Whisk to combine, then add hot sauce, if desired, and whisk to incorporate.

3. Add a few tenders at a time to flour, toss to coat, then remove from the bag, shaking off any excess flour. Dip tenders into buttermilk mixture, allowing any excess to drip off, then return tenders to flour and toss again to coat.

4. Transfer coated tenders to a wire rack to dry while you prepare remaining tenders.
5. In a 6- or 8-quart deep Dutch oven heat 3-inch oil over medium-high heat to 350°F (180°C), making sure there is a 3-inch air gap at the top of the pot. Once oil is hot add 3–4 tenders at a time and fry until golden brown and floating, about 3 minutes per side.
6. Transfer to a clean wire rack over a sheet pan to drain. You may store cooked tenders in a warm oven while you fry the rest.

Nutrition:

Carbohydrates: 11 g

Fat: 6 g

Protein: 14 g

Calories: 319

160. Fried Chicken

Preparation time: 20 minutes

Cooking time: 20 minutes

Servings: 4

Ingredients:

- 1 quart buttermilk
- ½ head garlic, peeled and minced
- 3 bay leaves
- 1 tablespoon chili powder
- ¼ cup sugar
- ¼ cup salt
- 2 tablespoons freshly ground black pepper
- 3½–4 pounds (1.59-1.8 kg) chicken pieces
- 4 cups all-purpose flour
- 1 large egg
- 1 teaspoon baking powder
- ½ teaspoon baking soda
- 1 cup whole milk
- 3 cups peanut or corn oil for frying

Directions:

1. In a gallon-sized, zip-top plastic bag combine buttermilk, garlic, bay leaves, chili powder, sugar, salt, and pepper. Trim off any

extra pieces of fat or skin from chicken.

2. Pat the pieces dry and nestle them into the bag. Squeeze out any excess air, seal bag, and refrigerate overnight or at least 3 hours.

3. Place a wire rack over a baking sheet and place chicken pieces on the rack. Drain 30 minutes.

4. Put flour in a shallow bowl. In a second bowl, whisk egg, baking powder, and baking soda. Once combined, add milk.

5. Place chicken pieces, one at a time, in flour and turn to coat. Shake off any excess and roll the pieces in egg mixture with your other hand.

6. Drain to remove any excess and place back in flour. Turn to coat. Place pieces on the rack.

7. Heat 2-inch oil in Dutch oven over medium-high heat to 360°F (182°C) making sure there is a 3-inch air gap at the top of the pot. Add a piece of chicken to the pan, skin side down.

8. Add in two more pieces of chicken, waiting 1 minute between each. Cover and cook 4 minutes, or until the bottom of the first piece is a deep golden brown. Turn over.

9. Turn over other pieces after waiting for intervals of 1 minute. Cook second side of each for 6 to 7 minutes.

10. Remove cooked chicken from pot and place on a paper towel–lined plate. Wait 4 to 5 minutes, or until oil has come back up to 375°F (190°C), before repeating Step 4 with the next batch of chicken. Serve warm or cold.

Nutrition:

Carbohydrates: 12 g

Fat: 6 g

Protein: 4 g

Calories: 288

161. Roast Chicken with Lemon

Preparation time: 15 minutes

Cooking time: 1 hour 40 minutes

Servings: 4

Ingredients:

- 1 (2–3 pound / 0.9-1.4 kg) whole chicken
- 2 teaspoons kosher salt
- 1 teaspoon freshly cracked black pepper
- 1 small bundle fresh thyme
- 1 small bundle fresh sage
- 2 sprigs fresh rosemary
- 1 medium lemon, cut into 4 wedges

Directions:

1. Heat oven to 450°F (235°C). Place a Dutch oven into oven to heat.
2. Pat chicken dry inside and out with paper towels, then coat the outside of chicken with salt and pepper, making sure to rub the spices into the skin evenly.
3. Stuff the cavity of the bird with fresh herbs and lemon wedges. Truss the bird by tying the legs together with butcher's twine, then wrapping twine around the base of the bird so the wings are held close to the body.
4. Carefully transfer chicken to the heated Dutch oven. Roast 50 to 60 minutes or until the juices from the thigh run clear and the internal temperature of the breast and thigh reach 160°F (71°C).
5. Allow chicken to rest 15 minutes. Remove and discard the twine and herbs and lemon from the chicken cavity and serve.

Nutrition:

Carbohydrates: 17 g

Fat: 6 g

Protein: 4 g

Calories: 326

162. Roast Chicken Drumsticks

Preparation time: 15 minutes

Cooking time: 45 minutes

Servings: 4

Ingredients:

- 2 cups buttermilk
- 1 tablespoon maple syrup
- 1 teaspoon smoked paprika
- ½ teaspoon salt
- ½ teaspoon freshly cracked black pepper
- ½ teaspoon poultry seasoning
- ½ teaspoon hot sauce
- 8 chicken drumsticks, about 1½ pounds (680g)

Directions:

1. In a large zip-top bag add all of ingredients except chicken. Close the bag and shake to combine then add chicken, seal the bag, and refrigerate 4 hours or overnight.
2. Remove chicken from the buttermilk and place in a colander 30 minutes to drain.
3. Heat oven to 400°F (205°C). Place an ovenproof 8- or 10-quart Dutch into oven to heat.
4. Once heated, lightly spray the Dutch oven with nonstick cooking spray. Arrange drumsticks in the bottom of the pan in a single layer.
5. Roast 35 to 45 minutes, turning the legs halfway through, or until chicken legs reach an internal temperature of 160°F (71°C) and the juices run clear.

Nutrition:

Carbohydrates: 19 g

Fat: 6 g

Protein: 18 g

Calories: 277

163. Chicken Thighs with Mushroom

Preparation time: 20 minutes

Cooking time: 1 hour

Servings: 4

Ingredients:

- 1–1½ pounds (454-680 g) bone-in, skin-on chicken thighs
- ½ teaspoon salt
- ½ teaspoon freshly ground black pepper
- ¼ cup vegetable oil
- 1 medium onion, peeled and finely chopped
- 1 pint sliced button mushrooms
- 1 clove garlic, peeled and minced
- ¼ teaspoon thyme
- ¼ teaspoon crushed red pepper flakes
- ½ cup red wine
- ½ cup chicken broth
- 1 tablespoon unsalted butter

Directions:

1. Season chicken thighs on all sides with salt and pepper. Place on a plate and refrigerate, uncovered, 2 hours or overnight, to dry out skin slightly.
2. In a Dutch oven over medium-high heat add oil. Once oil shimmers add chicken thighs skin side down, leaving ½-inch between each thigh. You may need to cook in batches.
3. Cook until skin is very brown and crisp, about 6 to 8 minutes. Remove thighs to a plate and rest skin side up. Repeat with any remaining thighs.
4. Heat oven to 400°F (205°C).
5. Reduce Dutch oven heat to medium and add onions and mushrooms. Sauté until vegetables are tender, about 5 minutes, then add garlic, thyme, and red pepper flakes; cook until garlic is fragrant, about 30 seconds more.
6. Add red wine to the pan and, with a wooden spoon or heatproof spatula, scrape any browned bits off the bottom of the pan.
7. Once wine has reduced by ¼, about 5 to 8 minutes, add chicken thighs back to the pot skin side up. Carefully pour in chicken broth until liquid reaches about halfway up the sides of the thighs. If you need more liquid use a little water.
8. Bake chicken uncovered 30 to 40 minutes, or until it is cooked through and reaches an internal temperature of 160°F (71°C). Remove thighs from the Dutch oven and return pan to medium heat.

9. Bring liquid to a boil and reduce by half, about 8 minutes, then reduce heat to medium-low and whisk in butter. Spoon sauce over thighs just before serving to preserve the crisp skin.

Nutrition:

Carbohydrates: 10 g

Fat: 6 g

Protein: 4 g

Calories: 368

164. Mushroom Chicken a la King

Preparation time: 10 minutes

Cooking time: 20 minutes

Servings: 4

Ingredients:

- 2 tablespoons unsalted butter
- 1 green onion, chopped
- 4 ounces (113 g) mushrooms, quartered
- 1 small red bell pepper, seeded and diced
- 2 tablespoons all-purpose flour
- 1½ cups chicken broth
- 1 cup light cream
- 2 cups diced cooked chicken
- ¼ teaspoon salt
- ¼ teaspoon freshly cracked black pepper
- 4 puff pastry shells or 4 slices toast

Directions:

1. In a Dutch oven melt butter over medium-high heat. Add green onion, mushrooms, and bell pepper, and cook until tender, about 5 minutes.
2. Add flour and stir to coat. Add broth and stir until flour dissolves. Bring mixture to boil;

cook, stirring often, 10 minutes or until the liquid is reduced by 1/3.

3. Reduce heat to medium-low. Stir in cream, chicken, salt, and pepper. Simmer 5 minutes, then remove from heat. Serve in puff pastry shells or over toast.

Nutrition:

Carbohydrates: 12 g

Fat: 6 g

Protein: 4 g

Calories: 326

165. Creamy Broccoli Chicken Noodles

Preparation time: 15 minutes

Cooking time: 25 minutes

Servings: 8

Ingredients:

- 1 tablespoon unsalted butter
- 1 tablespoon extra-virgin olive oil
- 1 large yellow onion, peeled and diced
- 1½ pounds (680 g) boneless, skinless chicken breasts, cut into bite-sized pieces
- 4 cloves garlic, peeled and minced
- ½ teaspoon salt
- ½ teaspoon freshly cracked black pepper
- 4 tablespoons Hungarian paprika, divided
- 4 cups chicken broth, divided
- 2 tablespoons all-purpose flour
- 1 (1-pound / 454-g) bag frozen broccoli stir-fry mix, thawed
- 16 ounces (454 g) sour cream
- 4 cups cooked egg noodles or spaetzle

Directions:

1. In a Dutch oven add butter and oil over medium-high heat. Once

the butter melts and starts to foam add onion and saute for 3 minutes. Add chicken to Dutch oven and stir-fry 5 minutes.

2. Stir in garlic, salt, pepper, 3 tablespoons of the paprika, and 3½ cups chicken broth; cover pan. Bring to a boil.

3. In a small bowl mix remaining ½ cup chicken broth with flour. Strain out any lumps then whisk broth mixture into the boiling broth. Boil 3 minutes.

4. Stir in broccoli stir-fry mix; lower the temperature, cover, and simmer 5 minutes.

5. Remove pan from the burner and stir in sour cream. Pour chicken and vegetable mixture over cooked noodles or spaetzle. Sprinkle remaining paprika over top. Serve immediately.

Nutrition:

Carbohydrates: 21 g

Fat: 6 g

Protein: 4 g

Calories: 290

166. Pineapple Chicken

Preparation time: 10 minutes

Cooking time: 1 hour

Servings: 6

Ingredients:

- 6 chicken breasts, sliced into strips
- ¼ cup flour
- 1 teaspoon salt
- ¼ teaspoon pepper
- 2 tablespoons oil
- 1 8-ounce can sliced pineapple, drained (retain the juice)
- 2/3 cup light molasses
- 1 tablespoon mustard
- 1 tablespoon cider vinegar
- 1 16-ounce can sweet potatoes, drained
- Rice or noodles, for serving

Directions:

1. Preheat the oven to 350°F.

2. In a bowl, combine the flour, salt, and pepper.

3. Dredge the chicken strips in flour. Shake off any excess.

4. Heat the oil in the Dutch oven on the stove top over medium.

5. Working in batches, brown the flour-coated chicken in the hot oil. Put the browned chicken on a plate and drain the oil from the Dutch oven. Wipe it clean.

6. In a bowl, whisk together the reserved pineapple juice, molasses, mustard, and vinegar.

7. Place the chicken back into the Dutch oven. Add the sweet potatoes, and toss to coat with about half of the pineapple mixture.

8. Cover and bake for 30 minutes.

9. Top with the pineapple and remaining sauce, and then bake for another 30 minutes.

10. Serve with rice or noodles.

Nutrition:

Calories 683

Carbs 41 g

Fat 29 g

Protein 61 g

Sodium 297 mg

167. Dutch Oven Chicken

Preparation time: 10 minutes

Cooking time: 45-60 minutes

Servings: 6

Ingredients:

- 6 boneless skinless chicken breasts
- 1 ½ cups sour cream
- 1 teaspoon salt
- ½ teaspoon paprika
- 1 teaspoon celery salt
- 1 teaspoon Worcestershire sauce
- 1 teaspoon lemon juice
- 2 cloves garlic, crushed
- 1 cup round, buttery crackers, crushed
- 3 tablespoons melted butter
- Cooking spray

Directions:

1. Preheat the oven to 350°F, and coat a large Dutch oven with cooking spray.

2. Combine the sour cream, lemon juice, salt, paprika, and celery salt.

3. Dip the chicken pieces in this mixture, turning to coat, and then press them into the crushed crackers.

4. Lay chicken pieces on slightly greased Dutch oven.

5. Drizzle melted butter over the chicken, and bake uncovered for 45-60 minutes.

Nutrition:

Calories 654

Carbs 5 g

Fat 42 g

Protein 62 g

Sodium 638 mg

168. Roast Chicken with Garlic and Truffles

Preparation time: 30 minutes

Cooking time: 2 hours

Servings: 8

Ingredients:

- 1 whole chicken
- ¼ cup butter, cut into small chunks about a teaspoon each
- ½ bulb garlic, peeled, crushed and minced
- 3 tablespoons extra virgin olive oil
- 1 teaspoon dried rosemary
- 2 teaspoons dried onion flakes
- ½ teaspoon fresh cracked pepper
- 2 cubes truffle bouillon
- ½ lemon, sliced
- Truffle Pan Gravy
- Drippings remaining in Dutch oven
- ¼ cup white wine
- ½ cup chicken stock
- 2 tablespoons flour

Directions:

1. Preheat the oven to 350°F.

2. Pat the chicken dry with paper towel and place it in a Dutch oven.

3. Surround the chicken with pats of butter, tucking pieces into the cavity and under the wings.

4. Drizzle the chicken with olive oil.

5. Sprinkle the chicken evenly with rosemary, garlic, onion flakes, and pepper.

6. Crush the bouillon cubes and rub them onto the chicken with your fingertips, massaging the spices into the surface.

7. Arrange the lemon slices around the chicken.

8. Bake, uncovered, for 45 minutes, and then baste. The chicken should be done after 1 ½ hours. It should be golden and the juices should run clear. If chicken browns too quickly on the outside, cover the bird with foil.

9. Baste the chicken a final time, then remove it from the pot and allow it to rest at room temperature for 30 minutes, loosely covered with foil.

10. To prepare the gravy, remove the lemon and skim off as much fat as possible from the chicken drippings in the Dutch oven.

11. Place the pot on the stove top over medium-high heat. Deglaze with the wine.

12. Mix the flour with the chicken stock until smooth, add it to the pot and stir. Bring to a boil, and simmer until the desired thickness is reached.

Nutrition:

Calories 216

Carbs 10 g

Fat 14 g

Protein 12 g

Sodium 725 mg

169. Chinese-Style One Pot Chicken

Preparation time: 20 minutes

Cooking time: 45-50 minutes

Servings: 6

Ingredients:

- ¼ cup soy sauce
- 1 ½ teaspoons sugar
- 2 teaspoons toasted sesame oil
- 2 teaspoons cornstarch
- 2 boneless, skinless chicken breasts, cut into ½-inch cubes
- 3 scallions, roughly chopped
- 3 garlic cloves, minced
- A thumb fresh ginger, roughly grated
- 2 ounces smoked sausage, cut into ¼-inch cubes
- 10 ounces fresh shiitake mushrooms, caps thinly sliced
- 1 tablespoon peanut oil
- 2 cups long-grain rice
- 1 teaspoon salt
- 4 cups chicken stock
- Scallions, chopped, for serving (optional)
- Soy sauce and chili garlic sauce, to serve on the side (optional)

Directions:

1. Preheat the oven to 350°F.
2. In a bowl, whisk the soy sauce, sugar, sesame oil, and cornstarch.
3. Add the chicken, scallions, garlic, and ginger. Toss well and let marinate for at least 15 minutes in the refrigerator.
4. Cook the sausage in the Dutch oven over medium-high heat. Lower the temperature to medium low and allow the sausage to release its fat.
5. When the oil from the sausage begins to coat the bottom of the Dutch oven, add the mushrooms. Raise the heat to high and cook mushrooms without stirring, for about 5 minutes. Flip over and cook for 3 minutes.
6. Add 1 tablespoon of peanut oil to the pot, and reduce the heat to medium. Sauté the rice very quickly to toast slightly in order to get a roasted flavor.
7. Add the marinated chicken (with the marinade) to the rice and mushrooms. Season with salt.

8. Pour in the stock and bring it to a boil. Turn off the burner and cover the pot.

9. Bake for 45 minutes. Check that the rice is done, and let it stand, covered, for 5 minutes.

10. Fluff the rice with a fork before serving to distribute chicken, sausage, and mushrooms.

11. Serve topped with scallions (optional) and with soy sauce and chili garlic sauce on the side.

Nutrition:

Calories 477

Carbs 64 g

Fat 11 g

Protein 28 g

Sodium 1326 mg

170. Moroccan Stew

Preparation time: 10 minutes

Cooking time: 20-30 minutes

Servings: 4

Ingredients:

- 3 tablespoons olive oil
- 2 onions, chopped
- 6 garlic cloves, minced
- 1 tablespoon ground coriander
- 1 tablespoon ground cumin
- 1 tablespoon paprika
- 1 teaspoon turmeric
- 4 cups low-sodium chicken broth
- 1 teaspoon finely grated lemon zest
- 2 ½ pounds boneless, skinless chicken breasts, cut into 1-inch cubes
- 1 pound frozen baby artichoke hearts
- 1 pound carrots, peeled, sliced
- Salt and pepper
- Steamed couscous
- Chopped flat-leaf parsley

Directions:

1. Heat the oil in a Dutch oven over medium heat.

2. Sauté the onions for about 8 minutes, or until they begin to caramelize.

3. Stir in the garlic, coriander, cumin, paprika, and turmeric. Cook for 1 minute or until fragrant.

4. Add the broth and lemon zest. Bring to a boil.

5. Reduce the heat to medium. Add the chicken, artichokes, and carrots. Simmer until vegetables are tender (about 10-15 minutes).

6. Season with salt and pepper.

7. Served spooned over couscous and garnished with parsley.

Nutrition:

Calories 242

Carbs 18 g

Fat 12 g

Protein 18 g

Sodium 746 mg

171. Chicken Risotto

Preparation time: 5 minutes

Cooking time: 35 minutes

Servings: 6

Ingredients:

- 2 chicken breasts, diced in 1-inch cubes
- 1 tablespoon vegetable oil
- 1 large onion, diced
- 1 bell pepper, diced
- 3 tablespoons butter
- 2 ½ cups Arborio rice
- ½ cup dry vermouth
- 2 packages chicken stock, reduced sodium
- Salt and pepper
- ¼ cup green onions, diced
- 1 cup water
- Salt and pepper
- Parmesan cheese, optional

Directions:

1. Heat the Dutch oven over high heat and add 1 tablespoon of oil.

2. Season the chicken with salt and pepper, and brown the chicken on all sides.

3. Add the onion and pepper, and cook, stirring occasionally, until slightly browned. Add the butter and stir.

4. Reduce the heat to medium-low. Add the rice to the pot and stir to toast slightly.

5. Pour in the vermouth and half the chicken stock; just enough to keep rice consistency liquid.

6. Simmer and stir until rice thickens. Keep adding stock in small amounts, just to prevent the rice from scorching. Keep doing this until rice is of desirable tenderness, using water if you run out of stock. The texture of risotto should be al dente. It shouldn't spread on a plate, neither should it be as thick as mashed potatoes.

7. Add green onions just before risotto is done.

8. Serve warm topped with grated Parmesan cheese.

Nutrition:

Calories 271

Carbs 40 g

Fat 5 g

Protein 9 g

Sodium 104 mg

Chapter 9. Turkey and Duck

172. Grilled Turkey

Preparation time: 10 minutes

Cooking time: 1 hour 30 minutes

Servings: 4

Ingredients:

- 1 pound turkey breast
- ¾ cup onion, chopped
- ¾ cup celery, chopped
- ¾ cup carrot, chopped
- ½ cup apple cider
- 1 ½ cups low sodium chicken broth
- 1 ½ cups cranberries, fresh or frozen
- 1 bay leaf
- 1 dash salt
- 1 dash pepper
- ¼ cup fresh sage, minced
- 1 tablespoon fresh thyme, minced
- 1 tablespoon olive oil
- ¼ teaspoon salt
- ¼ teaspoon pepper
- Cooking spray

Directions:

1. Coat a Dutch oven with cooking spray, and place it on the stove top over medium-high heat. Sauté the onion, celery, and carrot until tender. Add the apple cider and the chicken broth, and bring to a boil.
2. Add the cranberries, and bay leaf; and reduce the heat. Simmer, uncovered, for 1 hour.
3. Strain the mixture through a sieve into a large bowl, and discard the solids. Season the broth with salt and pepper and set it aside, covered.
4. Combine the sage, thyme, oil, salt and pepper and rub on both sides of the turkey breast.
5. Prepare a grill.
6. Place the turkey on the grill rack coated with cooking spray, and grill for 10 minutes on each side.
7. Slice thinly and serve with broth.

Nutrition:

Calories 270

Carbs 42 g

Fat 3 g

Protein 19 g

Sodium 380 mg

173. Peppers with Turkey Stuffing

Preparation time: 10 minutes

Cooking time: 35-40 minutes

Servings: 6

Ingredients:

- 2 tablespoons vegetable oil
- ½ pound ground turkey breast
- 1 clove garlic, minced
- 3 large red peppers, cut lengthwise in halves and cleaned
- 4 cups water
- ¼ cup shredded mozzarella
- ¾ cup brown rice, cooked
- ¾ cup wild rice, cooked
- 1/3 cup green onions, chopped
- 2 ounces pimiento, chopped
- 1/8 teaspoon cayenne pepper

Directions:

1. Preheat the oven to 350°.
2. On the stove top, heat the vegetable oil and cook the turkey and garlic in a skillet until browned.
3. Rinse cut, cleaned peppers.
4. Pour the water into a Dutch oven and bring to a boil. Carefully drop the bell peppers into the boiling water and cook for 2 minutes. Remove peppers and drain.
5. In a large bowl, stir together the mozzarella, brown rice, wild rice, green onions, pimiento, cayenne pepper, and the turkey mixture.
6. Dry the Dutch oven and coat with a minimal amount of oil.
7. Stuff the peppers loosely and arrange on bottom of Dutch oven.
8. Cover and bake for 30 minutes.
9. Uncover and sprinkle with cheese, and return to the oven until the cheese is melted.

Nutrition:

Calories 160

Carbs 20 g

Fat 8 g

Protein 4 g

Sodium 231 mg

174. Artichoke Turkey with Spinach Casserole

Preparation time: 10 minutes

Cooking time: 40 minutes

Servings: 10

Ingredients:

- 1 (14-ounce / 397-g) jar artichoke hearts, drained and chopped
- 3 (10-ounce / 283-g) packages frozen chopped spinach, thawed and well drained
- 2 cups finely chopped cooked turkey
- 2 (8-ounce / 227-g) packages cream cheese, cut into cubes
- 2 tablespoons mayonnaise
- ¼ cup unsalted butter or extra-virgin olive oil
- 6 tablespoons heavy cream or milk
- ½ teaspoon freshly cracked black pepper
- ½ cup freshly grated Parmigiano-Reggiano or Romano cheese

Directions:

1. Heat oven to 375°F (190°C).
2. Evenly spread artichoke hearts across the bottom of a Dutch oven. Top with spinach and turkey.
3. Add cream cheese, mayonnaise, butter or oil, and cream or milk to a food processor; process until smooth. Spread over top of turkey. Sprinkle with pepper, and then cheese.
4. Bake uncovered 40 minutes, or until the cheese is bubbly and the casserole is lightly browned on top. This dish can be assembled the night before and refrigerated; allow extra baking time if you move the casserole directly from the refrigerator to the oven.

Nutrition:

Carbohydrates: 22 g

Fat: 6 g

Protein: 4 g

Calories: 326

175. Turkey Pilaf with Cheese

Preparation time: 10 minutes

Cooking time: 30 minutes

Servings: 4

Ingredients:

- 2 tablespoons unsalted butter
- 1 small yellow onion, peeled and chopped
- 1 cup uncooked long-grain rice
- 2 cloves garlic, peeled and minced
- 1½ cups chicken broth
- ½ cup dry white wine
- ½ teaspoon salt
- 1 (12-ounce / 340-g) steam-in-the-bag frozen mixed vegetables
- 1 to 2 cups chopped cooked turkey
- Freshly grated Parmigiano-Reggiano cheese, for garnish

Directions:

1. Add the butter to a Dutch oven and melt over medium heat. Add the onion and saute 2 minutes. Add rice and brown it in butter, about 6 to 8 minutes. Watch carefully as the rice can burn easily. Add garlic and saute 30 seconds.
2. Pour in broth and wine. Bring to a boil and then add salt. Cover; simmer 20 minutes, or until rice is tender.
3. While the rice cooks, microwave vegetables in the bag 4 to 5 minutes.
4. Uncover the rice and add turkey and microwave-steamed vegetables. Stir to combine. Cover and cook on low 2 minutes. Remove the cover and stir. Cover and continue to cook until the turkey is warmed through, if necessary.
5. Serve warm topped with cheese.

Nutrition:

Carbohydrates: 20 g

Fat: 6 g

Protein: 24 g

Calories: 398

176. Turkey Breast with Asparagus

Preparation time: 20 minutes

Cooking time: 25 minutes

Servings: 4

Ingredients:

- 4 medium baking potatoes
- 2 tablespoons unsalted butter, softened
- 1 teaspoon Dijon mustard
- 1 (7-ounce / 198-g) jar roasted red sweet peppers, drained and chopped
- 4 teaspoons peeled, finely chopped red onion or shallot
- ¼ teaspoon dried tarragon, crushed
- ½ teaspoon dried parsley, crushed
- 1/8 teaspoon salt
- 1/8 teaspoon freshly cracked black pepper
- 1 pound (454 g) asparagus spears
- 2 tablespoons extra-virgin olive oil
- 4 (4-ounce / 113-g) boneless turkey breast cutlets

Directions:

1. Heat oven to 325°F (163°C).
2. Clean and pierce potatoes. Place on a microwave-safe plate and microwave on high 6 to 10 minutes, or until they can be pierced easily with a knife.
3. In a small bowl, combine butter, mustard, peppers, onion or shallot, tarragon, parsley, salt, and black pepper; set aside.
4. Clean asparagus and snap off and discard the woody bases. Carefully cut potatoes into quarters. Add potatoes, asparagus, and olive oil to a large zip-top plastic bag. Close the bag and shake to coat vegetables. Pour potatoes and asparagus out of the bag into a Dutch oven.
5. Evenly spread butter mixture over the top of turkey cutlets. Place cutlets on top of potatoes and asparagus. Bake 15 to 20 minutes, or until turkey is baked through and asparagus is tender.

Nutrition:

Carbohydrates: 19 g

Fat: 6 g

Protein: 12 g

Calories: 306

177. Savory Turkey Breast

Preparation time: 10 minutes

Cooking time: 15 minutes

Servings: 4

Ingredients:

- 1 pound (454 g) turkey breast cutlets
- 1/3 cup all-purpose flour
- 1 teaspoon seasoned salt
- 2 tablespoons unsalted butter
- 1 medium onion, peeled and thinly sliced
- 1 small red bell pepper, seeded and thinly sliced
- 1 small green bell pepper, seeded and thinly sliced
- 1 cup turkey or chicken broth
- 1 cup white wine
- ¼ teaspoon salt
- ¼ teaspoon freshly cracked black pepper

Directions:

1. Lightly pound turkey cutlets with a meat mallet. Combine flour and seasoned salt in a shallow dish, then dredge turkey in the mixture.
2. Heat butter in Dutch oven over medium-high heat. Place cutlets in butter and brown, about 3 minutes per side. Spread onions and peppers evenly over top of cutlets. Carefully add broth and wine to the Dutch oven.
3. Cover with the lid and cook until turkey is cooked through and vegetables are crisp-tender, about 10 minutes. Season with salt and pepper.

Nutrition:

Carbohydrates: 22 g

Fat: 6 g

Protein: 4 g

Calories: 326

178. Duck Breast with Olive

Preparation time: 15 minutes

Cooking time: 1 hour 30 minutes

Servings: 4

Ingredients:

- 1 tablespoon extra-virgin olive oil
- 6 duck breasts, skin scored
- 3 shallots, minced
- 2 garlic cloves
- 1 tablespoon roughly chopped fresh thyme leaves
- 1 bay leaf
- 1½ cups dry white wine
- Freshly ground black pepper, to taste
- ½ cup pitted Kalamata olives
- 1 bouillon cube
- 1 cup water

Directions:

1. Preheat the oven to 300°F (150°C).
2. In a Dutch oven over medium heat, heat the olive oil. Turn the heat to low, and sear half of the duck breasts, skin-side down, until crisp. Turn and lightly brown the other side. Using a slotted spoon, transfer the duck breasts to a platter. Repeat for the remaining breasts.
3. Strain the fat from the pot. Add the shallots and garlic. Brown lightly, Add the thyme and the bay leaf, and sauté for 1 minute.
4. Add the wine, season with pepper, and reduce by half. Add the olives and sauté for 1 minute.
5. Return duck breasts to the pot, skin-side up. Add the bouillon cube and the water, and bring to a boil. Cover, place in the heated oven, and simmer for 30 to 45 minutes, or until the duck breasts are tender.
6. Remove duck breasts and place on a platter. Reduce the sauce, skimming the fat from the top. Ladle the sauce over the duck breasts and serve.

Nutrition:

Carbohydrates: 21 g

Fat: 6 g

Protein: 24 g

Calories: 396

Chapter 10. Beef, Pork and Lamb

179. Jerk Pork Chops with Plantains

Preparation time: 1 hour

Cooking time: 35 minutes

Servings: 6

Ingredients:

- 8 pork chops
- 4 tablespoons extra-virgin olive oil, plus a splash for cooking
- 2 tablespoons onion powder
- 2 teaspoons thyme
- 1 teaspoon ground allspice
- ½ teaspoon ground cumin
- 2 teaspoons sea salt, divided
- 4 pounds ripe plantains, peeled and cut into 1-inch-thick slices
- ½ cup melted butter
- ½ cup honey

Directions:

1. Rub the pork chops evenly with the 4 tablespoons of olive oil, onion powder, thyme, allspice, cumin, and 1 teaspoon of salt. Let stand for 1 hour.
2. Preheat the oven to 350°F.
3. In a Dutch oven over medium heat, heat the remaining splash of olive oil. Add 4 pork chops, and cook for about 4 minutes. Turnover and cook for 4 minutes or until the pork is lightly browned on both sides. Transfer to a platter and repeat with the remaining 4 chops. Drain off all the fat. Cover to keep warm.
4. Combine the plantains, butter, honey, and the remaining 1 teaspoon of salt in the Dutch oven. Cover with the lid, place in the heated oven and bake for 20 minutes, or until tender and brown, turning once.
5. Serve with the pork chops.

Nutrition:

Calories 692

Total Fat 33.5g

Saturated Fat 13.9g

Cholesterol 79mg

Sodium 601mg

Total Carbohydrate 91.6g

Dietary Fiber 5.5g

Total Sugars 52g

Protein 16.1g

Calcium 42mg

Iron 2mg

Potassium 1364mg

180. Pork with Rice & Beans

Preparation time: 10 minutes

Cooking time: 3 hours

Servings: 6

Ingredients:

- 1 (15-ounce) can red kidney beans
- 1 smoked pork hock (about 1½ pounds)
- 12 ounces chorizo, cut into ½-inch pieces
- 2½ cups low-sodium chicken broth or stock
- 1 onion, chopped
- 1 stalk celery, chopped
- 1 tablespoon tomato paste
- 2 cloves garlic, minced
- ½ teaspoon crushed dried thyme
- ½ teaspoon crushed dried oregano

- 3 ½ cups precooked long-grain rice

Directions:

1. Preheat the oven to 300°F.
2. In a Dutch oven, combine the beans, pork hock, chorizo, broth, onions, celery, tomato paste, garlic, thyme, and oregano. Cover, place in the heated oven and cook for 2 to 2½ hours.
3. Remove the pork hock from the pot.
4. Slice the meat off the bone, and cut it into bite-size pieces.
5. Stir the meat back into the bean mixture, add the rice, and return to the oven. Stew for 10 to 15 minutes, or until the rice is heated through.

Nutrition:

Calories 823

Total Fat 66.9g

Saturated Fat 23.5g

Cholesterol 432mg

Sodium 1109mg

Total Carbohydrate 135.3g

Dietary Fiber 12.8g

Total Sugars 2.8g

Protein 158.5g

Calcium 134mg

Iron 16mg

Potassium 2878mg

181. Cajun Riblets

Preparation time: 20 minutes

Cooking time: 1 hours

Servings: 6

Ingredients:

- 2 pounds pork loin back ribs
- 1 tablespoon Cajun seasoning
- 1 cup chili sauce
- 1 onion, chopped
- 1 tablespoon cornstarch
- 1 jalapeño pepper, seeded and finely chopped
- 1 tablespoon lemon juice
- 1 teaspoon hot pepper sauce

Directions:

1. Preheat the oven to 300°F.
2. Sprinkle the pork ribs with the Cajun seasoning, cut them into single-rib portions, and place in the Dutch oven.
3. In a medium bowl, mix the chili sauce, onions, cornstarch, jalapeño pepper, lemon juice, and hot pepper sauce. Pour the mixture over the ribs.
4. Cover with the lid, place in the preheated oven, and cook for 1 to 1½ hours.

Nutrition:

Calories 366

Total Fat 25.6g

Saturated Fat 9.4g

Cholesterol 100mg

Sodium 1108mg

Total Carbohydrate 3.8g

Dietary Fiber 0.6g

Total Sugars 1.4g

Protein 27.2g

Calcium 8mg

Iron 1mg

Potassium 90mg

182. Pork Rib Casserole

Preparation time: 10 minutes

Cooking time: 2 hours

Servings: 6

Ingredients:

- 1 tablespoon vegetable oil
- 2 pounds boneless pork country-style ribs
- 1 red bell pepper, seeded and chopped
- 1 poblano chile, seeded and chopped
- 1½ teaspoons bottled minced garlic
- 2 (15-ounce) cans pinto beans, rinsed and drained
- 1 (28-ounce) can crushed tomatoes
- 1 medium onion, chopped
- 1 tablespoon chili powder
- 1 teaspoon ground cumin
- Salt
- Freshly ground black pepper

Directions:

1. Preheat the oven to 325°F.
2. Heat the vegetable oil in a Dutch oven over medium heat. Cook the pork ribs, in batches, until browned on both sides. Remove the ribs to a plate and drain off the fat from the pot.
3. In the Dutch oven, combine the bell and poblano peppers, garlic, beans, tomatoes, onions, chili powder, cumin, salt, and pepper. Add the ribs.
4. Cover with the lid, place in the oven, and cook for 2 to 2½ hours, or until the meat is tender.
5. On a clean work surface, break the ribs apart into serving-size pieces. Return to the pot, stirring to combine. Serve in the Dutch oven with a side of cornbread.

Nutrition:

Calories 775, Total Fat 10g

Saturated Fat 2.7g, Cholesterol 110mg

Sodium 222mg, Total Carbohydrate 98.8g

Dietary Fiber 24.8g, Total Sugars 8.4g

Protein 71.9g, Calcium 200mg

Iron 10mg, Potassium 3032mg

183. Beef Bourguignon

Preparation time: 30 minutes

Cooking time: 3 hours

Servings: 8

Ingredients:

- 2 ½ pounds chuck beef, cut into 1-inch cubes
- Salt
- Freshly ground black pepper
- ¾ cup gluten-free flour (made from fava beans or garbanzo beans), divided
- 4 tablespoons extra-virgin olive oil
- 6 ounces applewood-smoked bacon, diced
- 12 pearl onions, peeled
- 12 baby carrots, peeled and halved
- 1 pound mushrooms, sliced
- 2 tablespoons butter
- 2 onions, diced
- 6 cloves garlic, peeled and chopped
- 2 tablespoons tomato paste
- ½ teaspoon dried thyme
- 1 (750-milliliter) bottle dry red burgundy wine
- 1 quart beef broth or stock

Directions:

1. Preheat the oven to 325°F.
2. Sprinkle the beef cubes with salt and pepper, then lightly coat with ½ a cup of flour.
3. In a Dutch oven over medium heat, heat the olive oil. Cook the bacon until the fat is rendered. Transfer to a platter. Working in batches, sear the beef in the hot fat for 3 to 5 minutes, until brown on all sides. Transfer to the platter with the bacon, and continue searing until all the beef is browned.
4. Add the pearl onions, carrots, and mushrooms to the pot and cook for 2 to 3 minutes. Transfer to a platter.
5. Add the butter to the pot. Put the onions and garlic, and cook for 4 to 5 minutes, or until transparent.
6. Stir in the remaining ¼ cup of flour, the tomato paste, and the thyme. Cook for 2 minutes.
7. Deglaze the pot with the wine, and bring to a boil.

Pour in the broth, and return to a boil.

8. Return the bacon and beef cubes to the pot. Bring to a boil. Cover, place in the heated oven and cook for 2 to 2½ hours.
9. Return the pearl onions, carrots, and mushrooms to the pot. Cook for 30 minutes.

Nutrition:

Calories 1553

Total Fat 54g

Saturated Fat 21.5g

Cholesterol 175mg

Sodium 1011mg

Total Carbohydrate 46g

Dietary Fiber 4.8g

Total Sugars 16.9g

Protein 52.8g

Calcium 148mg

Iron 10mg

Potassium 1865mg

184. Herb-Crusted Roast Beef & Potatoes

Preparation time: 10 minutes

Cooking time: 1 hours

Servings: 6

Ingredients:

- 1½ pounds baby new potatoes
- 1 teaspoon sea salt
- 1 teaspoon black pepper
- 4 garlic cloves, minced
- 1 teaspoon dried thyme
- 1 teaspoon dried rosemary
- 2 tablespoons Dijon mustard
- 3 pounds eye round roast

Directions:

1. Preheat the oven to 325°F.
2. In a Dutch oven over medium heat, bring water to

a boil. Boil the potatoes until they are just barely cooked through. Transfer to a bowl.

3. Mix the salt, pepper, garlic, thyme, rosemary, and mustard into a paste, and spread it over the roast. Place the meat in the Dutch oven, fatty side up, and roast for about 20 minutes per pound or until the internal temperature registers 125°F for rare, 150°F for medium, or 160°F for well-done.

4. About 30 minutes before the beef is cooked to your liking, add the potatoes to the pot, turning them on all sides.

Nutrition:

Calories 621

Total Fat 8.3g

Saturated Fat 3g

Cholesterol 100mg

Sodium 502mg

Total Carbohydrate 72.1g

Dietary Fiber 4.6g

Total Sugars 0.1g

Protein 56.8g

Calcium 54mg

Iron 6mg

Potassium 23mg

185. Beef tenderloin

Preparation time: 15 minutes

Cooking time: 1 hour

Servings: 6

Ingredients:

- ¾ pound shallots, peeled and halved lengthwise
- 2 tablespoons extra-virgin olive oil, divided
- Salt
- Freshly ground black pepper
- 3 cups beef broth or stock
- 1½ teaspoon tomato paste
- 3 slices bacon, diced
- 1 (2-pound) beef tenderloin
- 1 teaspoon dried thyme
- 2 tablespoons softened butter
- 1 tablespoon all-purpose flour

Directions:

1. Preheat the oven to 350°F.
2. In a Dutch oven, combine the shallots and 1 tablespoon of olive oil. Season with salt and pepper. Cook in the heated oven for about 30 minutes, or until the shallots are browned. Transfer to a platter.
3. Boil the broth in the Dutch oven over high heat. Stir in the tomato paste, and transfer the mixture to a bowl.
4. Heat the remaining 1 tablespoon of olive oil in the pot over medium heat, and toast the bacon for 7 to 10 minutes, or until the bacon is browned and crispy.
5. Transfer to the platter with the shallots.
6. Season the tenderloin with the thyme, salt, and pepper. Add to the pot and cook over medium heat until browned on all sides, about 7 minutes.
7. Cover, put in the oven, and bake until medium-rare, or an internal thermometer registers 130-135°F, about 25 minutes.
8. Transfer the tenderloin to a platter. Skim away any excess fat from the pot, and place the pot back on the stovetop.
9. Pour the broth mixture to the pot and bring to a boil, scraping the bottom and sides of the pot with a wooden spoon to loosen any browned bits. Reduce the heat to low.
10. Whisk in the butter and flour, and cook for 2 to 3 minutes, or until the sauce thickens. Return the shallots and bacon to the pot. Season with salt and pepper.
11. Cut the tenderloin into ½-inch-thick slices. Place on a serving dish and spoon the sauce on top.

Nutrition:

Calories 506

Total Fat 27.1g

Saturated Fat 9.9g

Cholesterol 160mg

Sodium 756mg

Total Carbohydrate 12.2g

Dietary Fiber 0.3g

Total Sugars 1g

Protein 51.5g

Calcium 58mg

Iron 4mg

Potassium 941mg

186. Roast Beef with Root Vegetables

Preparation time: 20 minutes

Cooking time: 1 hour

Servings: 6

Ingredients:

- 6 garlic cloves, minced
- 2 tablespoons whole-grain Dijon mustard
- 2 tablespoons sea salt, plus a pinch, divided
- 2 tablespoons freshly ground black pepper, plus a pinch, divided
- 1 tablespoon dried thyme
- ¼ cup extra-virgin olive oil, plus 3 tablespoons, divided
- 1 (4-pound) boneless prime rib roast beef
- 1 ½ pounds baby or new potatoes, halved
- ½ pound beets, peeled and sliced
- ½ pound turnips, peeled and sliced
- ½ pound parsnips, peeled and sliced
- 1 cup champignons

Directions:

1. Preheat the oven to 325°F.
2. In a small bowl, mix the garlic, mustard, 2 tablespoons of salt, and 2 tablespoons of pepper, thyme, and ¼ cup of olive oil to create a rub. Spread the rub evenly over the prime rib, patting it well. Place the roast in the Dutch oven, fat-side up.
3. In a bowl, toss the potatoes, beets, turnips, champignons, and parsnips with the remaining 3 tablespoons of olive oil and the remaining salt and pepper. Arrange the vegetables around the prime rib.
4. Cover the pot, place in the heated oven, and roast for about 20 minutes per pound for medium-rare, or until the internal temperature becomes 130°F. If you prefer a medium roast, take it out at 150°F. Let the roast rest for 20 minutes before carving to seal in the juices.

Nutrition:

Calories 609

Total Fat 23.1g

Saturated Fat 6g

Cholesterol 140mg

Sodium 1675mg

Total Carbohydrate 50.8g

Dietary Fiber 11g

Total Sugars 4.9g

Protein 53.8g

Calcium 137mg

Iron 17mg

Potassium 1571mg

187. Stuffed Meatballs

Preparation time: 10 minutes

Cooking time: 6 hours

Servings: 8

Ingredients:

- 1 egg, lightly beaten
- ½ cup seasoned bread crumbs
- ¼ cup chopped fresh parsley
- 2 cloves garlic, minced
- Salt
- Freshly ground black pepper
- ½ pound ground beef
- ½ pound ground lamb
- 3 ounces feta cheese, cut into ½-inch cubes
- 1 (8-ounce) can tomato sauce

Directions:

1. Preheat the oven to 350°F.
2. In a large bowl, blend the egg, breadcrumbs, parsley, and garlic, and season with salt and pepper. Add the ground beef and ground lamb. Mix well.
3. To make the meatballs, shape some of the meat mixture into a ball around a cheese cube, being sure to enclose the cheese completely.
4. Place the meatballs in a Dutch oven, cover, and bake in the heated oven for 20 minutes. Drain off the fat.
5. Place the tomato sauce over the meatballs and gently toss to coat. Return to the oven and cook for 45 minutes to 1 hour.

Nutrition:

Calories 177

Total Fat 7.1g

Saturated Fat 3.3g

Cholesterol 81mg

Sodium 439mg

Total Carbohydrate 7.3g

Dietary Fiber 0.8g

Total Sugars 2.1g

Protein 20.2g

Vitamin D 2mcg

Calcium 80mg

Iron 7mg

Potassium 345mg

188. Lamb Shanks with Vegetables

Preparation time: 10 minutes

Cooking time: 3 hours

Servings: 6

Ingredients:

- 4 lamb shanks
- Salt
- Freshly ground black pepper
- 2 tablespoons extra-virgin olive oil
- 2 onions, chopped
- 2 carrots, chopped
- 2 parsnips, chopped
- 1 (28-ounce) can whole Italian plum tomatoes
- 1 cup chicken broth or stock
- 1 cup beef broth or stock
- 1 can chickpeas, drained and rinsed

- 1 teaspoon dried thyme
- Parsley, for garnish

Directions:

1. Sprinkle the lamb shanks with salt and pepper.
2. In a Dutch oven over medium-high heat, heat the olive oil. Brown the shanks, two at a time, about 2 minutes per side. Remove to a platter as they finish browning.
3. Add the onions, carrots, and parsnips to the pot, and sauté over medium heat for 5 to 7 minutes or until lightly browned.
4. Increase the heat to medium-high. Add the tomatoes, chicken broth, beef broth, chickpeas, and thyme. Bring to a boil.
5. Return the shanks to the pot. Briefly bring back to a boil, then cover and reduce the heat to low. Simmer for about 2 ½ hours, or until the meat is tender.
6. Open the lid, increase the heat to medium-high, and cook about 10 minutes, or until the juices thicken. Garnish with fresh parsley and serve.

Nutrition:

Calories 457

Total Fat 15.9g

Saturated Fat 4g

Cholesterol 102mg

Sodium 509mg

Total Carbohydrate 37.3g

Dietary Fiber 10.1g

Total Sugars 12.7g

Protein 42.5g

Calcium 112mg

Iron 7mg

Potassium 1235mg

189. Braised Beef Ribs

Preparation time: 10 minutes

Cooking time: 2 hours

Servings: 6

Ingredients:

- 3 pounds bone-in beef short ribs
- 2 tablespoons vegetable oil
- Salt and pepper to taste
- 1 large onion, sliced
- 4 cloves garlic, minced
- 3 cups cooking liquid (wine, beer, or low-sodium broth)
- 3–4 sprigs fresh rosemary or thyme

Directions

1. Coat the short ribs with oil and season with salt and pepper.
2. Add the ribs to the Dutch oven and heat it over medium-high heat.
3. Stir-cook for 7–8 minutes per side until evenly brown.
4. Add the onion and garlic; stir-cook for 4–5 minutes until softened and fragrant.
5. Add the cooking liquid and bring to a simmer.
6. Add the herb sprigs.
7. Cover and cook over medium heat for about 2 hours until the meat flakes easily.
8. Set aside for 20 minutes to settle.
9. Serve warm with onion sauce on top.

Nutrition:

Calories 1412,

Fat 130 g,

carbs 7 g,

Protein 50 g,

sodium 1310 mg

190. Dutch Oven Corned Beef

Preparation time: 10 minutes

Cooking time: 3 hours

Servings: 8

Ingredients:

- 1 (3–4 pound) corned beef brisket with a spice packet, trimmed
- 1 medium onion, sliced
- 1 celery rib, sliced
- ¼ cup butter, cubed
- 1 packed cup brown sugar
- 2/3 cup ketchup
- 1/3 cup white vinegar
- 2 tablespoons prepared mustard
- 2 teaspoons prepared horseradish

Directions

1. Add the seasoning pack and beef to the Dutch oven and cover with water.
2. Add the celery and onion. Bring to a boil.
3. Reduce heat to low, cover, and simmer for about 2½ hours until the meat is tender.
4. Drain the liquid and remove the vegetables.
5. Transfer the beef to a shallow greased roasting pan. Set aside to cool.
6. Clean the Dutch oven. Add the butter and melt it over medium-high heat.
7. Add the remaining ingredients; stir and cook for 25 minutes until the sauce is thickened.
8. Slice the beef, pour the sauce over it, and serve warm.

Nutrition:

Calories 484,

Fat 29 g,

carbs 35 g,

Protein 22 g,

sodium 1708 mg

191. Braised Pork Ribs

Preparation time: 15 minutes

Cooking time: 3 hours

Servings: 4

Ingredients:

- 3½–4 pounds country-style pork ribs, bone-in (or 2–2½ pounds boneless)
- Salt and pepper to taste
- 3 tablespoons olive oil (divided)
- 1 large onion, chopped
- 1 large carrot, diced
- 3–4 cloves garlic, minced
- ¾ cup apple cider
- ¼ cup apple cider vinegar
- 1 cup chicken broth
- 2 tablespoons tomato paste
- 2 bay leaves
- ½ teaspoon dried thyme

Directions

1. Preheat the Dutch oven to 300°F (150°C).
2. Season the pork ribs with salt and pepper.
3. Add 2 tablespoons of the olive oil to the Dutch oven and heat it over medium-high heat.
4. Add the pork ribs and stir-cook until evenly browned. Set aside.
5. Add the remaining olive oil to the Dutch oven along with the carrot and onion; stir-cook until softened.
6. Add the garlic and stir cook for 1–2 minutes until fragrant.
7. Mix in the pork ribs, thyme and bay leave.
8. To a mixing bowl, add the apple cider, chicken broth, and vinegar, and tomato paste. Mix well.
9. Pour over the pork.
10. Cover and cook for 3 hours until the meat is tender.
11. Season with salt and pepper.
12. Serve warm.

Nutrition:

Calories 826,

Fat 45 g,

carbs 20 g,

Protein 81 g,

sodium 379 mg

192. Pork BBQ Burger

Preparation time: 10 minutes

Cooking time: 2 hours

Servings: 6

Ingredients:

- 2–2½ pounds boneless pork shoulder roast, trimmed
- Salt and pepper to taste
- 1 large sweet onion, cut into thin wedges
- 1 (18-ounce) bottle hot and spicy barbecue sauce
- 1 cup carbonated beverage (beer or soda)
- 8 toasted hamburger buns, split, or 16 toasted French bread slices, baguette-style
- Lettuce leaves, sliced tomatoes, pickles, and/or mustard for topping (optional)

Directions

1. Season the pork roast with salt and pepper.
2. Arrange the onion and pork roast over the bottom of the Dutch oven.
3. Add the barbecue sauce and carbonated beverage.
4. Cover and cook for about 2 hours until the roast is tender.
5. Remove the onion and pork roast, shred, and set aside in a bowl.
6. Trim off the Fat. Add enough of the cooking liquid to the bowl to moisten the shredded roast.
7. Stuff the mixture between hamburger buns and add toppings of your choice.
8. Serve warm.

Nutrition:

Calories 378,

Fat 8 g,

carbs 45 g,

Protein 27 g,

sodium 1355 mg

193. Mushroom Sausage Pizza

Preparation time: 10 minutes

Cooking time: 20 minutes

Servings: 8

Ingredients:

- 1 tablespoon olive oil
- 1 cup marinara sauce
- ½ cup fresh mushrooms, sliced
- 1/3 Cup chopped onion
- 1 cup Italian cheese blend, shredded
- 1 pound frozen pizza dough, thawed
- ½ pound bulk spicy pork sausage, cooked and drained
- Red pepper flakes, minced basil, and grated Parmesan cheese for topping (optional)

Directions

1. Preheat the oven to 450°F (230°C).
2. Warm the Dutch oven in the heated oven for 2–3 minutes.
3. On a lightly floured surface, roll the dough into a 12-inch circle.
4. Fold an 18-inch piece of foil lengthwise into thirds to make a sling.
5. Place the crust over the sling and then lower it to the bottom of the Dutch oven; brush it with oil.
6. Spread the marinara sauce on top. Add the mushrooms, onions, pork, and cheese on top.
7. Bake for about 20 minutes until the crust is light brown.
8. Slice and serve warm with toppings of your choice.

Nutrition:

Calories 273,

Fat 13 g,

carbs 27 g,

Protein 11 g,

sodium 418 mg

194. Lentil Sausage Pasta

Preparation time: 10 minutes

Cooking time: 20 minutes

Servings: 4

Ingredients:

- 2 tablespoons olive oil
- ½ pound sweet Italian sausage, uncooked (optional to remove casings)
- ¾ pound farfalle pasta, dried
- 1 cup cooked lentils
- 1-quart chicken broth
- ½ cup dry red wine
- ½ cup of water
- Salt and pepper to taste
- Grated Parmesan cheese (optional)

Directions

1. Boil some water in the Dutch oven. Add the lentils and cook over medium heat for 18–20 minutes until tender but not mushy. Drain and set aside.
2. Add the oil to the Dutch oven and heat it over medium-high heat.
3. Add the sausage and stir-cook for 3 minutes until evenly browned. Break into pieces with a spatula.
4. Add the lentils, broth, pasta, red wine, and ½ cup water.
5. Bring to a boil and cook for about 14 minutes until the pasta is cooked well. Season with salt and pepper.
6. Serve warm with grated Parmesan on top.

Nutrition:

Calories 626,

Fat 16 g,

carbs 84 g,

Protein 30.5 g,

sodium 1125 mg

195. Beef Carrot Meal

Preparation time: 25 minutes

Cooking time: 2 hours

Servings: 6

Ingredients:

- ½ cup red wine or water
- ½ (6-ounce) can tomato pastes with garlic, basil, and oregano
- 1–1½ pounds boneless beef short ribs, fat trimmed and cut into bite-sized chunks
- Salt and pepper to taste
- 10 cloves garlic, peeled and smashed
- 1 pound Roma tomatoes, chopped
- ½ pound fresh baby carrots, peeled and chopped
- Fresh basil (optional)

Directions

1. Add the water/wine and tomato paste to a mixing bowl. Mix well.
2. Season the beef chunks with salt and pepper.
3. Add the beef chunks over the bottom of the Dutch oven.
4. Add the garlic, tomatoes, and carrots. Pour in the tomato paste mixture.
5. Cover and cook for 1½–2 hours until cooked to satisfaction.
6. Serve warm with basil leaves on top.

Nutrition:

Calories 509,

Fat 42 g,

carbs 15 g,

Protein 19 g,

sodium 568 mg

196. Bacon Ranch Pasta

Preparation time: 10 minutes

Cooking time: 20 minutes

Servings: 6

Ingredients:

- 6 slices bacon, diced
- 1 tablespoon olive oil
- 1 tablespoon butter
- 3 cloves garlic, minced
- 2 cups chicken broth
- 1¼ cups milk
- ½ pound spaghetti
- ½ teaspoon pepper
- ½ cup Parmesan cheese, shredded
- ¼ cup sour cream
- 1 tablespoon ranch seasoning mix
- Parsley to serve (optional)

Directions

1. Heat the Dutch oven over medium-high heat.
2. Add the diced bacon and cook until crisp. Drain over paper towels and set aside.
3. Clean the Dutch oven; add the oil and heat it over medium-high heat.
4. Add the garlic and stir cook for 1–2 minutes until fragrant.
5. Add the milk, chicken broth, spaghetti, and pepper. Stir and bring to a boil.
6. Reduce heat to low and simmer until the pasta is cooked well, stirring occasionally.
7. Mix in the bacon, sour cream, ranch dressing, and Parmesan.
8. Serve warm with parsley on top.

Nutrition:

Calories 397,

Fat 20 g,

carbs 29 g,

Protein 17 g,

sodium 864 mg

197. Zucchini Beef Meal

Preparation time: 10 minutes

Cooking time: 25 minutes

Servings: 4

Ingredients:

- 2 tablespoons dehydrated minced onion
- 2 cloves garlic, chopped
- 1 pound lean ground beef
- ½ teaspoon salt
- ¼ teaspoon pepper
- 1 teaspoon ground cumin
- 1 cup chunky salsa of your choice
- 2 cups medium fresh zucchini, cut into rounds and then half circles
- Fresh cilantro, chopped

Directions

1. Lightly grease the Dutch oven with cooking spray. Heat it over medium-high heat.
2. Add the onion and garlic and stir-cook until softened.
3. Add the ground beef, salt, and pepper and stir cook for 6–8 minutes until evenly browned.
4. Mix in the cumin and salsa.
5. Reduce heat to low, cover, and simmer for about 10 minutes, stirring occasionally.
6. Mix in the zucchini and simmer for 5–10 minutes until the zucchini is tender and softened.
7. Serve warm with chopped cilantro on top.

Nutrition:

Calories 198,

Fat 4.5 g,

carbs 10 g,

Protein 26 g,

sodium 838 mg

198. Cheddar Beef Gnocchi Bake

Preparation time: 10 minutes

Cooking time: 20 minutes

Servings: 4

Ingredients:

- 1½ pounds ground beef
- 1 pack taco seasoning
- 2 cups beef broth
- 2 (16-ounce) packs of gnocchi
- 1 (15-ounce) can petite tomatoes, diced
- 1 cup cheddar cheese
- Black olives, green onions, and sour cream for topping (optional)

Directions

1. Lightly grease the Dutch oven with cooking spray. Heat it over medium-high heat.
2. Add the ground beef and stir-cook until evenly browned; drain excess Fat.
3. Mix in the taco seasoning.
4. Add the broth, gnocchi, and tomatoes; stir gently.
5. Bring to a boil.
6. Reduce heat to low and simmer until the sauce is thickened and the gnocchi is tender, stirring occasionally.
7. Mix in the cheese.
8. Serve warm with optional toppings.

Nutrition:

Calories 555,

Fat 43 g,

carbs 32.5 g,

Protein 37 g,

sodium 757 mg

199. Pork Chops Potatoes

Preparation time: 10 minutes

Cooking time: 30 minutes

Servings: 4

Ingredients:

- Vegetable oil for cooking
- 6 pork chops
- 6 potatoes, peeled and thinly sliced
- 1 onion, sliced
- 2 cans cream of mushroom soup
- Cheddar or Parmesan cheese, shredded, to sprinkle

Directions

1. Add the oil to the Dutch oven and heat it over medium-high heat.
2. Add the pork chops and stir-cook until evenly browned. Discard excess oil.
3. Add the potatoes and onions. Pour on the mushroom soup.
4. Cover and cook for 20 minutes; continue cooking and check every 10 minutes until the pork chops are cooked well.
5. Serve warm with shredded cheddar or Parmesan cheese on top.

Nutrition:

Calories 291,

Fat 10 g,

carbs 7 g,

Protein 43 g,

sodium 459 mg

200. Bulgur Sausage Bean Meal

Preparation time: 10 minutes

Cooking time: 30 minutes

Servings: 8

Ingredients:

- ½ cup yellow onion, diced
- 1 pound ground sausage
- ½ cup green pepper, diced
- ¾ cup bulgur wheat
- 1 teaspoon salt
- 1 tablespoon chili powder
- 1 tablespoon cumin, ground
- 1¾ pounds tomatoes, diced
- 1½ cup fresh green beans
- Chopped cilantro (optional)

Directions

1. Lightly grease the Dutch oven with cooking spray. Heat it over medium-high heat.
2. Add the onion, sausage, green pepper, bulgur, and salt; stir-cook until the sausage is evenly browned.
3. Mix in the chili powder, cumin, tomatoes, and green beans.
4. Reduce heat to low and simmer for 20–25 minutes until the veggies are softened and tender, stirring occasionally.
5. Serve warm with chopped cilantro on top.

Nutrition:

Calories 248,

Fat 15 g,

carbs 16 g,

Protein 11 g,

sodium 682 mg

201. Succulent Braised Pork

Preparation time: 10 minutes

Cooking time: 3 hours

Servings: 4

Ingredients:

- 2 pounds pork shoulder, cut into 4 large chunks
- ¼ cup butter
- Salt and pepper to taste
- ¾ pound frozen vegetables
- 1 teaspoon garlic powder
- 2 tablespoons all-purpose flour
- 1 cup red wine
- 2½ cups water

Directions

1. Preheat the oven to 350°F (180°C).
2. Warm the butter in the Dutch oven on medium heat and brown the pork pieces for about 5 minutes on each side. Season with salt and pepper.
3. Remove the pork pieces and cook the frozen vegetables in the grease for 5 minutes.
4. Stir in the garlic powder and flour and mix well.
5. Return the pork shoulder to the Dutch oven and pour in the red wine and water.
6. Mix until a thick sauce forms. If necessary, season again with salt and pepper.
7. Cover and bake for about 1 hour.
8. Reduce heat to 320°F (160°C) and cook for 90 more minutes.
9. Remove the lid and cook for 30 more minutes uncovered.

Nutrition:

Calories 885,

Fat 60.2 g,

carbs 16.3 g,

Protein 55.9 g,

sodium 273 mg

202. Roasted Pork Loin in Mushroom Sauce

Preparation time: 10 minutes

Cooking time: 50 minutes

Servings: 4

Ingredients:

- 2½ pounds pork loin
- ¼ cup butter
- Salt and pepper to taste
- 1 small onion, diced
- 1 pound mushrooms, diced
- 1 teaspoon garlic powder
- 2 cups white wine
- 1 cup of water

Directions

1. Preheat the oven to 350°F (180°C).
2. Warm the butter in the Dutch oven over medium heat.
3. Cut the pork loin into smaller pieces and season them with salt and pepper.
4. Brown the pork for 8–10 minutes on each side. Remove it from the Dutch oven.
5. Cook the onion and mushrooms in the grease for about 7 minutes.
6. Season with salt and pepper and garlic powder.
7. Return the pork loin pieces to the Dutch oven and pour in the white wine and water.
8. Bring to a boil and then place the Dutch oven in the oven and bake for about 40 minutes.
9. If the meat gets too brown, cover loosely with the lid, letting the steam slowly escape on one side.

Nutrition:

Calories 920,

Fat 51.3 g,

carbs 9.1 g,

Protein 81.5 g,

sodium 273 mg

203. Korean Style Pork Chops

Preparation time: 10 minutes

Cooking time: 30 minutes

Servings: 4

Ingredients:

- 2 tablespoons olive oil
- ¼ cup of soy sauce
- 2 tablespoons light brown sugar
- ½ teaspoon grated ginger
- 1 tablespoon chili and garlic sauce
- 2 pounds pork chops
- 2 tablespoons butter
- Salt and pepper to taste

Directions

1. Preheat the oven to 350°F (180°C).
2. Warm the butter and olive oil in the Dutch oven over medium heat.
3. Mix the soy sauce, sugar, ginger, and chili and garlic sauce in a small bowl.
4. Season the pork chops with salt and pepper on each side.
5. Brush the pork chops on one side with the soy sauce mixture place them brushed side down in the warmed Dutch oven to brown them for about 5 minutes.
6. Meanwhile, brush the top side with the soy sauce glaze. Turn them over and cook for about 5 minutes on the other side.
7. Pour the remaining soy sauce liquid into the Dutch oven and cook in the preheated oven for 25–30 minutes.

Nutrition:

Calories 867,

Fat 69.3 g,

carbs 6.4 g,

Protein 52.2 g,

sodium 1124 mg

204. Slow Roasted Pork Shoulder with Rosemary

Preparation time: 10 minutes

Cooking time: 30 minutes

Servings: 4

Ingredients:

- 2 tablespoons butter
- 2 tablespoons olive oil
- 3 pounds boneless pork shoulder
- Salt and pepper to taste
- 2 teaspoons garlic powder
- 1 tablespoon chili flakes
- 1½ pounds of frozen vegetables
- 2 cups of water
- 3 sprigs rosemary

Directions

1. Preheat the oven to 350°F (180°C).
2. Warm the butter and olive oil in the Dutch oven over medium heat.
3. Season the pork shoulder with salt and pepper, garlic powder, and chili flakes.
4. Brown the pork shoulder for about 7 minutes on each side.
5. Remove the pork and cook the frozen vegetables for about 5 minutes.
6. Return the pork shoulder, pour in the water, and add the sprigs of rosemary.
7. Cover and cook for 1 hour in the preheated oven.
8. Reduce heat to 320°F (160°C), remove the lid, and cook for 60–70 minutes uncovered.

Nutrition:

Calories 721,

Fat 25.4 g,

carbs 25 g,

Protein 94.3 g,

sodium 300 mg

205. Sunday Pork Roast

Preparation time: 10 minutes

Cooking time: 30 minutes

Servings: 4

Ingredients:

- 3 tablespoons olive oil
- Salt and pepper to taste
- 2 teaspoons garlic powder
- 2 teaspoons onion powder
- 2 teaspoons dried paprika
- 3 pounds boneless pork butt
- 2 pounds baby potatoes
- ½ cup of water

Directions

1. Preheat the oven to 350°F (180°C).
2. Warm the olive oil in the Dutch oven over medium heat.
3. Season the pork butt with salt and pepper, garlic powder, onion powder, and dried paprika.
4. Brown the pork butt on each side for about 7 minutes.
5. Remove the pork and cook the baby potatoes for about 2 minutes.
6. Place the pork butt in the center of the Dutch oven, pour in the water, and season with salt and pepper.
7. Cover and cook for 60 minutes in the preheated oven.
8. Reduce heat to 320°F (160°C), remove the lid, and cook uncovered for 40 minutes.

Nutrition:

Calories 890,

Fat 33.6 g,

carbs 30.8 g,

Protein 112.2 g,

sodium 215 mg

206. Pulled Pork

Preparation time: 10 minutes

Cooking time: 1 hour 40 minutes

Servings: 4

Ingredients:

- 3 tablespoons olive oil
- 3 pounds boneless pork butt
- Salt and pepper to taste
- 1 tablespoon Dijon mustard
- ½ cup ketchup
- 2 tablespoons brown sugar
- 1 (12-ounce) can beer

Directions

1. Preheat the oven to 350°F (180°C).
2. Warm the olive oil in the Dutch oven over medium heat.
3. Season the pork butt with salt and pepper and Dijon mustard. Rub the ketchup all over. Sprinkle with the brown sugar.
4. Brown the pork butt for about 7 minutes on each side.
5. Pour in the beer. Cover the Dutch oven and place it in the preheated oven.
6. Cook for 60 minutes.
7. Reduce heat to 320°F (160°C), remove the lid, and cook uncovered for 40 minutes.

Nutrition:

Calories 832,

Fat 33.4 g,

carbs 15.2 g,

Protein 107 g,

sodium 574 mg

207. Classic Beef Stew

Preparation time: 10 minutes

Cooking time: 40 minutes

Servings: 4

Ingredients:

- ¼ cup olive oil
- 2 medium onions, chopped
- 2 pounds beef chuck
- Salt and pepper to taste
- 1 pound potatoes, peeled and diced into 1-inch chunks
- 1 pound carrots, peeled and diced into 1-inch chunks
- 2 teaspoons Herbs de Provence
- 1½ quarts water

Directions

1. Warm the olive oil in the Dutch oven over medium heat.
2. Add the diced onion and cook for around 5 minutes until tender, stirring occasionally.
3. Meanwhile, cut the beef chuck into 1–1½-inch chunks.
4. Stir the diced beef into the Dutch oven and cook for about 5 minutes until well browned on all sides.
5. Stir in the potatoes and carrots and cook for 5 more minutes.
6. Season with salt and pepper and Herbes de Provence. Cover and let the flavors marry together.
7. Stir in the water and bring to a boil.
8. Cook for about 40 minutes.
9. Serve warm or store for later use.

Nutrition:

Calories 688,

Fat 28.3 g,

carbs 34.1 g,

Protein 72.3 g,

sodium 247 mg

208. Braised Short Ribs

Preparation time: 10 minutes

Cooking time: 2 hours

Servings: 4

Ingredients:

- 3 tablespoons vegetable oil
- 1 large onion, sliced
- 4 cloves garlic, minced
- 3 pounds bone-in beef short ribs
- Salt and pepper to taste
- 3 cups beef broth
- 4 sprigs rosemary

Directions

1. Warm the vegetable oil in the Dutch oven over medium heat.
2. Add the diced onion and cook for around 5 minutes until tender, stirring occasionally. Stir in the minced garlic and cook for 1 more minute. Season with salt and pepper.
3. Remove the onion and garlic to a plate.
4. Season the short ribs well with salt and pepper. Add them to the greasy Dutch oven and brown them for about 5 minutes on each side.
5. Return the onion and garlic to the Dutch oven with the meat.
6. Stir in the beef broth and bring to a boil. Cover and transfer the Dutch oven to a preheated oven at 350°F (180°C) and bake for 120–150 minutes. The ribs are ready when the meat can be easily pulled from the bone.
7. Let rest for 20 minutes before serving.

Nutrition:

Calories 1474,

Fat 135.2 g,

carbs 7.3 g,

Protein 52.6 g,

sodium 742 mg

209. Dutch Oven Chili

Preparation time: 10 minutes

Cooking time: 40 minutes

Servings: 4

Ingredients:

- 2 tablespoons olive oil
- 1 onion, diced
- 2 pounds stewing beef, diced
- Salt and pepper to taste
- 1 (30-ounce) can bean and chili mix
- 1 (15-ounce) can diced tomatoes
- 7 ounces diced green chilies
- ½ cup of water

Directions

1. Warm the olive oil in the Dutch oven over medium heat.
2. Add the diced onion and cook for around 5 minutes until tender, stirring occasionally.
3. Stir in the diced stewing beef and season with salt and pepper.
4. Cook for about 10 minutes until well browned.
5. Stir in the bean and chili mix, tomatoes, and green chilies.
6. Pour in the water and cook for 25–30 minutes with the lid on.

Nutrition:

Calories 753,

Fat 31.3 g,

carbs 25.4 g,

Protein 88.1 g,

sodium 1247 mg

210. Lemony Rib Lamb Chops

Preparation time: 5 minutes

Cooking time: 10 minutes

Servings: 4

Ingredients:

- Juice of 1 large lemon
- 2 tablespoons extra-virgin olive oil, divided
- 1 teaspoon dried oregano
- 1 teaspoon garlic powder
- 1 teaspoon seasoned salt
- 8 rib lamb chops (about 2 pounds / 907 g total)
- Freshly ground black pepper, to taste
- 2 tablespoons chopped fresh parsley

Directions:

1. In a large zip-top bag, mix together the lemon juice, 1 tablespoon of the olive oil, and the oregano, garlic powder, and seasoned salt.
2. Add the lamb chops, seal the bag, and turn the bag so the lamb chops are well coated with the marinade. Let the lamb sit for 15 minutes at room temperature, turning the bag halfway through.
3. In a Dutch oven over medium-high heat, heat the remaining 1 tablespoon of olive oil. Remove the lamb chops from the marinade and add them to the pot.
4. Cook for about 3 minutes per side, until they reach the desired doneness.
5. Season the chops with salt and pepper, and garnish with the chopped parsley before serving.

Nutrition:

Carbohydrates: 21 g

Fat: 16 g

Protein: 34 g

Calories: 626

Chapter 11. Seafood and Fish Recipes

211. Shrimp and Wild Rice in a Pot

Preparation time: 10 minutes

Cooking time: 40-45 minutes

Servings: 4

Ingredients:

- ¾ pound raw shrimp, cleaned and shelled
- 5 ounces pancetta, diced
- 2 cups chicken broth
- 1 cup wild rice medley
- 2 tablespoons olive oil, divided
- 5 cups kale, chopped
- ¼ teaspoon chili flakes
- Salt and pepper

Directions:

1. Heat a Dutch oven over medium and cook the pancetta until crisp. Transfer the pancetta to a paper-lined plate.
2. Add 1 tablespoon of olive oil to the Dutch oven and cook the kale until wilted. Season with the chili flakes, and salt and pepper to taste. Set it aside, covered.
3. Prepare the shrimps. Dry with towels and season with salt and pepper.
4. Add another tablespoon of oil to the Dutch oven and cook the shrimp until it's pink. Transfer to a plate and set aside.
5. Add the chicken broth to the pot. Add the rice and raise the heat to high. Bring to a boil.
6. Reduce the heat to low and simmer for 30 minutes, until the rice absorbs the liquid.
7. Remove the pot from the heat and let it sit for 5 minutes.
8. Return the pancetta to Dutch oven, and stir it into the rice. Place the shrimp and kale on top, to heat through.

Nutrition:

Calories 374

Carbs 20 g

Fat 19 g

Protein 30 g

Sodium 1578 mg

212. Baked Trout

Preparation time: 5 minutes

Cooking time: 45 minutes

Servings: 6

Ingredients:

- 6 10-inch trout, cleaned and cut in halves
- 1 14.5-ounce can tomatoes
- 2 medium onions, sliced
- ½ teaspoon oregano
- ½ teaspoon basil
- 1 bay leaf
- Cooking spray

Directions:

1. Preheat the oven to 350°F. Coat a Dutch oven with cooking spray.
2. Arrange the trout and tomatoes in the Dutch oven. Layer the onions on top, and add the bay leaf.
3. Cover and bake for 45 minutes. Discard the bay leaf before serving.

Nutrition:

Calories 275

Carbs 5 g

Fat 12 g

Protein 34 g , Sodium 242 mg

213. Poached Fish

Preparation time: 5 minutes

Cooking time: 45 minutes

Servings: 4

Ingredients:

- 2 pounds fish of choice, filleted
- 6 cups water
- 1 small onion, sliced
- 1 teaspoon black peppercorns
- 3 whole allspice, or a pinch of ground
- 3 tablespoons lemon juice
- 1 bay leaf
- 1 teaspoon salt
- ½ cup dry wine

Directions:

1. To prepare the poaching liquid, combine the water, onion, peppercorns, allspice, lemon juice, bay leaf, salt, and wine in a Dutch oven.
2. Simmer the liquid for 20-30 minutes.
3. Carefully lower the fish into the hot liquid, pressing gently so all the fillets are immersed. (You may add a little boiling water if necessary.)

4. Cover and simmer on low for 15-20 minutes. The fish is done when it flakes easily with a fork.

5. Remove the fish carefully and drain well before serving.

Nutrition:

Calories 166

Carbs 1 g

Fat 6 g

Protein 22 g

Sodium 172 mg

214. Chili Catfish

Preparation time: 10 minutes

Cooking time: 35-55 minutes

Servings: 4

Ingredients:

- 2 pounds catfish fillets, cut into 1-inch by 2-inch strips
- 1 cup whole wheat flour
- 1 cup yellow cornmeal
- ½ teaspoon chili powder (or more to taste)
- 1 teaspoon paprika
- 1 teaspoon onion powder
- 1 teaspoon sugar
- 1 teaspoon garlic powder
- 1 teaspoon seasoned salt
- ½ teaspoon celery salt
- ½ lemon, squeezed
- 1 cup onion, chopped
- Handful of mixed chili peppers: tepins, Bolivians and cayennes
- Salt to taste
- Vegetable oil

Directions:

1. Dry the fish with paper towels and drizzle with lemon juice.

2. In a mixing bowl, combine the flour, cornmeal, chili powder, paprika, onion powder, sugar, garlic powder, hickory smoke salt, and celery powder.

3. Roll each piece of fish in the dry mix, one at a time, to avoid too much sticking and lumping of the mix.

4. Heat 2 inches of oil in a Dutch oven over medium-high heat, to 350°F.

5. Fry the fish in the oil. As soon as the fish floats to the top, add the chilies and onion chunks.

6. Cover and fry for about 5 minutes. The fish should be golden brown and floating.

7. Drain the fried fish chunks on paper towels.

Nutrition:

Calories 370

Carbs 34 g

Fat 16 g

Protein 24 g

Sodium 317 mg

215. Beer Batter Shrimp

Preparation time: 10 minutes

Cooking time: 10 minutes

Servings: 20

Ingredients:

- 1 pound unpeeled, fresh shrimp
- ¼ cup all-purpose flour
- ¼ cup cornstarch
- 1/8 teaspoon salt
- ¼ cup beer
- 2 tablespoons butter, melted
- 1 egg yolk
- Vegetable oil

Directions:

1. Peel the shrimp, leaving the tails on.

2. Combine the flour, cornstarch, and salt. Add the beer, butter, and egg yolk. Stir until smooth.

3. Heat 2 inches of oil in a Dutch oven over medium-high, to 350°F.

4. Dip the shrimps in the batter and fry until golden brown.

Nutrition:

Calories 48

Carbs 5 g

Fat 2 g

Protein 1 g

Sodium 134 mg

216. Pasta with Clams and Pancetta

Preparation time: 10 minutes

Cooking time: 55 minutes

Servings: 4

Ingredients:

- 3 tablespoons extra-virgin olive oil
- 2 ounces pancetta, thinly sliced and chopped
- 1 medium onion, finely chopped
- 4 cloves garlic, thinly sliced
- ¾ teaspoon red pepper flakes, crushed
- 1 (28-ounce) can whole tomatoes, peeled and crushed
- 2 cups of water
- 24 littleneck clams, scrubbed
- 4 ounces (about 1 cup) ditalini pasta or other short cut pasta
- A handful of torn basil leaves (optional)

Directions

1. Add the oil to the Dutch oven and heat it over medium heat.
2. Add the pancetta and stir-cook for 4–5 minutes until it begins to crisp.
3. Add the onion and stir cook for 6–8 minutes until softened.

4. Add the garlic and stir cook for 4–5 minutes until fragrant.

5. Mix in the red pepper flakes.

6. Add the crushed tomatoes.

7. Over medium-high heat, simmer and cook for 12–15 minutes until liquid is reduced to half.

8. Add the water and clams. Cover and simmer over low heat for 8–10 minutes.

9. Uncover and remove the opened clams.

10. Cover again and cook the remaining clams for 15 more minutes. Discard any unopened ones; remove the opened clams.

11. Add the pasta and cook for 8–10 minutes until al dente.

12. Mix the clams back into the Dutch oven. Add the fresh basil if desired.

13. Serve warm.

Nutrition:

Calories 407,

Fat 16 g,

carbs 35 g,

Protein 30 g,

sodium 414 mg

217. Beer Mustard Shrimp

Preparation time: 10 minutes

Cooking time: 15 minutes

Servings: 4

Ingredients:

- 1 cup whole-wheat pastry flour or all-purpose flour
- 1 teaspoon Dijon mustard
- 1 cup pale ale or light-colored beer
- ½ teaspoon salt (divided)
- 2 tablespoons canola oil
- 1 pound (13–15 pieces) raw shrimp, peeled and deveined, tails left on
- Pepper to taste

Directions

1. Add the flour, mustard, beer, and ¼ teaspoon of the salt to a mixing bowl. Mix well to make a smooth batter.

2. Cook shrimp in two batches.

3. Add 1 tablespoon of the canola oil to the Dutch oven and heat it over medium-high heat.

4. Dip the shrimp in the batter, holding them by their tails.

5. Add the shrimp one at a time and stir-cook for 3–4 minutes until

evenly brown. Drain over paper towels.

6. Repeat with the remaining 1 tablespoon of oil and the other half of the shrimp.

7. Season with the remaining salt and pepper.

8. Serve warm.

Nutrition:

Calories 173,

Fat 8.5 g,

carbs 6.5 g,

Protein 16 g,

sodium 825 mg

218. Tilapia Nuggets

Preparation time: 10 minutes

Cooking time: 15 minutes

Servings: 6

Ingredients:

- 1½ cups all-purpose flour
- 2 pounds tilapia fillets, cut into bite-sized chunks
- 1 tablespoon onion powder
- 2 cups dry pancake mix
- 1-pint club soda
- 1 tablespoon seasoned salt
- 2 cups of vegetable oil
- Tartar sauce to taste

Directions

1. Add the flour to a bowl. Coat the fish chunks with flour. Place them over paper towels and set aside for 5 minutes.

2. Add the onion powder, pancake mix, soda, and seasoned salt to a mixing bowl. Mix well to make a smooth batter.

3. Coat the fish chunks with the batter.

4. Add the oil to the Dutch oven and heat it to 400°F (200°C).

5. Add the coated fish chunks and fry for 3 minutes per side until evenly brown.

6. Drain over paper towels and serve warm.

Nutrition:

Calories 308,

Fat 3 g,

carbs 42 g,

Protein 28 g,

sodium 1198 mg

219. Lobster Bisque

Preparation time: 10 minutes

Cooking time: 70 minutes

Servings: 4

Ingredients:

- 2 (1-pound) live lobsters
- 3 tablespoons butter
- 1 medium onion, chopped
- 2 medium carrots, peeled and chopped
- 2 tablespoons tomato paste
- 2 cloves garlic, minced
- ¾ cup sherry or white wine
- 1-quart seafood stock
- 2/3 cup long-grain rice, uncooked
- 2 cups heavy whipping cream
- 1½ teaspoons salt
- 1 teaspoon pepper
- Minced fresh parsley(optional)

Directions

1. Boil 2 inches of water in the Dutch oven. Add the lobsters and cook, covered, for 8 minutes. Remove the lobsters and reserve the water.

2. Remove the meat from the lobsters. Reserve the juice and shells; discard the claws and tail.

3. Add the butter to the Dutch oven and melt it over medium-high heat.

4. Add the onion and carrots and stir-cook for 6–8 minutes until softened and translucent.

5. Mix in the tomato paste and cook for 5 minutes.

6. Add the garlic and stir cook for 50–60 seconds until fragrant.

7. Pour in the wine and cook until the liquid reduces to half.

8. Pour in the seafood stock along with the reserved water, juice, and shells. Reserve the meat.

9. Simmer for 1 hour; strain to remove solids and shells.

10. Heat the strained liquid in the Dutch oven. Add the rice and cook for 25–30 minutes until softened.

11. Puree the rice in a blender until it becomes smooth.

12. Mix in the pepper, salt, and cream.

13. Add the lobster meat and simmer over low heat until cooked well.

14. Season with parsley and pepper.

15. Serve warm.

Nutrition:

Calories 373,

Fat 26 g,

carbs 20 g,

Protein 10 g,

sodium 942 mg

220. Baked Salmon with Herbs

Preparation time: 10 minutes

Cooking time: 35 minutes

Servings: 4

Ingredients:

- 2 tablespoons olive oil
- 1 lemon, sliced
- 2 bunches of dill
- 2 pounds salmon fillet
- ¾ cup white wine
- Salt and pepper to taste

Directions

1. Arrange the lemon slices on the bottom of the Dutch oven.
2. Arrange the dill on top of the lemon and place the salmon fillet on top of that.
3. Pour in the white wine and season with salt and pepper.
4. Cover and cook at 350°F (180°C) for about 10 minutes.
5. Remove the lid and continue cooking for another 20–25 minutes.

Nutrition:

Calories 405,

Fat 21.1 g,

carbs 3.4 g,

Protein 44.5 g,

sodium 106 mg

221. Baked Trout with Cherry Tomatoes

Preparation time: 10 minutes

Cooking time: 45 minutes

Servings: 4

Ingredients:

- 2 tablespoons olive oil
- 2 tablespoons butter
- 1 pound potatoes, sliced
- 1 pound cherry tomatoes
- 2 pounds whole trout
- Salt and pepper to taste
- 1 lemon, sliced

Directions

1. Coat the Dutch oven with butter.
2. Arrange the potato slices and cherry tomatoes in the Dutch oven and season with salt and pepper.
3. Bake at 350°F (180°C) for about 20 minutes.
4. Meanwhile, season the cleaned trout with salt and pepper and stuff it with lemon slices.
5. Place the trout on top of the potatoes and cherry tomatoes and drizzle some olive oil on top of the fish.
6. Cover and bake for about 20 minutes more.
7. Remove the lid and cook for another 10 minutes.

Nutrition:

Calories 597,

Fat 29.5 g,

carbs 23.6 g,

Protein 58.2 g,

sodium 149 mg

222. Tilapia Cacciatore

Preparation time: 10 minutes

Cooking time: 30 minutes

Servings: 4

Ingredients:

- 2 tablespoons olive oil
- 2 pounds tilapia fillets
- Salt and pepper to taste
- 2 cups tomato sauce
- 2 teaspoons Italian seasoning
- ¼ cup white wine
- ¾ cup diced Kalamata olives

Directions

1. Warm the olive oil in the Dutch oven over medium heat.
2. Season the fish fillets with salt and pepper. Add them to the heated oil and cook for about 5 minutes on each side.
3. Pour in the white wine and cook uncovered for about 5 minutes.
4. When half of the wine has evaporated, pour in the tomato sauce and season with Italian seasoning.
5. Stir in the diced Kalamata olives and cook, covered, for 15–20 minutes.
6. When the tomato sauce has thickened and the fish is cooked, serve on plates.

Nutrition:

Calories 302,

Fat 10.5 g,

carbs 7.7 g,

Protein 43.8 g,

sodium 774 mg

223. Seafood Risotto

Preparation time: 10 minutes

Cooking time: 40 minutes

Servings: 4

Ingredients:

- 2 tablespoons olive oil
- 2 tablespoons butter
- 1 onion, diced finely
- ½ pound frozen seafood mix
- 1½ cups arborio rice
- Salt and pepper to taste
- ½ cup white wine
- 3 cloves garlic, minced
- 1-quart water

Directions

1. Warm the olive oil and butter in the Dutch oven over medium heat.
2. Stir in the onion and cook for about 5 minutes or until tender.
3. Stir in the seafood mix and cook for about 5 minutes.
4. Stir in the rice and cook for 5 more minutes.
5. Season with salt and pepper and pour in the white wine.
6. While stirring constantly, pour in the water, ½ cup at a time, mixing well so the mixture remains creamy but not too watery.
7. The risotto is done when the rice is cooked through.
8. Serve while it's still creamy with a dash of pepper on top.

Nutrition:

Calories 457,

Fat 13.7g,

carbs 62.1g,

Protein 13.3 g,

sodium 233 mg

224. Calamari Fra Diavolo

Preparation time: 10 minutes

Cooking time: 40 minutes

Servings: 4

Ingredients:

- 2 tablespoons olive oil
- 2 pounds fresh squid, cut into rings
- Salt and pepper to taste
- ½ cup red wine
- ½ cup of water
- 1 (28-ounce) can tomato sauce
- 2 teaspoons chili flakes
- 3 cloves garlic, minced

Directions

1. Warm the olive oil and butter in the Dutch oven over medium heat.
2. Stir in the squid rings and cook for about 5 minutes.
3. Season with salt and pepper and chili flakes.
4. Pour in the wine, water, and tomato sauce.
5. Cover and cook for 30 minutes.
6. When the mixture is almost thick and most of the liquid has evaporated, serve alone or on top of pasta or crusty bread.

Nutrition:

Calories 344,

Fat 10.5 g,

carbs 19.3 g,

Protein 38.1 g,

sodium 1143 mg

225. Seafood Stew

Preparation time: 10 minutes

Cooking time: 40 minutes

Servings: 4

Ingredients:

- 2 tablespoons olive oil
- 1 medium onion, diced
- 3 cloves garlic, minced
- 1 (14-ounce) bag of frozen vegetables
- 2 pounds seafood mix
- 2 tablespoons tomato paste
- Salt and pepper to taste
- 1-quart water

Directions

1. Warm the olive oil in the Dutch oven over medium heat.
2. Cook the diced onion and garlic for about 5 minutes until tender.
3. Stir in the frozen veggies and seafood and cook for 10 minutes.
4. Stir in the tomato paste and season with salt and pepper.
5. Pour in the water and cook for 30 minutes.
6. Serve with bread if desired.

Nutrition:

Calories 348,

Fat 9.3 g,

carbs 22.9 g,

Protein 36 g,

sodium 760 mg

226. Lemony Salt Snapper

Preparation time: 15 minutes

Cooking time: 40 minutes

Servings: 4

Ingredients:

- 2 pounds (907 g) sea salt
- ¾ to 1 cup water
- Cooking spray, for frying
- 1 large orange, sliced, divided
- 1 large lemon, sliced, divided
- 1 large grapefruit, sliced, divided
- 1 (4-pound / 1.8-kg) whole red snapper, cleaned and scaled

Directions:

1. Preheat the oven to 375°F (190°C).
2. In a large bowl, combine the salt and water, and stir until it forms a pastelike consistency.
3. Coat a Dutch oven with cooking spray, then pour a 1-inch-thick layer of the salt mixture into the bottom of the pot. Layer half of the orange, lemon, and grapefruit slices on top of the salt.
4. Place the red snapper on top of the slices. Press the remaining salt on top of the fish to form a thick crust. Top with the remaining fruit slices.
5. Cover, place in the heated oven, and bake for 35 to 40 minutes, or until the fish is done and the salt is lightly browned.

227. Baked Salmon Fillet

Preparation time: 10 minutes

Cooking time: 20 minutes

Servings: 4

Ingredients:

- 1 teaspoon kosher salt
- 1 teaspoon chili powder
- 1 teaspoon cumin
- 4 (6-ounce / 170-g) salmon fillets, skin on
- 1 tablespoon extra-virgin olive oil

Directions:

1. Preheat the oven to 375°F (190°C).
2. In a small bowl, combine the salt, chili powder, and cumin. Rub the salmon fillets with the spice mixture, coating them evenly.
3. Heat the olive oil in a Dutch oven over medium-high heat. Place the salmon fillets in the pot, skin-side up. Cook for 3 minutes, or until the tops are evenly browned. For medium-rare, flip and cook for 3 minutes. For medium to well-done, cover, place in the preheated oven, and bake for 5 to 10 minutes.

Nutrition:

Carbohydrates: 23 g, Fat: 6 g

Protein: 24 g, Calories: 326

228. Lemon Halibut with Salsa

Preparation time: 25 minutes

Cooking time: 15 minutes

Servings: 4

Ingredients:

- 6 halibut fillets
- Juice and zest of 1 lemon
- 1 tablespoon roughly chopped fresh thyme leaves
- 1 tablespoon chopped fresh parsley
- 6 tablespoons extra-virgin olive oil, divided
- Salt and freshly ground black pepper, to taste
- 1 fennel bulb, sliced
- ½ teaspoon sea salt
- 1½ cups arugula
- ¼ cup fresh tarragon leaves
- ¼ cup chives, cut into ½-inch pieces
- ¼ cup fresh mint leaves
- ¼ cup fresh basil leaves
- Salsa verde, for garnish

Directions:

1. Season the halibut fillets with the lemon zest, thyme, and parsley.

Cover and refrigerate for at least 4 hours.

2. Remove the fish from the refrigerator 15 minutes before cooking to bring it to room temperature. Brush with 2 tablespoons of olive oil, and season with salt and pepper.

3. Heat 1 tablespoon of olive oil in a Dutch oven over medium heat, and add the fish. Cook for 2 to 3 minutes, until it's nicely colored on the first side.

4. Turn the fish over and cook a few minutes, until it's almost cooked through, and remove the pot from the heat (the fish will continue to cook).

5. In a large bowl, toss the sliced fennel with the sea salt, the remaining 3 tablespoons of olive oil, and 1 tablespoon of lemon juice. Add the arugula, tarragon, chives, mint, and basil, and toss, then season with salt and pepper.

6. Arrange the salad on a large platter, place the fish on top, and garnish each fillet with a spoonful of salsa verde.

Nutrition:

Carbohydrates: 12 g

Fat: 6 g

Protein: 14 g

Calories: 312

229. Quick Swordfish Steaks

Preparation time: 10 minutes

Cooking time: 10 minutes

Servings: 4

Ingredients:

- 4 tablespoons extra-virgin olive oil, divided
- 2 teaspoons chili powder
- 2 teaspoons dried oregano, crumbled
- 1 teaspoon sea salt
- ½ teaspoon freshly ground black pepper
- 4 swordfish steaks, cut ¾-inch thick

Directions:

1. Mix 3 tablespoons of olive oil with the chili powder, oregano, salt, and pepper. Brush the swordfish steaks with the oil mixture.

2. In a Dutch oven over medium heat, heat the remaining 1 tablespoon of olive oil. Add the swordfish steaks and cook for about 4 minutes.

3. Turn and cook for a few minutes, until browned on both sides but still moist. It's best if the fish is slightly undercooked in the center, as it will continue to cook a bit after you've removed it from the heat.

230. Salmon with Spinach

Preparation time: 10 minutes

Cooking time: 15 minutes

Servings: 6

Ingredients:

- 3 tablespoons unsalted butter
- 2 pounds (907 g) fresh baby spinach
- 4 shallots, minced
- 6 salmon fillets
- 3 tablespoons fresh lemon juice
- Sea salt and freshly ground black pepper, to taste
- 2 teaspoons finely chopped fresh rosemary leaves
- 6 lemon wedges, for garnish
- Horseradish cream sauce, for garnish

Directions:

1. Preheat the oven to 325°F (163°C).
2. Coat the bottom of a Dutch oven, with the butter. Spread the spinach leaves evenly over the butter, and sprinkle with the minced shallots.
3. Place the salmon fillets on the spinach, skin-side down, and drizzle with the lemon juice. Season with the salt, pepper, and rosemary.

Nutrition:

Carbohydrates: 19 g

Fat: 6 g

Protein: 24 g

Calories: 326

4. Cover, place in the heated oven, and bake for 8 to 10 minutes. Uncover the pot and check the fish for doneness. If needed, finish the cooking with the pot uncovered for 3 to 5 minutes, or until the fish is opaque and the salmon flakes.
5. Garnish with lemon wedges or a dollop of horseradish sauce.

Nutrition:

Carbohydrates: 21 g

Fat: 6 g

Protein: 20 g

Calories: 398

231. Buttery Grouper

Preparation time: 20 minutes

Cooking time: 50 minutes

Servings: 4

Ingredients:

- 2 pounds (907 g) grouper
- 2 tablespoons extra-virgin olive oil
- 1 fennel bulb, thinly sliced
- 2 celery stalks, thinly sliced
- 6 shallots, skinned and chopped
- Salt and freshly ground black pepper, to taste
- 4 ounces (113 g) butter, cut into small chunks
- 2 teaspoons chopped fresh dill

Directions:

1. Remove the fine membrane covering the grouper. Remove the central bone (if the fish is not already deboned), and cut the fish into 1½-inch-thick diagonal slices.
2. In a Dutch oven over medium heat, heat the olive oil. Add the fennel, celery, and shallots, and cook until they begin to soften. Transfer to a small bowl.
3. Brown the fish in the oil and transfer to a plate. Return the vegetables to the pot, then lay the

fish on top. Season with salt and pepper.

4. Cover the Dutch oven and cook over a low heat for 5 minutes. Transfer the vegetables to a serving platter, and cover to keep warm. Cover the Dutch oven, and cook the fish for 30 to 40 minutes, or until tender.
5. Transfer the fish to the serving platter with the vegetables.
6. Place the Dutch oven back over the heat. Return the liquid to a boil, and stir in the butter. Add the dill and cook, stirring until thickened. Season with salt and pepper, and pour the butter sauce over the fish.

Nutrition:

Carbohydrates: 19 g

Fat: 6 g

Protein: 14 g

Calories: 326

232. Whitefish and Oyster Bouillabaisse

Preparation time: 30 minutes

Cooking time: 1 hour

Servings: 4

Ingredients:

- 3 tablespoons extra-virgin olive oil
- 6 garlic cloves, minced
- 1 to 2 onions (about ¾ pound / 340 g), diced
- 1 shallot, minced
- 1 celery stalk, minced
- 1 carrot, diced
- 1½ tablespoons tomato paste
- ½ teaspoon saffron
- 1 teaspoon minced basil or 1 fresh basil leaf
- 2 tablespoons minced fresh parsley
- Salt and freshly ground black pepper, to taste
- 1 (28-ounce / 794-g) can diced tomatoes, undrained
- 2 cups clam juice
- 1 (8-ounce / 227-g) jar fresh oysters, juice reserved

- 1 pound (454 g) whitefish (cod, halibut, or trout), cut into bite-size pieces
- 2½ pounds (1.1 kg) seafood mix (shrimp, clams, mussels, lobsters, scallops, crab meat, or squid)
- 2 tablespoons chopped fresh parsley, for garnish

Directions:

1. In a Dutch oven over medium heat, heat the olive oil. Add the garlic, onion, shallot, celery, and carrot, and sauté until lightly golden, about 20 minutes.
2. Add the tomato paste, saffron, basil, minced parsley, salt, and pepper. Mix well.
3. Add the tomatoes, clam juice, and juice from the jar of oysters. Bring the pot to a boil, lower the heat, and simmer for 15 minutes.
4. Add the oysters, whitefish, and seafood mix. Bring the pot back to a boil. Skim off any scum or fat. Lower the heat and simmer for 15 minutes.
5. Garnish with the chopped parsley.

Nutrition:

Carbohydrates: 20 g

Fat: 6 g

Protein: 22 g

Calories: 299

233. Lemon Halibut with Tomato

Preparation time: 10 minutes

Cooking time: 30 minutes

Servings: 4

Ingredients:

- 4 tablespoons unsalted butter
- Juice from 2 medium lemons
- Several dashes Tabasco sauce
- 4 (8-ounce / 227-g) halibut steaks
- Pinch salt
- Pinch pepper
- 1 small onion, peeled and chopped
- ½ large red bell pepper, seeded and chopped
- 3 large tomatoes, peeled, seeded, and chopped

Directions:

1. Heat oven to 400°F (205°C).
2. Place a Dutch oven over medium heat. Add butter, lemon juice, and Tabasco sauce. Stir until butter has melted. Turn off heat.
3. Season fish on each side with salt and pepper. Sprinkle onion and bell pepper over the bottom of the Dutch oven. Add fish and scatter tomatoes over the top.
4. Bake 20 to 25 minutes or until the thickest part of fish is opaque.

Spoon the pan juices over fish every 10 minutes. Remove fish from pan and spoon sauce over it to serve.

Nutrition:

Carbohydrates: 12 g

Fat: 6 g

Protein: 14 g

Calories: 376

234. Roast Fish with Lemon

Preparation time: 20 minutes

Cooking time: 40 minutes

Servings: 4

Ingredients:

- 1 (4-pound / 1.8-kg) whole fish, such as snapper or sea bass, cleaned and scaled
- 1 tablespoon olive oil
- ½ teaspoon sea salt
- ½ teaspoon freshly cracked black pepper
- 2 medium lemons, sliced 1/8-inch thick
- 4 dill fronds
- 2 sprigs thyme
- 1 clove garlic, peeled and thinly sliced

Directions:

1. Heat oven to 450°F (235°C) and lightly spray an ovenproof 12-inch Dutch oven with nonstick cooking spray.
2. Brush the outside of the fish with olive oil and season with salt and pepper. Open the fish slightly and fill the center with 3 slices of lemon, along with dill, thyme, and garlic slices.
3. Place fish into the Dutch oven and top with a few slices of lemon. Roast 30 minutes,

occasionally spooning juices in the bottom of the Dutch oven over fish.

4. The fish is ready when the flesh flakes easily and reaches an internal temperature of 130°F (54°C). Let fish rest 10 minutes, and then carefully transfer to a platter to serve.

Nutrition:

Carbohydrates: 13 g

Fat: 6 g

Protein: 19 g

Calories: 326

235. Beer Catfish Fillet

Preparation time: 25 minutes

Cooking time: 15 minutes

Servings: 8

Ingredients:

- 2 pounds (907 g) catfish fillets, about 4 ounces (113 g) each
- 2 (12-ounce / 340-g) beers, lager or ale preferred
- Oil, for frying
- 1 cup all-purpose flour
- 1 teaspoon salt
- ½ teaspoon freshly cracked black pepper
- 2 large eggs, beaten
- 1 cup buttermilk
- 1 teaspoon hot sauce
- 1 cup yellow cornmeal
- 1 cup fine saltine cracker crumbs

Directions:

1. In a large bowl combine catfish fillets and beer. Refrigerate 1 hour, then drain well and pat the fillets dry.
2. In a 6- or 8-quart deep Dutch oven add 3-inch oil, making sure there is at least a 3-inch air gap at the top of the pot. Heat oil to 350°F (180°C).

3. In a large zip-top bag combine flour, salt, and pepper. Seal the bag and shake to mix. In a shallow dish combine eggs, buttermilk, and hot sauce. Whisk to combine. Finally, in a second large zip-top bag combine cornmeal and cracker crumbs. Seal and shake to combine.

4. Working in batches, add a few fillets to flour and toss to coat. Remove from flour and tap off any excess. Dip fillets into egg mixture, allowing any excess to drip off. Finally, add fillets to cornmeal mixture and toss to coat. Transfer coated fillets to a wire rack to hold.

5. Fry fillets 2 to 3 at a time until they are golden brown on both sides, about 3 minutes per side. While first batch is frying, heat oven to 175°F (79°C). Transfer cooked fillets to a wire rack over a sheet pan and place in warm oven to hold while you fry remaining fillets. Serve hot.

Nutrition:

Carbohydrates: 13 g

Fat: 6 g

Protein: 11 g

Calories: 278

236. Cod Fillet with Beer

Preparation time: 20 minutes

Cooking time: 25 minutes

Servings: 4

Ingredients:

- 2 cups all-purpose flour
- 1 teaspoon salt
- ½ teaspoon freshly cracked black pepper
- ½ teaspoon smoked paprika
- ½ teaspoon garlic powder
- ¼ teaspoon onion powder
- 1 large egg, beaten
- 1 (12-ounce / 340-g) beer, lager preferred
- Oil, for frying
- 2 pounds (907 g) cod fillets, about 4 ounces (113 g) each

Directions:

1. In a large bowl combine flour, salt, pepper, paprika, garlic powder, and onion powder. Whisk to combine, then add egg and beer and whisk until a smooth batter forms. Allow to rest at room temperature for 1 hour.

2. In a 6- or 8-quart deep Dutch oven add 3-inch oil, making sure there is a 3-inch air gap at the top

of the pot. Heat oil to 350°F (180°C).

3. Heat oven to 175°F (79°C). Pat the fish fillets dry. Working with one fillet at a time, dip into batter and immediately add to hot oil. Fry until fish is golden brown on both sides, about 5 to 6 minutes.
4. Remove fillet from the oil and transfer to a wire rack over a sheet pan to drain, then transfer to warm oven to keep warm while you fry remaining fish. Serve hot.

Nutrition:

Carbohydrates: 11 g

Fat: 6 g

Protein: 14 g

Calories: 302

237. Salmon Fillet with Lemon

Preparation time: 10 minutes

Cooking time: 30 minutes

Servings: 4

Ingredients:

- 1 tablespoon extra-virgin olive oil
- 1 (1½-pound / 680-g) skin-on salmon fillet
- 1 teaspoon salt
- ¼ teaspoon freshly ground black pepper
- 1 teaspoon dried dill
- 2 tablespoons melted butter
- 2 lemons, sliced, divided

Directions:

1. Preheat the oven to 400°F (205°C).
2. In a Dutch oven over medium heat, heat the olive oil. Add the salmon, skin-side down, and let it sear for 5 to 10 minutes, so the skin gets crispy.
3. Remove the pot from the heat, and sprinkle the salmon with the salt, pepper, and dill. Pour the melted butter evenly over the salmon. Place half of the lemon slices on top of the salmon.

4. Cover and bake in the oven for 15 to 20 minutes, until the salmon flakes easily with a fork.
5. Transfer the salmon to a serving dish. Throw away the cooked lemons and replace them with the fresh sliced ones before serving. Season with salt, if needed.

Nutrition:

Carbohydrates: 12 g

Fat: 6 g

Protein: 19 g

Calories: 278

238. Arugula Cod with Cherry Tomato

Preparation time: 5 minutes

Cooking time: 15 minutes

Servings: 4

Ingredients:

- 4 (6-ounce / 170-g) cod fillets
- 1 teaspoon salt
- ½ teaspoon freshly ground black pepper
- 2 tablespoons extra-virgin olive oil
- 2 cups grape or cherry tomatoes
- 2 garlic cloves, chopped
- 1/3 cup Italian salad dressing
- 6 cups baby arugula

Directions:

1. Pat the fish dry with paper towels, and season with salt and pepper. In a Dutch oven over medium-high heat, heat the olive oil. Sear the fish for 2 to 3 minutes on each side, until browned. Transfer the fish to a plate to rest.
2. Add the tomatoes and garlic to the pot. Cook for 3 minutes or until the tomatoes start to soften. Stir in the salad dressing. Add the arugula and toss well. Cook for 2 more minutes or until the arugula is wilted.

3. Place the cod fillets on top of the greens and tomatoes. Spoon some of the sauce over the fish. Cover and cook for 2 to 3 more minutes, until the cod easily flakes with a fork.
4. Serve the fish with the vegetables and sauce, all in one pot.

Nutrition:

Carbohydrates: 11 g

Fat: 6 g

Protein: 14 g

Calories: 226

239. Olive Cod with Lemon

Preparation time: 5 minutes

Cooking time: 15 minutes

Servings: 4

Ingredients:

- 4 (6-ounce / 170-g) cod fillets
- Kosher salt and freshly ground black pepper, to taste
- 12 thin lemon slices
- ¼ cup pitted, chopped kalamata olives
- ¼ cup capers, drained and chopped
- 2 teaspoons chopped fresh rosemary leaves
- ¼ cup olive oil

Directions:

1. Arrange the fish fillets in a single layer in the Dutch oven and season with salt and pepper. Top each piece of fish with 3 lemon slices and then scatter the olives, capers, and rosemary evenly over the top. Drizzle the olive oil evenly over all of the fish. Place the lid on the pot.
2. Place the Dutch oven on a bed of 10 hot coals and then place 24 hot coals on the lid. Cook for about 15 minutes, until the fish is cooked through. Serve hot.

Nutrition: Carbohydrates: 16 g, Fat: 6 g

Protein: 20 g, Calories: 326

240. Mussels with Bacon

Preparation time: 10 minutes

Cooking time: 15 minutes

Servings: 4

Ingredients:

- 2 to 3 tablespoons extra-virgin olive oil, plus more for garnish
- ½ cup bacon, diced
- 4 cloves garlic, thinly sliced
- 1 onion, chopped
- 1 cup dry white wine
- 2 teaspoons paprika
- 2 dozen mussels, cleaned and beards removed
- Cayenne pepper, for garnish
- Handful fresh oregano, chopped, for garnish

Directions:

1. In a Dutch oven over medium heat, heat the olive oil and cook the bacon. Once the bacon fat begins to render, 2 minutes, add the garlic and onion. Cook, stirring, until they are translucent.
2. Add the wine and stir in the paprika.
3. Add the mussels. Increase the heat to high, and cook for about 30 seconds, or until the alcohol has evaporated.
4. Reduce the heat to medium-low. Cover the pot and steam for 5 to 8 minutes, until all the mussels have opened. Discard any mussels that haven't opened.
5. Garnish with a drizzle of olive oil, a sprinkle of cayenne pepper, and chopped oregano.

Nutrition:

Carbohydrates: 19 g

Fat: 6 g

Protein: 4 g

Calories: 326

241. Chives Mussels

Preparation time: 25 minutes

Cooking time: 20 minutes

Servings: 6

Ingredients:

- 6 tablespoons unsalted butter, divided
- 2 shallots, peeled and minced
- 2 cloves garlic, peeled and minced
- ½ teaspoon salt
- ½ teaspoon freshly cracked black pepper
- 3 cups white wine
- 3 pounds (1.4 kg) cultivated mussels, scrubbed and beards removed
- ¼ cup chopped fresh chives
- 1 tablespoon chopped fresh tarragon

Directions:

1. In a Dutch oven over medium heat add 2 tablespoons butter. Once butter melts and starts to foam add shallots and cook until tender, about 1 minute. Add garlic, salt, and pepper and cook until the garlic is fragrant, about 30 seconds.
2. Add white wine and bring to a boil, then add mussels and stir to combine. Cover and cook 6 to 8 minutes.
3. With a slotted spoon remove and discard any mussels that did not open. Transfer remaining mussels to a serving bowl.
4. Bring the cooking liquid to a simmer and whisk in remaining butter and herbs. Pour liquid over the mussels and serve immediately.

Nutrition:

Carbohydrates: 12 g

Fat: 6 g

Protein: 4 g

Calories: 288

242. Shrimp and Mussels Paella

Preparation time: 20 minutes

Cooking time: 45 minutes

Servings: 4

Ingredients:

- 2 to 3 tablespoons extra-virgin olive oil
- 2 pounds (907 g) chicken thighs, skinned, boned, and cut into 2-inch pieces
- 5½ cups low-sodium chicken broth or stock
- ½ pound (227g) shrimp, peeled and shells reserved
- 1½ pounds (680g) paella rice, or any Spanish-style medium-grain rice
- ¼ teaspoon saffron
- 1 (15-ounce / 425-g) can cannellini beans, drained and rinsed
- 1 to 2 tomatoes (about ¾ pound), peeled, halved, seeded, and finely chopped
- 1 tablespoon smoked paprika
- 1 dozen mussels, scrubbed
- Sea salt, to taste

Directions:

1. In a Dutch oven over medium heat, heat the olive oil. Add the chicken pieces and sauté until golden. Using a slotted spoon, transfer the chicken to a platter. Pour off the fat from the pot.
2. Return the pot to the heat, add the broth, and bring to a boil. Add the shrimp shells (reserving the shrimp), and simmer for 15 to 20 minutes. Remove the shells with a slotted spoon and discard.
3. Stir in the rice and cook on medium heat for 10 minutes. Add the chicken pieces, saffron, cannellini beans, tomato, and paprika. Cook, covered, for 10 minutes.
4. Add the shrimp and mussels. Cook, covered, for 5 minutes, or until the mussels have opened.
5. Season with salt.

Nutrition:

Carbohydrates: 11 g

Fat: 6 g

Protein: 24 g

Calories: 234

243. Crab and Clam Cioppino

Preparation time: 20 minutes

Cooking time: 2 hours 30 minutes

Servings: 8

Ingredients:

- ¼ cup unsalted butter or olive oil
- 2 medium onions, peeled and chopped
- 4 cloves garlic, peeled and minced
- ¼ cup parsley leaves
- ¼ cup oregano leaves
- 2 (28-ounce / 794-g) cans whole tomatoes, peel removed
- 2 (10-ounce / 283-g) cans of clams
- 2 bay leaves
- 2 tablespoons dried basil leaves
- 2 cups dry white wine
- 16 fresh clams
- 16 mussels
- 1½ pounds (680g) salmon, cut into bite-sized chunks
- 1 pound (454 g) fresh crab meat or imitation crab stick, cut into chunks
- 1½ pounds (680g) small bay scallops
- ½ teaspoon salt
- ¼ teaspoon freshly cracked black pepper

Directions:

1. Place a Dutch oven over medium heat. Once it's heated through add butter and onion. Cook 10 to 12 minutes. Add the garlic and stir continually 1 minute. Stir in parsley and oregano.
2. Add juice from the tomatoes to the Dutch oven. Squeeze each tomato in your hand to break apart. Add to pan and press each tomato against the side to break it into smaller pieces. Pour clam juice into pan and refrigerate clams for later. Stir in dried herbs and wine.
3. Cover with a lid, reduce the heat to low, and simmer 2 hours. (If necessary, you can complete this part up to 2 days ahead and refrigerate. Return it to the pan and bring to a boil before turning the flame to low.)
4. Scrub clams and mussels with a bristle brush. Remove beards from mussels. Soak in cold water 20 minutes. Gently add shellfish and reserved canned clams to the pan. Stir them into the sauce.
5. Stir in fish chunks, then crab meat. Stir in scallops. Cover and steam 5 to 8 minutes until clams and mussels have opened.
6. Remove bay leaves and season dish with salt and pepper. Serve directly from the Dutch oven while hot.

Nutrition:

Carbohydrates: 11 g

Fat: 6 g

Protein: 21 g

Calories: 226

244. Breaded Crab Fish Cheese Casserole

Preparation time: 10 minutes

Cooking time: 50 minutes

Servings: 4

Ingredients:

- 2 tablespoons unsalted butter
- 1 medium onion, peeled and minced
- 3 cloves garlic, peeled and minced
- 1 (16-ounce / 454-g) jar Alfredo sauce
- ½ pound (227g) fish fillets
- 3 tablespoons orange juice
- ½ cup ground almonds
- 1 cup shredded Havarti cheese
- ½ pound (227g) crab meat
- 1 cup soft whole-wheat bread crumbs
- 3 tablespoons grated Parmesan cheese
- 3 tablespoons unsalted butter, melted

Directions:

1. Heat oven to 350°F (180°C).
2. In a Dutch oven melt butter over medium heat. Once melted add onion and garlic, and cook 5 minutes or until tender. Add Alfredo sauce and bring to a simmer. Add fish fillets and simmer 4 to 5 minutes, or until fish flakes. Stir to break up fish.

3. Stir in orange juice and almonds and remove from heat. Add Havarti cheese and crab meat.
4. In a small bowl, combine the bread crumbs, Parmesan cheese, and melted butter; mix well. Sprinkle over fish mixture. Bake 30 to 40 minutes, or until the bread crumbs have browned. Serve immediately.

Nutrition:

Carbohydrates: 19 g

Fat: 6 g

Protein: 14 g

Calories: 234

245. Panko Shrimp Scampi

Preparation time: 10 minutes

Cooking time: 25 minutes

Servings: 4

Ingredients:

- ½ cup Panko bread crumbs
- 6 tablespoons salted butter, divided
- 1 shallot, peeled and minced
- 1 clove garlic, peeled and minced
- 1 tablespoon finely chopped fresh chives
- 1 teaspoon finely chopped fresh parsley
- ½ teaspoon finely chopped fresh dill
- ¼ teaspoon smoked paprika
- ¼ teaspoon salt
- ¼ teaspoon freshly cracked black pepper
- 1 pound (454 g) (23 to 30 counts) tail-on shrimp

Directions:

1. Heat oven to 350°F (180°C).
2. In a small bowl add bread crumbs. Melt 2 tablespoons butter and toss until the crumbs are evenly coated. Set aside.
3. In a Dutch oven over medium heat add remaining butter. Once

it melts and starts to foam add shallots and cook until tender, about 1 minute. Add remaining ingredients except the shrimp and cook until fragrant, about 30 seconds. Remove the Dutch oven from heat.

4. Add shrimp and toss to coat, then sprinkle the bread crumbs over the shrimp and bake 15 to 20 minutes, or until the shrimp are cooked through and the bread crumbs are golden brown. Serve immediately.

Nutrition:

Carbohydrates: 12 g

Fat: 6 g

Protein: 14 g

Calories: 256

246. Creamy Shrimp Mushrooms Stroganoff

Preparation time: 15 minutes

Cooking time: 15 minutes

Servings: 8

Ingredients:

- 4 tablespoons unsalted butter
- 2 shallots, peeled and minced
- 2 cloves garlic, peeled and minced
- 4 plum tomatoes, diced
- 1 pound (454 g) chanterelle mushrooms, separated into individual pieces
- 4 ounces (113 g) portobello mushrooms, finely chopped
- 1 cup dry white wine
- 1 cup heavy cream
- 3 pounds (1.4 kg) shrimp, peeled and deveined
- 1 tablespoon chopped fresh tarragon
- 1 cup sour cream, room temperature
- ½ teaspoon salt
- ¼ teaspoon freshly cracked black pepper

Directions:

1. Melt butter in a Dutch oven over medium-high heat. Add shallots

and garlic and cook until just tender, about 2 minutes.

2. Add diced tomatoes and cook an additional 2 minutes. Add mushrooms and cook, stirring frequently, until the mushrooms soften, about 5 minutes.

3. Add white wine and heavy cream to mushroom mixture. Bring to a boil and stir well. Add shrimp and cook just until they begin to turn opaque, about 2 minutes.

4. Remove the Dutch oven from heat; stir in chopped tarragon, sour cream, salt, and pepper. Serve immediately.

Nutrition:

Carbohydrates: 10 g

Fat: 6 g

Protein: 4 g

Calories: 386

247. Oysters and Shrimp Cream Salad

Preparation time: 10 minutes

Cooking time: 30 minutes

Servings: 8

Ingredients:

- 1 pound (454 g) dried penne pasta
- 2 tablespoons peanut or vegetable oil
- 2 tablespoons all-purpose flour
- 1 large yellow onion, peeled and diced
- 1 teaspoon anchovy paste
- 1 cup milk
- 1 cup heavy cream
- ½ teaspoon hot sauce
- 1 teaspoon Worcestershire sauce
- Pinch dried thyme
- 2 pints small oysters, drained, liquid reserved
- 2 pounds (907 g) medium shrimp, cooked, peeled, and deveined
- ½ teaspoon salt
- ½ teaspoon freshly cracked black pepper
- 8 cups salad mix
- 8 green onions, chopped

Directions:

1. In a Dutch oven, cook penne according to package directions; drain, set aside, and keep warm.
2. Wipe out the Dutch oven; add oil over medium heat. Once the oil is hot, stir in flour and cook until it begins to turn light brown, about 5 to 6 minutes. Add onion and saute for 3 minutes or until soft. Whisk in anchovy paste, milk, and cream.
3. Bring to a simmer and stir in hot sauce, Worcestershire sauce, and thyme; simmer 10 minutes.
4. Stir oysters and shrimp into the cream sauce. Simmer just long enough to heat the seafood, about 2 minutes, then stir in pasta. If pasta mixture is too thick, stir in a little extra milk, cream, or liquid drained from the oysters. Taste for seasoning and add salt and pepper if needed.
5. To serve, spread 1 cup salad mix over the top of a plate, ladle pasta mixture over the salad greens, and garnish with chopped green onion.

Nutrition:

Carbohydrates: 19 g

Fat: 6 g

Protein: 20 g

Calories: 290

248. Shrimp and Tomato Provencal

Preparation time: 20 minutes

Cooking time: 1 hour

Servings: 4

Ingredients:

- 1 tablespoon olive oil
- 3 tablespoons unsalted butter
- 2 medium onions, peeled and chopped
- 4 cloves garlic, peeled and minced
- 1 (14-ounce / 397-g) can diced tomatoes, undrained
- 1 (8-ounce / 227-g) can tomato sauce
- ¼ cup dry sherry, if desired
- ½ teaspoon fennel seeds
- 1 teaspoon sugar
- ½ teaspoon salt
- 1/8 teaspoon cayenne pepper
- 1 teaspoon dried thyme leaves
- 1½ pounds (680 g) raw medium shrimp, shelled
- 3 cups hot cooked brown rice
- ½ cup crumbled Goat cheese

Directions:

1. In large Dutch oven combine olive oil and butter over medium heat. Once butter melts add onion and garlic; cook 5 to 6 minutes or until tender.
2. Add all remaining ingredients except shrimp, rice, and cheese. Bring to a simmer, stirring frequently. Reduce heat to low, partially cover, and simmer 50 minutes, stirring occasionally.
3. Just before serving, stir in shrimp and cook until shrimp curl and turn pink, about 3 to 4 minutes. Serve over rice and sprinkle with cheese.

Nutrition:

Carbohydrates: 13 g

Fat: 6 g

Protein: 14 g

Calories: 246

249. Savory Calamari

Preparation time: 15 minutes

Cooking time: 20 minutes

Servings: 3

Ingredients:

- 1 pound (454 g) frozen calamari, cleaned
- ¼ cup fine cornmeal
- 2 tablespoons cornstarch
- 2 teaspoons seafood seasoning, such as Old Bay
- ½ teaspoon salt
- 1 quart canola or safflower oil

Directions:

1. Thaw calamari. Slice off the tentacles. Slice the tubes into ½-inch-wide rings. Pat dry with paper towels.
2. Combine cornmeal, cornstarch, seasoning, and salt in a plastic bag. Add calamari to the bag and shake until coated evenly.
3. Heat oven to 175°F (79°C). Place a wire rack over a baking sheet in the middle of the oven.
4. Place 2-inch oil in a Dutch oven over medium-high heat. Once oil reaches 350°F (180°C), carefully add a handful of calamari pieces. Cook 2 to 3 minutes or until they're lightly golden brown.

5. Remove cooked calamari with a slotted spoon or wire skimmer and place on wire rack in warm oven to drain.

Nutrition:

Carbohydrates: 19 g

Fat: 6 g

Protein: 19 g

Calories: 312

250. Buttery Tomato Shrimp

Preparation time: 5 minutes

Cooking time: 15 minutes

Servings: 4

Ingredients:

- ¼ cup (½ stick) unsalted butter
- 2½ pounds shrimp, peeled and deveined
- 6 garlic cloves, minced
- Juice of 1 large lemon
- ¼ cup white wine (or substitute broth or water)
- 1 cup chopped tomatoes
- ½ teaspoon kosher salt
- ½ teaspoon freshly ground black pepper

Directions:

1. Melt the butter in the Dutch oven place on a bed of 6 hot coals. Add the shrimp, garlic, lemon juice, wine (or broth or water), tomatoes, salt, and pepper and cover the pot.
2. Add 20 hot coals to the lid and bake for about 10 minutes, until the shrimp are cooked through. Serve hot.

Nutrition: Carbohydrates: 19 g, Fat: 6 g

Protein: 18 g, Calories: 290

251. Mango Shrimp

Preparation time: 5 minutes

Cooking time: 10 minutes

Servings: 4

Ingredients:

- 2 tablespoons cooking oil
- 1 large onion, chopped
- 2 medium mangos, cubed
- ¼ cup soy sauce
- Juice of 2 limes
- 2 pounds (907 g) peeled and deveined shrimp

Directions:

1. Heat the oil in the Dutch oven set over a bed of 10 hot coals. Add the onion and cook, stirring, until soft and beginning to brown, about 5 minutes.
2. Add the mango, soy sauce, lime juice, and shrimp and cook, stirring occasionally, until the shrimp are cooked through, about 5 more minutes. Serve hot.

Nutrition:

Carbohydrates: 16 g

Fat: 6 g

Protein: 14 g

Calories: 321

252. Panko Crab Cakes

Preparation time: 10 minutes

Cooking time: 30 minutes

Servings: 4

Ingredients:

- 1 pound (454 g) crab meat
- 1/3 cup mayonnaise
- 1 teaspoon seasoned salt, plus more to taste
- ½ cup Panko bread crumbs
- 1 egg, beaten
- ½ cup roasted red bell peppers, finely chopped
- 2 to 3 tablespoons extra-virgin olive oil
- Freshly ground black pepper, to taste
- Optional:
- Buns
- Tartar sauce and/or cocktail sauce

Directions:

1. In a medium bowl, mix together the crab meat, mayonnaise, seasoned salt, Panko crumbs, egg, and roasted red peppers. Divide the mixture and use your hands to form 6 patties. Place the patties a plate, cover with plastic wrap, and chill in the refrigerator for 30 minutes.

2. Heat enough oil to coat the bottom of a Dutch oven over medium heat. Gently add the crab cakes to the pot, and cook for 5 to 6 minutes on each side, until the cakes are cooked through and golden brown.
3. You may want to do this in batches, as all the crab cakes will probably not fit in the pot at once. Add another tablespoon of oil to the pot, if needed, for the second batch.
4. Season with seasoned salt and pepper before serving—on buns with sauce, if using.

Nutrition:

Carbohydrates: 19 g

Fat: 6 g

Protein: 20 g

Calories: 378

253. Sausage Corn Chowder

Preparation time: 5 minutes

Cooking time: 10 minutes

Servings: 4

Ingredients:

- 1 pound bulk breakfast sausage
- 1 cup chopped onion
- 3/4 cup chopped celery
- 3 cups 1/2-inch diced red potatoes
- 2 cups chicken broth
- salt and ground black pepper to taste
- 1 (14 ounce) can whole kernel corn
- 1 (14 ounce) can cream-style corn
- 1 (12 fluid ounce) can evaporated milk
- 1/2 teaspoon paprika
- 1/4 teaspoon cayenne pepper, or to taste

Directions

1. Heat a Dutch oven over medium-high heat. Cook and stir sausage, onion, and celery in the hot Dutch oven until sausage is browned and crumbly, 5 to 7 minutes; drain and discard grease.
2. Mix potatoes, chicken broth, salt, and pepper into sausage mixture; bring to a boil. Reduce heat and simmer until potatoes are soft, about 10 minutes.

Add whole kernel corn, cream-style corn, evaporated milk, paprika, and cayenne pepper; simmer until heated through, 5 to 10 more minutes.

Nutrition:

Carbohydrates: 11 g

Fat: 6 g

Protein: 20 g

Calories: 278

Chapter 12. Breads and Rolls

254. No-Knead Bread

Preparation time: 9 hours

Cooking time: 45 minutes

Servings: 10

Ingredients:

- 3 cups all-purpose flour
- 3/4 teaspoon active yeast
- 2 teaspoons salt
- 1 1/2 cups water, lukewarm

Directions:

1. Take a large bowl, place flour in it, and stir in yeast and salt until combined.
2. Make a well in the center, pour in water, whisk well until the dough comes together, then cover it with a plastic wrap and let it stand for 8 hours in a warm place until doubled in size.
3. Then take a parchment sheet, dust it flour, place dough on it, fold it into a round shape, cover with a kitchen towel and let it stand for 1 hour in a warm place.
4. Switch on the oven, then set it to 450 degrees F and let it preheat.
5. After 30 minutes, place the Dutch oven in it along with its lid and bring it to 450 degrees F.
6. Then carefully transfer the dough into the Dutch oven by using a parchment sheet as a sling, make a slash on top of the dough and bake for 30 minutes, covering the pan.
7. Uncover the lid, continue baking for 15 minutes until the internal temperature of the bread reaches 210 degrees F, and when done, transfer bread to a wire rack and cool for 15 minutes.
8. Slice the bread and serve.

Nutrition: Per Serving:

Calories: 229;

Total Fat: 0.7 g;

Saturated Fat: 0.1 g;

Protein: 6.7 g;

Carbs: 47.9 g;

Fiber: 1.8 g;

Sugar: 0.2 g

255. Sourdough Bread

Preparation time: 11 hours

Cooking time: 55 minutes

Servings: 12

Ingredients:

- 5 cups all-purpose flour
- 2 teaspoons instant yeast
- 1 tablespoon salt
- 1 tablespoon honey
- 1 1/2 cups warm water
- 1 cup Greek yogurt

Directions:

1. Take a large bowl, add all the ingredients in it, beat well by using an electric mixer until incorporated, then cover with plastic wrap and let it stand for 2 hours at warm environment until doubled in size.
2. Then punch the dough, cover it with a kitchen towel and let it stand for 8 hours.
3. When ready to cook, switch on the oven, then set it to 475 degrees F and let it preheat.
4. Transfer dough onto a surface dusted with flour, shape it in a dough ball, then place it into the Dutch oven lined with parchment sheet and let it rest for 1 hour in a warm environment.
5. Bake the bread for 25 minutes, covering the pan, then uncover the pan and continue baking for 30 minutes until the crust is golden brown.
6. When done, lift out the bread, let cool for 2 hours on a wire rack and then slice to serve.

Nutrition: Per Serving:

Calories: 174;

Total Fat: 1.5 g;

Saturated Fat: 0.3 g;

Protein: 7 g;

Carbs: 33 g;

Fiber: 1.4 g;

Sugar: 3 g

256. 5 Seeds Bread

Preparation time: 3 hours

Cooking time: 35 minutes

Servings: 8

Ingredients:

- 3 cups bread flour
- 1 tablespoon flax seeds
- 2 tablespoon toasted sunflower seeds and more for topping
- 1 teaspoon poppy seeds
- 2 tablespoons toasted pumpkin seeds and more for topping
- 1 tablespoon cornmeal
- 3/4 tablespoon active yeast
- 1/2 tablespoons salt
- 2 tablespoons honey
- 1 tablespoon toasted sesame seeds and more for topping
- 1 1/2 cups warm water, at 100 degrees F

Directions:

1. Take a 9-inches piece of parchment sheet, sprinkle with cornmeal and set aside until required.
2. Pour water in a large bowl, stir in salt and honey until the honey has dissolved, then stir in yeast and let it stand for 5 minutes.
3. Then whisk in flour in four batches along with all the seeds until incorporated, cover with plastic wrap and let the dough rest for 2 hours until tripled in size.
4. After 2 hours, sprinkle flour on two, then fold it in half twice, sprinkle again with some flour and shape the dough into a ball. Place the dough onto the prepared parchment sheet, sprinkle with sunflower and pumpkin seeds, and let it stand for 40 minutes, don't cover the bread.
5. When ready to bake, switch on the oven, set it to 450 degrees F, place Dutch oven with lid in it and let it preheat for 30 minutes.
6. Then place the dough in it along with parchment sheet, cover with the lid, bake for 30 minutes, then uncover the lid and continue baking for 5 minutes.
7. When done, lift the bread by using a parchment sheet, transfer it onto a wire rack and cool for 2 hours. Slice to serve.

Nutrition:

Per Serving: Calories: 218; Total Fat: 4.7 g; Saturated Fat: 1.1 g; Protein: 7 g; Carbs: 36.5 g; Fiber: 3.1 g; Sugar: 0.8 g

257. Focaccia

Preparation time: 3 hours

Cooking time: 42 minutes

Servings: 4

Ingredients:

- 3 cups bread flour
- 1 envelope of active yeast
- 1 1/2 teaspoon salt
- 3 teaspoons chopped rosemary
- 3 tablespoons grated parmesan cheese
- 1 tablespoon olive oil
- 1 1/2 cups lukewarm water

Directions:

1. Take a medium bowl, add yeast and water in it, stir until mixed and let it stand for 10 minutes.
2. Whisk flour in the yeast mixture in four batches along with salt, rosemary, oil, and cheese until incorporated, then cover with plastic wrap and let it stand at a warm place for 3 hours until doubled in size.
3. Then transfer the dough onto a working space dusted with flour, shape it into a boule, then place it on a parchment sheet, return dough with it in a bowl, cover with a kitchen towel, and let it stand for 20 minutes.
4. When ready to bake, switch on the oven, set it to 450 degrees F, place Dutch oven with lid in it and let it preheat for 30 minutes.
5. Then place the dough in the Dutch oven by using parchment sheet as a sling, make some slashes across the top, sprinkle with some flour, cover with the lid, bake for 30 minutes, then uncover the lid and continue baking for 12 minutes.
6. When done, lift the bread by using a parchment sheet, transfer it onto a wire rack and cool for 2 hours.
7. Slice to serve.

Nutrition: Per Serving:

Calories: 182;

Total Fat: 6.1 g;

Saturated Fat: 0.7 g;

Protein: 4.4 g;

Carbs: 27 g;

Fiber: 1.1 g;

Sugar: 0.45 g

258. Oven Tomato and Olive Focaccia

Preparation time: 3 hours

Cooking time: 35 minutes

Servings: 8

Ingredients:

- 4 cups all-purpose flour
- 1 tablespoon cornmeal
- 2 teaspoons active yeast
- 1/2 teaspoon sea salt
- 1/2 teaspoon sugar
- 2 tablespoons and 1 teaspoon olive oil
- 1 cup of warm water

For The Topping:

- 6 whole Campari tomatoes
- 6 black olives, pitted
- ½ teaspoon of sea salt
- Fresh basil for garnish
- 1 teaspoon Italian herbs mix
- 3 tablespoons grated parmesan cheese

Directions:

1. Take a medium bowl, add yeast, sugar, and water in it, stir until sugar has dissolved, and let it stand for 10 minutes.
2. Whisk flour in the yeast mixture in four batches until incorporated, then knead for 10 minutes, cover the dough with plastic wrap and let it stand at a warm place for 3 hours until doubled in size.
3. Then knead the dough for 5 minutes, place it in the Dutch oven by using parchment sheet as a sling, poke the dough by using a fork, sprinkle with herb and salt, and top with olives.
4. Let the dough stand for 4 minutes, then switch temperature of the oven to 400 degrees F, bake for 20 minutes, cover with the lid, then uncover the lid, remove tomatoes and continue baking for 15 minutes until the crust turns golden brown.
5. When done, lift the bread by using a parchment sheet, return tomatoes on the bread, transfer it onto a wire rack, cool for 10 minutes, and sprinkle with cheese.
6. Slice to serve.

Nutrition:

Per Serving: Calories: 120; Total Fat: 2 g; Saturated Fat: 1 g; Protein: 5 g; Carbs: 20 g; Fiber: 0.5 g; Sugar: 0.5 g

259. Cheddar Sage Bread

Preparation time: 6 hours

Cooking time: 40 minutes

Servings: 10

Ingredients:

- 3 cups bread flour
- 2¼ teaspoons instant yeast
- 1 cup whole-wheat flour
- 1 tablespoon salt
- 1 teaspoon dried sage
- 1¾ cups and 2 tablespoons warm water 110 degrees F
- 8-ounce block of Cheddar cheese
- Corn flour as needed for dusting

Directions:

1. Place both flours in a large bowl, add salt and yeast, pour in water and stir until wet dough comes together, scraping the sides of the bowl.
2. Cover the dough with foil, let it stand for 2 hours at room temperature, and then refrigerate for 2 hours.
3. Meanwhile, cut cheese into half, cut one block into ½-inch cubes, grate the other block, add sage in it and stir until mixed.
4. Transfer prepared dough onto a dusted working space, roll it into 1-inch thickness, sprinkle with two-third of grated cheese mixture and cheese cubes, then fold the edges of the dough towards the center in the clockwise direction, starting from the left side.
5. Then reroll the dough to 1-inch thickness, sprinkle with remaining cheese mixture and cheese cubes, repeat folding the dough in the same manner, turn it into a ball, cup it and pull it towards you.
6. Turn the dough to ninety degrees, repeat the folding and rolling of dough until a tight dough comes together, place it onto the parchment sheet sprinkled with cornflour, seam side down, cover with a kitchen towel and let it stand for 1 hour at the warm environment.
7. Meanwhile, switch on the oven, set it to 500 degrees F, place Dutch oven with lid in it, and let it preheat.
8. Then place the prepared dough in it using parchment as a sling, use a knife to score the top, cover with the lid and bake for 25 to 40 minutes at 450 degrees F until the internal temperature of the bread reaches to 190 degrees F.
9. When done, lift the bread by using a parchment sheet, transfer it onto a wire rack, and cool for 2 hours.

10. Slice to serve.

Nutrition: Per Serving:

Calories: 170;

Total Fat: 5 g;

Saturated Fat: 3 g;

Protein: 8 g;

Carbs: 24 g;

Fiber: 1 g;

Sugar: 1 g

260. Chocolate, Walnut, and Cranberry Bread

Preparation time: 10 hours

Cooking time: 35 minutes

Servings: 12

Ingredients:

- 3 cups all-purpose flour
- 1/2 teaspoon active yeast
- 1 cup white whole wheat flour
- 1/2 teaspoon ground nutmeg
- 2 teaspoons salt
- 1 1/2 teaspoons cinnamon
- 1/4 cup brown sugar
- 3 ounces dark chocolate, chopped
- 3/4 cup chopped walnuts
- 1/2 teaspoon ground cardamom
- 1/2 cup dried cranberries
- 1 3/4 cup warm water

Directions:

1. Take a bowl, place both flours in it, stir in, yeast all the spices, salt, and brown sugar, then whisk in warm water until combined and fold in chocolate, cranberries, and walnuts until mixed.

2. Shape the dough into a ball, place it in a bowl, cover with plastic wrap, and

let it stand for 8 hours in a warm environment until doubled in size.

3. Then place the dough onto a piece of parchment sheet, shape it into a circular dough and then place it into a Dutch oven by using parchment by a sling.

4. Score the top of the dough, then cover it with plastic wrap and let it stand in a warm environment for 2 hours until doubled in size.

5. Meanwhile, switch on the oven, then set it to 450 degrees F, place Dutch oven with lid in it, and let it preheat.

6. Then remove the plastic wrap from the risen dough, place it into the Dutch oven by using parchment as a sling, cover the pan with lid, bake for 25 minutes, then uncover the pan and continue baking for 15 minutes until the top is golden brown.

7. When done, lift the bread by using a parchment sheet, transfer it onto a wire rack, and cool for 2 hours. Slice to serve.

Nutrition:

Per Serving: Calories: 273; Total Fat: 8 g; Saturated Fat: 2 g; Protein: 6 g; Carbs: 46 g; Fiber: 4 g; Sugar: 12 g

261. Honey Sunflower Bread

Preparation time: 5 minutes

Cooking time: 30 minutes

Servings: 8

Ingredients:

- 1 1/2 cups whole wheat flour
- 2 teaspoons active yeast
- 1 1/2 cups all-purpose flour
- 1/2 tablespoon salt
- 1/2 cup sunflower seeds, chopped
- 2 tablespoons honey
- 2 tablespoons olive oil
- 1 egg
- 1 1/4 cups warm water

Directions:

1. Take a bowl, add yeast, honey, and warm water in it, stir until mixed and let it stand for 5 minutes until frothy. Meanwhile, place sunflower seeds in a large bowl, add 1 cup of whole wheat flour, and then stir in salt until combined.

2. Stir oil into the yeast mixture, pour it into the flour-sunflower seeds mixture until smooth, then whisk in all-purpose flour in a four batched until incorporated, transfer the dough onto a clean and dusted working space, and knead remaining whole wheat flour for 5 minutes until soft.

3. Return dough into the bowl, wrap with plastic wrap, and let it stand at the warm environment for 1 hour and 30 minutes until doubled in size.

4. Then deflate the dough, shape it into a ball, place it onto a piece of parchment paper, cover the ball with a kitchen towel and let it stand at the warm environment for 1 hour and 30 minutes.

5. Meanwhile, switch on the oven, then set it to 450 degrees F, place Dutch oven with lid in it, and let it preheat.

6. Separate the egg yolk and white, whisk 1 tablespoon water into the egg white, then brush it all over the loaf and score an X on the top.

7. Then place the dough into the Dutch oven by using parchment as a sling, cover the pan with lid, bake for 25 minutes, then uncover the pan and continue baking for 15 minutes until the top is golden brown.

8. When done, lift the bread by using a parchment sheet, transfer it onto a wire rack, and cool for 2 hours. Slice to serve.

Nutrition:

Per Serving: Calories: 110; Total Fat: 2 g; Saturated Fat: 1 g; Protein: 4 g; Carbs: 19 g; Fiber: 3 g; Sugar: 3 g

262. Rosemary and Lemon Bread

Preparation time: 14 hours

Cooking time: 45 minutes

Servings: 12

Ingredients:

- 3 cups all-purpose flour
- 1/4 teaspoon active yeast
- 2 teaspoons chopped lemon zest
- 2 teaspoons chopped rosemary
- 1 3/4 teaspoon salt
- 1 5/8 cups water
- Cornmeal as needed

Directions:

1. Place flour in a bowl, stir salt, rosemary, yeast, and lemon zest until combined, then whisk in water until blended, cover with plastic wrap and let it stand at the warm environment for 12 hours.

2. Transfer the dough on a clean and dusted working space, roll dough twice, then cover with plastic wrap and let it stand at room temperature for 15 minutes.

3. Shape the dough into a ball, cover with a kitchen towel, turn the dough on the towel seam side down, dust

with cornmeal, then cover with another towel and let it stand at the warm environment for 2 hours until doubled in size.

4. Meanwhile, switch on the oven, then set it to 450 degrees F, place Dutch oven with lid in it, and let it preheat.

5. Then turn the dough seam side up, place it into the Dutch oven by using parchment as a sling, cover the pan with lid, bake for 30 minutes, then uncover the pan and continue baking for 15 minutes until the top is golden brown.

6. When done, lift the bread by using a parchment sheet, transfer it onto a wire rack, and cool for 2 hours.

7. Slice to serve.

Nutrition: Per Serving:

Calories: 118;

Total Fat: 3.4 g;

Saturated Fat: 0.5 g;

Protein: 3.1 g;

Carbs: 19 g;

Fiber: 0.8 g;

Sugar: 0.5 g

263. Rosemary Cheese Bread

Preparation time: 3 hours

Cooking time: 40 minutes

Servings: 8

Ingredients:

- 3 3/4 cups bread flour
- 2 teaspoons salt
- 2 1/4 teaspoon active yeast
- 1 teaspoon sugar
- 2 teaspoons chopped rosemary
- 1/4 cup olive oil
- 1/2 cup grated Parmesan cheese
- 2 cups shredded mozzarella cheese
- 1 1/3 cup warm water

Directions:

1. Place yeast, sugar, and water in a small bowl, stir until combined and let it stand for 5 minutes until foamy.

2. Then place flour in a bowl, whisk in salt and yeast mixture until thoroughly combined, sprinkle with half of the parmesan, continue whisking for 12 to 15 minutes until the smooth and elastic dough comes together.

3. Transfer prepared dough onto a dusted space, knead for 2 minutes, shape it into a ball, brush with some

of the oil, return the dough into a bowl, brush the dough with some of the oil, cover with a kitchen towel and let it stand for 2 hours until doubled in size.

4. When ready to bake, switch on the oven, then set it to 450 degrees F, and let it preheat.

5. Place remaining parmesan cheese on a plate, stir in ¼ cup of mozzarella and set aside until required.

6. Punch down the risen dough, knead it for 5 minutes on clean working space, roll the dough into a 12-inches long log, cut it into six equal pieces and then knead 2 tablespoons of mozzarella into each piece until thoroughly combined.

7. Roll each piece into a ball, coat with cheeses mixture until lightly coated, place the prepared balls into a greased Dutch oven, arranging nine dough balls around the pan and three in the center.

8. Cover the dough balls with plastic wrap, and then let it stand for 40 minutes in a warm environment.

9. Then sprinkle remaining cheeses and rosemary on dough balls, make a ¼-inch deep cut in the top of each dough ball and bake for 10 minutes, covering the pan.

10. Then continue baking for 30 minutes until bread is crusty, uncovering the pan, and when done, transfer the pan onto the wire rack and cool for 10 minutes.

11. Lift out the bread, cool for 1 hour, and serve.

Nutrition: Per Serving:

Calories: 150;

Total Fat: 2 g;

Saturated Fat: 1 g;

Protein: 6 g;

Carbs: 24 g;

Fiber: 1 g;

Sugar: 0 g

264. Rosemary Bread

Preparation time: 12 hours

Cooking time: 45 minutes

Servings: 12

Ingredients:

- 3 cups all-purpose flour
- 1/2 teaspoon active yeast
- 3/4 cup chopped rosemary
- 1 3/4 teaspoon sea salt
- 1 1/2 cups water

Directions:

1. Place flour in a large bowl, stir in yeast, salt, and rosemary and yeast, then whisk in water until well combined, cover with plastic wrap and let it stand for 12 hours.

2. When ready to bake, switch on the oven, then set it to 450 degrees F, place Dutch oven with lid in it, and let it preheat.

3. Shape the risen dough into a ball, folding a couple of times, then place it into the heated Dutch oven by using parchment sheet as a sling, bake for 30 minutes, covering the pan, then uncover the pan and bake for 15 minutes until the top is golden brown.

4. When done, lift the bread by using a parchment sheet, transfer it onto a wire rack, and cool for 2 hours.

5. Slice to serve.

Nutrition: Per Serving:

Calories: 118;

Total Fat: 3.4 g;

Saturated Fat: 0.5 g;

Protein: 3.1 g;

Carbs: 19 g;

Fiber: 0.8 g;

Sugar: 0.5 g

265. Zucchini Bread

Preparation time: 20 minutes

Cooking time: 60 minutes

Servings: 20

Ingredients:

- 2 cups zucchini, peeled, grated
- 3 cups all-purpose flour
- 1 teaspoon baking soda
- 1 teaspoon salt
- 3 teaspoons cinnamon
- 1 teaspoon baking powder
- 2 cups of sugar
- 1 teaspoon vanilla extract, unsweetened
- 1 cup olive oil
- 3 eggs

Directions:

1. Take forty charcoal briquettes, and let them heat until white and glowing.
2. Then prepare the dough and for this, crack eggs in a bowl, beat in sugar, oil, flour in four batches, salt, cinnamon, vanilla, baking powder, and soda until incorporated and then fold in zucchini until just mixed and the smooth dough comes together.
3. Take a 4-quart Dutch oven, line its bottom with parchment paper, place dough in it, cover the pan with the lid and place the pan over fifteen hot charcoals.
4. Place twenty-five hot charcoals on the lid of the pan, bake the bread for 15 minutes, then remove charcoals from the bottom and continue baking for 45 minutes until done, rotating the pan and charcoals every 5 minutes.
5. When done, lift the bread by using a parchment sheet, transfer it onto a wire rack, and cool for 2 hours.
6. Slice to serve.

Nutrition: Per Serving:

Calories: 154;

Total Fat: 8 g;

Saturated Fat: 0.7 g;

Protein: 2.1 g;

Carbs: 19 g;

Fiber: 0.6 g;

Sugar: 11 g

266. Cornbread with Green Chiles

Preparation time: 20 minutes

Cooking time: 20 minutes

Servings: 8

Ingredients:

- 4 ounces green chilies, sliced
- 1/2 cup all-purpose flour
- 1 teaspoon salt
- 1 cup cornmeal
- 1 tablespoon baking powder
- 2 tablespoons honey
- 2 tablespoons unsalted butter
- 1 egg
- 1 cup milk, unsweetened
- 1/4 cup grated cheddar cheese

Directions:

1. Take twenty-four charcoal briquettes, and let them heat until white and glowing.
2. Then prepare the dough and for this, crack eggs in a bowl, beat in milk and honey until combined and then beat in remaining ingredients except for chilies and cheese until incorporated and smooth batter comes together.
3. Take a 4-quart Dutch oven, grease its bottom with melted butter, pour in the prepared batter and sprinkle with chilies and cheese on top.
4. Cover the pan with lid, place it over seven hot charcoals, place remaining charcoals on the lid of the pan, bring the temperature of the pan to 425 degrees F and bake the bread for 20 minutes until bread is baked and the top is golden, rotating the pan and charcoals every 5 minutes.
5. When done, lift the bread, transfer it onto a wire rack, and cool for 30 minutes.
6. Slice to serve.

Nutrition: Per Serving:

Calories: 176.8;

Total Fat: 6.7 g;

Saturated Fat: 3.8 g;

Protein: 5.1 g;

Carbs: 25.4 g;

Fiber: 1.7 g;

Sugar: 2.5 g

267. Buttermilk Cornbread

Preparation time: 15 minutes

Cooking time: 30 minutes

Servings: 6

Ingredients:

- 12-ounce creamed corn
- 2 cups cornmeal
- 1 teaspoon salt
- 1/2 teaspoon baking soda
- 1 1/2 teaspoons baking powder
- 2 tablespoons lard
- 2 eggs
- 1 cup buttermilk

Directions:

1. Take twenty-five charcoal briquettes, and let them heat until white and glowing.
2. Then prepare the dough and for this, place cornmeal in a bowl, stir in salt, baking powder, and soda and then whisk in remaining ingredients, except for lard, until incorporated and smooth batter comes together.
3. Take a 4-quart Dutch oven, grease its bottom with lard, pour in prepared batter, cover the pan with lid, and place it over fifteen hot charcoals.
4. Place remaining charcoals on the lid of the pan, and bake the bread for 30 minutes until bread is firm, rotating the pan and charcoals every 5 minutes.
5. When done, lift the bread, transfer it onto a wire rack, and cool for 30 minutes.
6. Slice to serve.

Nutrition: Per Serving:

Calories: 141.5;

Total Fat: 6.1 g;

Saturated Fat: 3.7 g;

Protein: 3.5 g;

Carbs: 19.1 g;

Fiber: 1.6 g;

Sugar: 1.6 g

268. Sweet Honey Corn Bread

Preparation time: 15 minutes

Cooking time: 40 minutes

Servings: 6

Ingredients:

- 1 cup all-purpose flour
- 1 teaspoon salt
- 1 cup cornmeal
- 3 1/2 teaspoons baking powder
- ½ cup honey
- 1/3 cup olive oil
- 1 egg
- 1 cup milk, unsweetened

Directions:

1. Switch on the oven, then set it to 375 degrees F and let it preheat.
2. Prepare the dough and for this, place flour in a bowl, stir in cornmeal, salt, blacking powder and honey until mixed and then whisk in remaining ingredients until incorporated and smooth batter comes together.
3. Pour the batter into a greased Dutch oven, cover with the lid, bake for 30 minutes, then uncover it and continue baking for 10 minutes until the top is golden.
4. When done, lift the bread, transfer it onto a wire rack, and cool for 30 minutes.
5. Slice to serve.

Nutrition: Per Serving:

Calories: 208.8;

Total Fat: 6.4 g;

Saturated Fat: 0.8 g;

Protein: 2.8 g;

Carbs: 27 g;

Fiber: 2 g;

Sugar: 12.1 g

269. Corn Muffins

Preparation Time: 10 minutes

Cooking time: 30 minutes

Servings: 8

Ingredients:

- 3/4 cup yellow cornmeal
- 1 1/4 cups self-rising flour
- 1/2 cup sugar
- 2 large eggs
- 2 tablespoons honey
- 3/4 cup buttermilk
- 1/2 cup unsalted butter, melted and cooled

Directions:

1. Preheat the oven to 350°F.
2. Line a muffin pan with muffin liners or grease thoroughly.
3. Combine the cornmeal, flour, and sugar in a mixing bowl.
4. Beat the eggs in a medium bowl. Add the honey and buttermilk and whisk until well combined.
5. Slowly add the buttermilk to the cornmeal mixture, stirring as you add. There will be some lumps, but don't over-mix.
6. Transfer the batter to the muffin pan and fill holes to the 3/4, and bake for 18–20 minutes or until set.
7. Remove from dutch oven and allow to cool slightly before serving.

Nutrition:

Calories: 181

Total Fat: 30g

Carbs: 32g

Protein: 71g

Fiber: 0g

270. Breadsticks

Preparation Time: 60 minutes

Cooking Time: 15 minutes

Servings: 16

Ingredients:

- 1 1/2 cups warm water
- 2 tablespoons sugar
- Breadsticks 1/4 cup butter
- 1 teaspoon garlic powder
- 1 packet (1 tablespoon/3/4 ounce) yeast
- 2 tablespoons butter, softened
- 2 teaspoons fine sea salt (and a bit extra to sprinkle on top)
- 4–5 cups bread flour (you can also use all-purpose flour, but the breadsticks will turn out denser)
- Topping

Directions:

1. To make the breadsticks, combine the warm water, sugar, and yeast in a large bowl. Proof for 10 minutes. Mix in the salt, softened butter, and 3 cups of bread flour. Mix in the rest of the bread flour to get a soft dough.
2. Cover the bowl with a damp towel and set aside in a warm place. Let dough rise for 1 hour. Gently knead the dough and separate into 14–16 balls.
3. Roll each ball into a log of your desired length. Place on two cookie sheets and let rise for 15–30 minutes.
4. To make the topping, melt the butter and mix with the garlic powder. Brush the topping mixture over the breadsticks and finish with sprinkles of sea salt.
5. Bake in the Dutch oven for 12–14 minutes. Brush the remaining garlic butter on top of the breadsticks.

Nutrition:

Calories 190,

Total Fat 4.4 g,

Cholesterol 0 mg,

Sodium 328 mg,

Potassium 57 mg,

Total Carbohydrate 31 g,

Dietary fiber 1.4 g,

Sugar 0.6 g,

Protein 6 g

271. Buttermilk Biscuits

Preparation Time: 15 minutes

Cooking Time: 15 minutes

Servings: 10

Ingredients:

- 2 cups all-purpose flour
- 2 teaspoons baking powder
- 1/2 teaspoon baking soda
- 1/2 teaspoon salt
- 1/4 cup shortening
- 3/4 cup buttermilk

Directions:

1. Preheat oven to 450°.
2. In a bowl, combine flour, baking powder, baking soda and salt; cut in shortening until the mixture resembles coarse crumbs.
3. Stir in buttermilk; knead dough gently.
4. Roll out to 1/2-in. thickness.
5. Cut with a 2-1/2-in. biscuit cutter and place on a lightly greased baking sheet.
6. Transfer to Dutch oven and Bake until golden brown, 10-15 minutes.

Nutrition: Calories: 142, Fat: 5g, Cholesterol: 1mg, Sodium: 281mg, Carbohydrate: 20g, Protein: 3g

272. Cinnamon Bread

Preparation Time: 10 minutes

Cooking Time: 45 minutes

Servings: 7

Ingredients

- 1 and ½ cups of flour
- ¾ Teaspoon of baking soda
- ½ Teaspoon of baking powder
- ¼ Teaspoon of salt
- 1 Teaspoon of cinnamon
- ½ Teaspoon of ground all spice
- 4 Tbsp of butter
- 2 Large organic eggs
- 1 Cup of avocado puree
- ½ Cup of heavy cream
- ½ Tbsp of grated lemon zest

Directions:

1. Preheat your oven to 340° F and place a 6-quart Dutch oven in it to heat for at least 30 minutes
2. In a deep bowl, combine all together the flour, the baking powder, the salt, the lemon zest, the all spice and the cinnamon and mix very well.
3. Pour the butter in a bowl and with a hand mixer beat it until it becomes soft and very smooth.
4. Add in the eggs and the avocado puree then carry on mixing the ingredients
5. Add your dry mixture and the heavy cream into your batter and Mix it very well until it is very well combined.
6. Remove the Dutch oven from the oven and line it with a baking paper

7. Grease the Dutch oven with a little bit of oil; then pour in the batter and cover it with the lid
8. Place the Dutch oven back in the oven and bake for about 45 minutes at a temperature of 400° F
9. Remove the Dutch oven from the oven and set it aside to cool for 5 minutes
10. Slice the bread; then serve and enjoy it!

Nutrition:

Calories: 174,

Fat: 17g,

Carbohydrates: 5g,

Protein: 4.8g,

Dietary Fiber: 1.9g

273. Cashew Bread

Preparation Time: 7 minutes

Cooking Time: 50 minutes

Servings: 5

Ingredients

- 2 Tablespoons of vegetable oil
- 2 and ½ cups of whole raw cashews
- 7 Tablespoons of flour
- 8 Beaten large eggs
- ½ Cup of milk
- 4 Teaspoons of apple cider vinegar
- 4 teaspoons of baking powder
- 1 Teaspoon of salt

Directions:

1. Put a 6-quart Dutch oven in the oven at a temperature of 325° F about ½ hour before baking the bread
2. Mix the flour, the cashews, the eggs, the milk, the apple cider vinegar, the salt and the baking powder and process the mixture for around 30 to 40 seconds
3. Once the mixture becomes very thick, add 1 to 2 tbsp of water and process again until the mixture becomes smooth
4. Remove the Dutch oven from the oven and line it with a parchment paper; then grease with a little bit of oil
5. Pour the batter into the Dutch oven and cover with a lid
6. Place the Dutch oven in the preheated oven and bake for about 45 to 50 minutes

7. Once the bread gets a golden brown color, remove the Dutch oven from the oven and discard it from the parchment paper.
8. Slice the bread; serve and enjoy it mesmerizing taste!

Nutrition:

Calories: 201.5,

Fat: 15.6g,

Carbohydrates: 12.3g,

Protein: 5.8g,

Dietary Fiber: 1.4g

274. Sesame Seeds Bread

Preparation Time: 10 minutes

Cooking Time: 60 minutes

Servings: 4

Ingredients

- 1 Cup of almond flour
- ¼ Cup of sesame seeds
- ½ Cup of golden flaxseed meal
- ½ Cup of pumpkin seeds
- 1 Cup of sunflower seeds
- 2 Tbsp of chia seeds
- ¼ Cup of water
- 1 and ¼ teaspoon of salt
- 5 Beaten eggs
- 2 Tbsp of sesame seeds to sprinkle it on the top of batter

Directions:

1. Preheat your oven to around 350° F and line a 6-quart Dutch oven with parchment paper.
2. Place the Dutch oven in the oven about ½ hour before baking the bread
3. In a deep and large bowl; combine all together the almond meal, the sesame seeds, the flaxseed meal, the pumpkin seeds, the sunflower seeds, and the chia seeds
4. Add the salt and mix very well.
5. Pour in the water and the eggs all at once, and stir your ingredients very well until you obtain a smooth batter
6. Remove the Dutch oven from the oven; then pour the batter into it already and sprinkle with 1

pinch of sesame seeds on top of your bread
7. Cover the Dutch oven with the lid and place it in the preheated oven
8. Bake the bread for around 55 to 60 minutes
9. Remove the Dutch oven from the oven and discard it from the parchment paper
10. Slice the bread into pieces, then serve and enjoy it!

Nutrition:

Calories: 144.7,

Fat: 9.8g,

Carbohydrates: 11.5g,

Protein: 3.8g,

Dietary Fiber: 1.2g

Chapter 13. Sauces

275. Cream and Butter Sauce

Preparation time: 5 minutes

Cooking time: 10 minutes

Servings: 1 cup

Ingredients:

- ¼ cup salted butter
- 1 cup light brown sugar
- ½ cup heavy (whipping) cream

Directions:

1. In a small saucepan over medium heat, melt the butter. Mix in the sugar, and whisk vigorously to combine.
2. When the sugar is dissolved, add the cream. Bring the mixture to a boil, reduce the heat to low, and simmer for 5 minutes, stirring frequently. Serve warm or allow the mixture to cool before storing it in the refrigerator. The sauce will get much thicker when chilled.
3. Stir really well before putting this sauce in the refrigerator. Store it in an airtight container in the refrigerator for up to 2 weeks.

Nutrition:

Carbohydrates: 19 g, Fat: 6 g

Protein: 4 g, Calories: 326

276. Honey and Soy Sauce

Preparation time: 5 minutes

Cooking time: 5 minutes

Servings: 1 cup

Ingredients:

- ½ cup water, divided
- 2 teaspoons cornstarch
- ½ cup low-sodium soy sauce
- 3 tablespoons honey
- 1 tablespoon rice wine vinegar

Directions:

1. Put ¼ cup of the water in a small saucepan, and whisk in the cornstarch until blended to a paste. Add the soy sauce, honey, vinegar, and remaining ¼ cup of water.
2. Turn the heat to medium-high and cook for 5 minutes or until the sauce comes to a simmer, whisking constantly. Mix well, and remove from the heat.
3. Store in an airtight container in the refrigerator for up to 2 weeks.

Nutrition:

Carbohydrates: 10 g

Fat: 6 g

Protein: 4 g

Calories: 231

277. Syrupy Sauce with Ketchup

Preparation time: 5 minutes

Cooking time: 15 minutes

Servings: 2 cups

Ingredients:

- 1½ cups ketchup
- ¼ cup pure maple syrup
- 2 tablespoons cider vinegar
- 2 teaspoons paprika
- 1 teaspoon seasoned salt
- 1 teaspoon garlic powder
- ¼ cup water

Directions:

1. In a small saucepan, whisk together the ketchup, maple syrup, vinegar, paprika, seasoned salt, garlic powder, and water.
2. Set the pan over medium heat, bring the sauce to a simmer, and cook for 10 more minutes or until it reaches your desired thickness.
3. Let the sauce cool to room temperature, then store it in an airtight container in the refrigerator. It will keep for 1 week.

Nutrition: Carbohydrates: 11 g, Fat: 6 g Protein: 4 g, Calories: 234

278. Tomato Marinara Sauce

Preparation time: 10 minutes

Cooking time: 50 minutes

Servings: 3 cup

Ingredients:

- 1 tablespoon extra-virgin olive oil
- ½ cup chopped onion
- 3 garlic cloves, minced
- 1 (28-ounce / 794-g) can crushed tomatoes with Italian seasoning
- 1 tablespoon sugar
- 1 tablespoon dried basil
- Salt and freshly ground black pepper, to taste

Directions:

1. In a Dutch oven over medium heat, heat the olive oil. Add the onion and garlic. Sauté for 5 to 7 minutes, until the onion is slightly translucent.
2. Add the tomatoes, sugar, and basil to the pot and stir well. Cover and simmer on low for 45 minutes. If the sauce gets too thick, add a little water to thin it out. Season with salt and pepper.
3. Store in an airtight container in the refrigerator for 3 to 4 days.

Nutrition: Carbohydrates: 19 g, Fat: 6 g Protein: 4 g, Calories: 306

279. Enchilada Tomato Sauce

Preparation time: 10 minutes

Cooking time: 10 minutes

Servings: 3 cups

Ingredients:

- 2 tablespoons lard, such as bacon grease
- ¼ cup mild chili powder
- 1 tablespoon ground cumin
- 1 teaspoon garlic powder
- ½ teaspoon dried oregano
- 1 (15-ounce / 425-g) can tomato sauce
- 1½ cups beef stock
- 2 teaspoons cornstarch
- 1 teaspoon salt

Directions:

1. Gently warm the spices. In a Dutch oven over medium heat, melt the lard. Add the chili powder, cumin, garlic powder, and oregano.
2. Cook, stirring, for about 1 minute to let the lard get hot, then add the tomato sauce.
3. Thicken the sauce. In a liquid measuring cup, whisk the beef stock and cornstarch well to create a slurry.
4. Immediately add the slurry to the tomato mixture. Increase the heat to medium-high and cook for about 5 minutes, stirring well, until the sauce bubbles and thickens slightly.
5. Add the salt and use right away, or cool and refrigerate for up to 4 days.

Nutrition:

Carbohydrates: 16 g

Fat: 6 g

Protein: 4 g

Calories: 267

280. Cream Sauce with Lemon

Preparation time: 5 minutes

Cooking time: 5 minutes

Servings: 1 cup

Ingredients:

- 3 tablespoons unsalted butter
- ½ teaspoon grated lemon zest
- 2½ teaspoons smoked paprika
- ½ teaspoon salt
- ¼ cup chicken stock
- 2 tablespoons freshly squeezed lemon juice
- 1/3 cup heavy cream, plus more as needed

Nutrition:

Carbohydrates: 19 g

Fat: 6 g

Protein: 12 g

Calories: 287

Directions:

1. Start the sauce. In a Dutch oven over medium heat, melt the butter until bubbly, then add the lemon zest, paprika, and salt. Cook, stirring, for 1 minute, then add the chicken stock and bring to a simmer.
2. Incorporate the cream. Turn off the heat and add the lemon juice and heavy cream. At this point, if you want to thicken the sauce, simmer while whisking for a few minutes; for a thinner sauce, add more cream. Serve warm. Refrigerate leftovers for up to 5 days.

281. Chile and Cheese Sauce

Preparation time: 10 minutes

Cooking time: 10 minutes

Servings: 1 cup

Ingredients:

- 2 tablespoons unsalted butter
- 2 tablespoons all-purpose flour
- 1½ cups whole milk
- 1 cup shredded Cheddar cheese
- ¾ teaspoon salt
- 1 (4-ounce / 113-g) can diced Hatch chiles

Nutrition:

Carbohydrates: 11 g

Fat: 6 g

Protein: 4 g

Calories: 245

Directions:

1. Make a roux. In a Dutch oven over medium heat, melt the butter. Add the flour and cook, stirring constantly, for 1 minute, until the mixture turns tan in color.
2. Add the milk and cook, stirring, for about 1 minute, just until the mixture thickens.
3. Melt the cheese. Turn off the heat and add the cheese and salt. Stir until the cheese is melted and the sauce is smooth.
4. Stir in the chiles. For the best texture, serve the sauce immediately over tortilla chips or as a dip for bread.

Chapter 14. Desserts

282. Heavenly Peach Cobbler

Preparation time: 10 minutes

Cooking time: 20 minutes

Servings: 6

Ingredients:

- ½ pack vanilla cake mix
- 1 cup lemon-lime soda (Sprite/7 Up)
- 4 cups fruit (peaches, apples, berries, etc.)
- 2 tablespoons unsalted butter, cold, diced
- 2 tablespoons sugar (optional)
- Whipped cream

Directions

1. Lightly grease the Dutch oven with cooking spray.
2. Add the cake mix and soda to a mixing bowl. Mix well to make a thick batter.
3. Arrange the fruit in the Dutch oven; pour the batter over it.
4. Top with the diced butter and sugar.
5. Heat the Dutch oven to 350°F (175°C).
6. Cover and cook for 20 minutes until the top is golden brown and the juices are bubbling.
7. Serve warm with whipped cream.

Nutrition:

Calories 282,

Fat 6 g,

carbs 57 g,

Protein 3 g,

sodium 304 mg

283. Chocolate Cake

Preparation time: 10 minutes

Cooking time: 35 minutes

Servings: 8

Ingredients:

- 1 (21-ounce) can cherry pie filling
- 1 (12-ounce) can evaporate milk
- 1 regular-size pack chocolate cake mix
- 1/3 cup almonds, sliced
- ¾ cup butter, melted
- Vanilla ice cream (optional)

Directions

1. Heat the Dutch oven to 350°F (175°C). Line it with parchment paper and lightly grease with cooking spray.
2. Add the pie filling and evaporated milk to a mixing bowl. Mix well.
3. Pour it over the Dutch oven and spread evenly.
4. Add the cake mix and almonds on top.
5. Drizzle the melted butter on top.
6. Cover and cook for 35–40 minutes until the cake springs back when prodded.
7. Serve warm with ice cream.

Nutrition:

Calories 515,

Fat 24 g,

carbs 68 g,

Protein 7 g,

sodium 605 mg

284. Pecan Pralines

Preparation time: 10 minutes

Cooking time: 20 minutes

Servings: 18 pralines

Ingredients:

- 1 cup whipping cream
- 3 cups light brown sugar
- ¼ cup butter
- 2 tablespoons corn syrup
- 2 cups pecan halves
- 1 teaspoon vanilla extract
- Wax paper

Directions

1. Preheat the Dutch oven to 350°F (175°C).
2. Spread the pecan halves in the Dutch oven and cook for 5 minutes. Stir-cook for another 5 minutes. Set aside.
3. Clean the Dutch oven and add the whipping cream, brown sugar, butter, and corn syrup.
4. Boil over high heat for 4–6 minutes until the sugar melts completely, stirring occasionally.
5. Remove from heat and add the pecans and vanilla; stir for 1–2 minutes. Let cool for a while.
6. Place a spoonful of the mixture on a wax paper; allow to firm up for 10–15 minutes.
7. Serve warm.

Nutrition:

Calories 228,

Fat 14 g,

carbs 25 g,

Protein 2 g,

sodium 31 mg

285. Quick and Easy Pop Brownies

Preparation time: 10 minutes

Cooking time: 45 minutes

Servings: 8

Ingredients:

- 1 box brownie mix
- 1 can soda pop
- ¾ pound chocolate chips

Directions

1. Line the Dutch oven with parchment paper.
2. Add the brownie mix and soda to a mixing bowl. Mix well until you get a smooth mixture.
3. Pour the batter over the parchment paper. Sprinkle the chocolate chips on top.
4. Heat to 350°F (175°C) and bake for 45–60 minutes until well set. Check by inserting a toothpick; it should come out clean. If not, cook for a few more minutes.
5. Slice and serve warm.

Nutrition: Calories 241, Fat 13 g, carbs 35 g, Protein 2 g, sodium 16 mg

286. Chocolate Chip Cookies

Preparation time: 10 minutes

Cooking time: 10 minutes

Servings: 24

Ingredients:

- 1 cup butter, softened
- ¾ cup granulated sugar
- ¾ cup packed brown sugar
- 1 egg
- 1 teaspoon vanilla
- ½ teaspoon of sea salt
- 1 teaspoon baking soda
- 2¼ cups flour
- 1–2 cups semisweet chocolate chips

Directions

1. Add the butter and both sugars to a mixing bowl. Mix well.
2. Beat the eggs in another bowl. Add the vanilla. Mix well.
3. Add the sea salt, baking soda, and flour; mix again.
4. Combine the mixtures until smooth.
5. Mix in the chocolate chips.
6. Divide into 24 balls.
7. Line the Dutch oven with parchment paper and lightly grease it with cooking spray.

8. Arrange the balls on the bottom.

9. Cover and cook for 6 minutes. If cookies have turned light brown, take them out. If not, cook for 2–4 more minutes. Do not overcook.

10. Let cool for a while.

11. Serve warm.

Nutrition:

Calories 220,

Fat 11 g,

carbs 29 g,

Protein 2 g,

sodium 100 mg

287. Dutch Oven Brownies

Preparation time: 10 minutes

Cooking time: 30 minutes

Servings: 9

Ingredients:

- 1 box brownie mix
- ½ cup melted butter
- 2 large eggs
- 3 tablespoons water
- 1 cup of chocolate chips
- 1 teaspoon vanilla extract

Directions

1. Add the brownie mix to a large mixing bowl and stir in the melted butter, eggs, and water, and chocolate chips until just combined, being careful not to over-mix the batter.

2. Line the Dutch oven with a piece of parchment paper and pour in the brownie mixture.

3. Bake at 350°F (180°C) for 25–30 minutes.

4. Let the brownies cool slightly and then cut into squares and serve.

Nutrition: Calories 502, Fat 27 g, carbs 63.2 g, Protein 5.7 g, sodium 308 mg

288. Cinnamon Rolls

Preparation time: 10 minutes

Cooking time: 30 minutes

Servings: 6

Ingredients:

- 8 canned cinnamon rolls
- 2 cups powdered sugar
- 5 ounces cream cheese, softened
- 1 teaspoon vanilla extract
- Zest of 1 orange

Directions

1. Place a piece of parchment paper in the Dutch oven and arrange the cinnamon rolls on it.
2. Bake at 350°F (180°C) for 30–35 minutes until golden brown.
3. Add the softened cream cheese to a medium mixing bowl and mix it well with the powdered sugar, vanilla extract, and lemon zest.
4. Make sure that the mixture is pourable. If it's too thick, add a little bit of water.
5. Spread the cream cheese mixture on top of the cinnamon rolls while they are still warm.
6. Let cool slightly and then serve with a cup of coffee or chocolate milk.

Nutrition:

Calories 281,

Fat 9.9 g,

carbs 46.1 g,

Protein 2.9 g,

sodium 282 mg

289. Very Berry Swirl

Preparation time: 10 minutes

Cooking time: 30 minutes

Servings: 6

Ingredients:

- 1 (14-ounce) pizza dough
- 3 cups frozen or fresh mixed berries
- ¾ cup granulated sugar
- ½ teaspoon cinnamon
- 2 tablespoons all-purpose flour
- ¼ cup powdered sugar for dusting

Directions

1. Roll out the pizza dough into a ¼-inch-thick square.
2. Sprinkle the mixed berries, granulated sugar, cinnamon, and all-purpose flour on top. Ensure that every berry is coated with flour so that a nice thick sauce will form during baking.
3. Roll up the dough with the berries inside and cut diagonally with a sharp knife.
4. Carefully twist both parts of the dough together to make one long braid.
5. Shape the braid into a circle and place it in the Dutch oven on top of a piece of parchment paper.
6. Bake at 350°F (180°C) for 30–40 minutes.
7. Let cool slightly and then dust with powdered sugar when ready to serve.

Nutrition:

Calories 473,

Fat 20.7 g,

carbs 68.6 g,

Protein 4.6 g,

sodium 319 mg

290. Peach Cobbler

Preparation time: 10 minutes

Cooking time: 30 minutes

Servings: 4

Ingredients:

- 2 tablespoons butter
- 6 tablespoons butter, melted
- 6 peaches, stoned and cut in wedges
- 1 cup sugar (divided)
- 1 cup all-purpose flour
- 1 tablespoon baking powder
- ½ cup whole milk
- Powdered sugar for dusting

Directions

1. Grease the Dutch oven well on every side with the two tablespoons of butter.
2. Arrange the peach slices in the Dutch oven and sprinkle with ¾ cup of the sugar.
3. To a bowl, add the flour, baking powder, melted butter, milk, and remaining sugar.
4. Mix until combined and then use an ice cream scoop to deposit the batter on top of the peaches in the Dutch oven.
5. Bake at 350°F (180°C) for 30–35 minutes.
6. Let cool slightly and then dust with powdered sugar when ready to serve.

Nutrition:

Calories 615,

Fat 25 g,

carbs 98 g,

Protein 6.6 g,

sodium 180 mg

291. Apple Crisp

Preparation time: 10 minutes

Cooking time: 30 minutes

Servings: 6

Ingredients:

- 6 apples, cored and cut into wedges
- ¼ cup of water
- 1 cup all-purpose flour
- ½ cup of sugar
- ¾ cup butter
- 1 teaspoon cinnamon

Directions

1. Grease the Dutch oven and place the apple wedges in the bottom.
2. Pour in the water and let sit for 5 minutes.
3. Meanwhile, blend the flour, sugar, butter, and cinnamon in a food processor until a crumbly dough forms.
4. Distribute the dough on top of the apples, making sure you fill every hole, and bake, covered, for about 25 minutes at 350°F (180°C).
5. Remove the lid and cook uncovered for another 10–15 minutes until golden brown.
6. Serve warm with a scoop of ice cream.

Nutrition:

Calories 459,

Fat 23.6 g,

carbs 63.7 g,

Protein 3 g,

sodium 166 mg

292. All in One Apple Cake

Preparation time: 10 minutes

Cooking time: 40 minutes

Servings: 8

Ingredients:

- 3 apples, cored and cut into wedges
- ½ cup butter softened
- ½ cup of sugar
- 2 large eggs
- 1¼ cups self-rising flour
- ½ cup whole milk
- Powdered sugar for sprinkling

Directions

1. Grease the Dutch oven with a small piece of butter.
2. Add the butter and the sugar to a large mixing bowl and beat with a hand mixer until fluffy.
3. Stir in the eggs one at a time, mixing well after each addition.
4. Stir in the flour and mix until just combined.
5. Stir in the apple wedges and mix with a spatula.
6. Pour the cake mixture into the buttered Dutch oven and bake at 350°F (180°C) for about 40 minutes.
7. Let the cake cool slightly before serving with a sprinkle of powdered sugar.

Nutrition:

Calories 290,

Fat 13.6 g,

carbs 39.8 g,

Protein 4.4 g,

sodium 106 mg

293. Dutch Oven Chocolate Chip Cookies

Preparation time: 10 minutes

Cooking time: 20 minutes

Servings: 4

Ingredients:

- ½ cup butter, melted
- ¾ cup light brown sugar
- 2 teaspoons vanilla extract
- 2 large eggs, room temperature
- 1½ cups self-rising flour
- 1 cup of chocolate chips

Directions

1. Grease the Dutch oven with a little bit of butter.
2. Add the melted butter, sugar, vanilla extract, and eggs to a large mixing bowl.
3. Mix until combined and stir in the flour.
4. Mix in the chocolate chips and transfer the cookie dough to the buttered Dutch oven.
5. Bake at 350°F (180°C) for about 20 minutes.

Nutrition: Calories 496, Fat 25.6 g, carbs 58.6 g, Protein 7.7 g, sodium 160 mg

294. Fruity Doughnuts

Preparation time: 30 minutes

Cooking time: 30 minutes

Servings: 12

Ingredients:

- 3 1/2 cup all-purpose flour
- 0.25-ounce dry yeast
- 2 tablespoons white sugar
- 1 3/4 teaspoon salt, divided
- 1/2 cup confectioners' sugar
- 1/3 cup unsalted butter
- 1 tablespoon corn syrup
- 1/2 teaspoon vanilla extract, unsweetened
- 1 cup whole milk
- 4 large egg yolks
- 5 tablespoons warm water, at 105 degrees F, divided
- 6 cups peanut oil
- 1 1/2 cup Fruity Pebbles cereal

Directions:

1. Take a small bowl, pour in 3 tablespoons warm, stir in yeast and let it stand for 6 minutes until foamy.
2. Then take a bowl, add flour in it along with sugar, butter, and 1 ½ teaspoon

salt, pour in milk and yeast mixture, and then beat with an electric beater at low speed until a soft dough comes together.

3. Beat the dough for 3 minutes at medium-high speed, then transfer it to a bowl dusted with flour, cover it with plastic wrap and let it stand for 2 hours in a warm environment until doubled in size.

4. Then transfer the dough to a working space dusted with flour, roll the dough into ½-inch thick crust and use a 3-inch round cutter to cut out 12 rounds for doughnuts.

5. Use a 1-inch round cutter to cut a hole in the middle of each doughnut, then transfer doughnuts onto a large baking sheet dusted with flour, cover with a kitchen towel and let it stand for 30 minutes in a warm environment until slightly puffed.

6. When ready to cook, take a 4-quart Dutch oven, place it over medium-high heat, add oil, heat it to 350 degrees F, then drop in doughnuts and cook for 3 minutes per side until golden brown.

7. Transfer fried doughnuts to a wire rack covered with paper towels to soak oil and cook remaining doughnuts in the same manner.

8. Prepare glaze, and for this, take a shallow dish, pour in remaining warm water and stir in remaining salt, vanilla, confectioner's sugar, and corn syrup until combined.

9. Take another shallow dish, and then place cereal in it.

10. Dip one side of the doughnut into the glaze, then dredge into cereal and let it stand for 20 minutes until the glaze has set.

11. Prepare doughnuts in the same manner and then serve.

Nutrition: Per Serving:

Calories: 260;

Total Fat: 10 g;

Saturated Fat: 7 g;

Protein: 19 g;

Carbs: 25 g;

Fiber: 4 g;

Sugar: 9 g

295. Cobbler

Preparation time: 10 minutes

Cooking time: 30 minutes

Servings: 6

Ingredients:

- 1/2 box of vanilla cake mix
- 1 ½ cups blueberries
- 1 ½ cup diced peaches
- 1 cup diced apples
- 2 tablespoons sugar
- 2 tablespoons cold butter, grated bits
- 1 cup lemon-lime soda
- Whipped cream, as needed for serving

Directions:

1. Take forty-five charcoal briquettes, and let them heat until white and glowing.
2. Then take a 4-quart Dutch oven, grease it with oil and place all the fruits in it.
3. Place cake mix in a bowl, whisk in soda until thick batter comes together, and then drop the batter on top of fruits.
4. Top with butter, then sprinkle with sugar and cover the pan with lid.
5. Take fifteen hot charcoal briquettes, place the Dutch oven over them, use a tong to transfer remaining hot charcoal briquettes on the lid of the pan and bake for 10 minutes.
6. Then rotate the lid of pan clockwise, and charcoals counter clockwise and continue baking for 20 minutes until cobbler has cooked and the top is golden brown.
7. Serve cobbler with whipped cream.

Nutrition: Per Serving:

Calories: 282;

Total Fat: 6 g;

Saturated Fat: 3 g;

Protein: 3 g;

Carbs: 57 g;

Fiber: 3 g;

Sugar: 36 g

296. Apple Cobbler

Preparation time: 15 minutes

Cooking time: 25 minutes

Servings: 6

Ingredients:

For The Topping:

- 3/4 cup all-purpose flour
- 1/4 cup almond meal
- 1/4 teaspoon salt
- 2 tablespoons brown sugar
- 2 teaspoons baking powder
- 1/4 cup butter, chilled, ¼-inch cubed
- 1/3 cup milk, unsweetened

For The Filling:

- 6 medium apples, cored
- 1/4 teaspoon ground nutmeg
- 1/4 cup brown sugar
- 1 teaspoon ground cinnamon
- 2 tablespoons rum

Directions:

1. Take twenty-four charcoal briquettes, and let them heat until white and glowing.
2. Then prepare the topping and for this, place flour in a bowl, stir in almond meal, salt, sugar and baking powder, and this whisk in butter until milk until a crumbly dough comes together.
3. Prepare the filling, and for this, take a 4-quart Dutch oven, place it over medium heat and let it heat.
4. Cut cored apples into ½-inch pieces, add them to the pan along with remaining ingredients, cook for 5 minutes until the sugar has dissolved, and then remove from heat.
5. Prepare the cobbler and for this, take six hot coals, place the Dutch oven on it, then top with eighteen hot coals and bake for 20 minutes until cobbler has cooked and the top is golden brown.
6. Serve straight away.

Nutrition: Per Serving:

Calories: 437;

Total Fat: 22 g;

Saturated Fat: 14 g;

Protein: 4 g;

Carbs: 57 g;

Fiber: 4.2 g;

Sugar: 33 g

297. Upside Down Peach Cake

Preparation time: 10 minutes

Cooking time: 15 minutes

Servings: 6

Ingredients:

- 2 cups all-purpose flour
- 1 teaspoon baking powder
- 1 cup white sugar
- 1 teaspoon baking soda
- 1 teaspoon cinnamon
- 1 teaspoons salt
- 3/4 cup brown sugar
- 1/2 cup unsalted butter, softened
- 1/4 cup canola oil
- 1 cup buttermilk
- 3 eggs

For the Base:

- 3 cups sliced peaches
- 1/4 cup melted butter, unsalted
- 1/2 cup brown sugar

Directions:

1. Take nineteen charcoal briquettes, and let them heat until white and glowing.
2. Then place butter in a bowl, beat in both sugars and oil until combined, and then beat in eggs until smooth.
3. Gradually whisk in flour, cinnamon, baking powder, and soda until incorporated and then whisk in buttermilk until well combined.
4. Prepare the base layer and for this, take a 4-quart Dutch oven, spread melted butter in the bottom, and then spread peach slices and brown sugar in a single layer.
5. Top with prepared cake batter, then place the Dutch oven on top of seven hot charcoal, cover the pan with lid, place twelve hot charcoals on the lid and bake for 12 minutes, rotating the pan and charcoals every 5 minutes.
6. Then remove the lid, check the cake by inserting the wooden skewer in it, and if it comes out clean, then the cake is ready, else continue baking the cake for another 3 minutes.
7. Serve straight away.

Nutrition:

Per Serving: Calories: 139.3; Total Fat: 3.5 g; Saturated Fat: 1.4 g; Protein: 2.1 g; Carbs: 25 g; Fiber: 1.2 g; Sugar: 11.5 g

298. Double Chocolate Cake

Preparation time: 10 minutes

Cooking time: 30 minutes

Servings: 10

Ingredients:

- 1 1/2 cups flour
- 1 cup white sugar
- 1/4 cup dried buttermilk
- 1/4 cup cocoa, unsweetened
- 1 teaspoon baking soda
- 1/2 teaspoon salt
- 1 cup chocolate chips, divided
- 1/3 cup olive oil
- 2 teaspoons vanilla extract, unsweetened
- 1 cup of water

Directions:

1. Take twenty-two charcoal briquettes, and let them heat until white and glowing.
2. Then take a bowl, add flour in it, stir in cocoa, sugar, salt, baking soda, buttermilk, and ½ cup chocolate chips and then whisk in water, oil, and vanilla until incorporated.
3. Take a 4-quart Dutch oven, grease it well with oil, line the inner bottom with parchment paper and oil paper, and then spread with the prepared batter.
4. Sprinkle remaining chocolate chips on top, cover with the lid, then place the pan over eight hot charcoal, place fourteen hot charcoals on the lid, and bake for 25 to 30 minutes until the cake has cooked, rotating the pan and charcoals every 5 minutes.
5. When done, let the cake cool in the pan for 15 minutes, then cut it into wedges and serve.

Nutrition: Per Serving:

Calories: 537;

Total Fat: 23 g;

Saturated Fat: 7 g;

Protein: 6.1 g;

Carbs: 83 g;

Fiber: 3.3 g;

Sugar: 8 g

299. Coconut and Pineapple Upside Down Cake

Preparation time: 20 minutes

Cooking time: 35 minutes

Servings: 6

Ingredients:

For the Cake:

- 1 1/3 cups all-purpose flour
- 1/2 cup coconut flakes, sweetened
- 1/4 teaspoon salt
- 1/4 cup white sugar
- 1 1/4 teaspoons baking powder
- 1/3 cup olive oil
- 1/2 cup coconut cream
- 2 eggs

For the Topping:

- 2 cups pineapple chunks
- 1/4 cup white sugar
- 1/3 cup melted butter, unsalted

Directions:

1. Take forty charcoal briquettes, and let them heat until white and glowing.
2. Then prepare the cake batter, and for this, place flour in a bowl, stir in coconut flakes, salt, sugar, and baking powder until mixed and then whisk in oil, cream, and eggs until incorporated.
3. Take a 4-quart Dutch oven, line its bottom with aluminum foil, then grease its bottom and all the sides with melted butter, sprinkle with white sugar, and scatter with pineapple chunks.
4. Cover the pineapple pieces with prepared batter, cover the pan with the lid and place the pan over fifteen hot charcoals.
5. Place twenty-five hot charcoals on the lid of the pan and bake the cake for 35 minutes, rotating the pan and charcoals every 5 minutes.
6. When done, cool the cake in pan for 10 minutes, then lift it cool, peel the foil, cut it into slices, and serve.

Nutrition: Per Serving:

Calories: 401;

Total Fat: 23 g;

Saturated Fat: 11 g;

Protcin: 4.4 g;

Carbs: 47 g;

Fiber: 1.7 g;

Sugar: 8 g

300. Brownies

Preparation time: 10 minutes

Cooking time: 30 minutes

Servings: 10

Ingredients:

- 1 box of brownie mix
- Ice cream for serving

Directions:

1. Take twenty-four charcoal briquettes, and let them heat until white and glowing.
2. Then prepare brownie batter according to the instruction on the brownie mix box.
3. Take a 4-quart Dutch oven, line it with parchment sheet, pour in the prepared batter and cover with the lid.
4. Place the Dutch oven onto four hot charcoals, then place remaining charcoals on the lid and bake for 20 minutes, rotating the pan and charcoals every 5 minutes.
5. Then check the brownies by inserting a wooden skewer, and if it doesn't come out clean, continue baking for 10 minutes.
6. When done, lift out the brownies, cut it into squares, and then serve with ice cream.

Nutrition: Per Serving:

Calories: 87;

Total Fat: 3 g;

Saturated Fat: 0.8 g;

Protein: 1.3 g;

Carbs: 15 g;

Fiber: 1.1 g;

Sugar: 5.8 g

301. Monkey Bread

Preparation time: 10 minutes

Cooking time: 30 minutes

Servings: 6

Ingredients:

- 1/3 cup white sugar
- 3 tablespoons cinnamon
- 1/3 cup brown sugar
- 2 rolls of buttermilk biscuits
- 1 stick of unsalted butter, melted

Directions:

1. Take twenty-five charcoal briquettes, and let them heat until white and glowing.
2. Then take a plastic bag, add cinnamon and both sugars, seal it, and shake well.
3. Cut buttermilk biscuits into bite-size pieces, add to the plastic bag, and toss until well coated.
4. Take a 4-quart Dutch oven, line it with parchment sheet, add biscuits in it, and then pour in melted butter.
5. Place the Dutch oven onto four hot charcoals, then place remaining charcoals on the lid and bake for 30 minutes, rotating the pan and charcoals every 5 minutes.
6. Serve straight away.

Nutrition: Per Serving:

Calories: 210;

Total Fat: 10 g;

Saturated Fat: 2.5 g;

Protein: 3 g;

Carbs: 26 g;

Fiber: 1 g;

Sugar: 8 g

302. Chocolate and Cherry Dump Cake

Preparation time: 10 minutes

Cooking time: 30 minutes

Servings: 6

Ingredients:

- 21 ounces of cherry pie filling
- 15.25 ounces of chocolate cake mix
- 1/2 cup chocolate chips
- 1 1/4 cups lemon and lime soda

Directions:

1. Take a 4-quart Dutch oven, grease it with oil, then line it with parchment sheet and spread the cherry pie filling in the bottom in an even layer.
2. Sprinkle with chocolate cake mix, then pour in soda, mix by dragging a spoon over the top to the bottom of the mixture until slightly combined, and then sprinkle chocolate chips over the top.
3. Bring the Dutch oven to 375 degrees F and then let it cook for 30 minutes until cake is cooked.
4. When done, let the cake cool for 10 minutes and then serve.

Nutrition: Per Serving:

Calories: 282;

Total Fat: 12 g;

Saturated Fat: 5 g;

Protein: 2 g;

Carbs: 44 g;

Fiber: 2 g;

Sugar: 28 g

303. Apple Dump Cake

Preparation time: 10 minutes

Cooking time: 60 minutes

Servings: 8

Ingredients:
- 42 ounces apple pie filling
- 15.25 ounces yellow cake mix
- 1 stick of unsalted butter, sliced

Directions:
1. Take a 4-quart Dutch oven, grease it with oil, then line it with parchment sheet and spread the apple pie filling in the bottom in an even layer.
2. Spread yellow cake mix in an even layer and then scatter butter slices on top.
3. Bring the Dutch oven to 350 degrees F and then let it cook for 1 hour until the cake is cooked.
4. When done, let the cake cool for 10 minutes and then serve.

Nutrition:

Per Serving: Calories: 285.5; Total Fat: 10 g; Saturated Fat: 6 g; Protein: 1.6 g; Carbs: 46.7 g; Fiber: 1.3 g; Sugar: 27 g

304. Cherry Dump Cake

Preparation time: 10 minutes

Cooking time: 45 minutes

Servings: 6

Ingredients:
- 8 ounces pineapple tidbits
- 15.25 ounces yellow cake mix
- 21 ounces cherry pie filling
- ¼ stick of butter, melted

Directions:
1. Take twelve charcoal briquettes, and let them heat until white and glowing.
2. Take a 4-quart Dutch oven, grease it with oil, line it with parchment sheet, spread pineapple tidbits, and then spread cherry pie filling.
3. Cover with yellow cake mix, drizzle with melted butter and then place the Dutch oven onto twelve hot charcoals.
4. Place remaining charcoals on the lid, bring the Dutch oven to 350 degrees F and then bake for 35 to 45 minutes until cake is cooked, rotating the pan and charcoals every 5 minutes.
5. Serve straight away.

Nutrition: Per Serving: Calories: 259.1; Total Fat: 2.4 g; Saturated Fat: 0.6 g; Protein: 2.9 g; Carbs: 56.4 g; Fiber: 1.2 g; Sugar: 4.9 g

305. Cinnamon Rice Pudding

Preparation time: 15 minutes

Cooking time: 50 minutes

Servings: 6

Ingredients:

- 1 Tbsp butter
- 2 cups cooked white rice
- ½ tsp ground cinnamon
- ¾ cup sugar
- 5 large eggs, beaten
- 2 cups heavy cream
- 1 tsp vanilla extract
- Sprinkle of ground cinnamon, for garnish

Directions:

1. Preheat the oven to 350°F.
2. Butter the inside of a 2-quart Dutch oven and put the rice in the pot.
3. In a large bowl, mix the cinnamon, sugar, and eggs until well blended.
4. Whisk in the cream and vanilla.
5. Pour the mixture gently over the rice. Cover with the lid and place Dutch oven in the oven. Bake for 50 minutes, or until the custard is set. Remove from the oven and sprinkle lightly with cinnamon.
6. Serve warm.

Nutrition:

Carbohydrates – 38 g

Fat – 7.5 g

Protein – 3.9 g

Calories – 228

306. Banana Clafouti

Preparation time: 15 minutes

Cooking time: 45 minutes

Servings: 8

Ingredients:

- 1 cup whole milk
- ¼ cup whipping cream
- 3 eggs
- ½ cup granulated sugar
- 1 tsp vanilla extract
- 2 Tbsp butter, melted
- ¼ tsp salt
- ½ cup all-purpose flour
- 2 bananas, peeled and thinly sliced
- 2 tsp fresh lemon juice

Directions:

1. Preheat the oven to 350°F.
2. Whisk together milk, cream, eggs, sugar, extract, butter and salt.
3. Add the flour and whisk gently until incorporated.
4. Place sliced bananas in a bowl with lemon juice.
5. Lightly grease Dutch oven and heat in oven for 5 minutes. Remove and pour in batter.
6. Scatter bananas over batter and bake until golden and puffed, about 35 minutes.

Nutrition:

Carbohydrates – 27.2 g

Fat – 8.2 g

Protein – 4.5 g

Calories – 194

307. Lemon Cake Pudding with Blueberries

Preparation time: 20 minutes

Cooking time: 40 minutes

Servings: 6

Ingredients:

- 3 eggs, separated
- 3 Tbsp all-purpose flour
- 1 cup sugar
- 1 Tbsp butter, melted
- 6 Tbsp freshly squeezed lemon juice
- 1 tsp grated lemon zest
- 1¼ cups milk
- Whipped cream, for garnish
- Fresh blueberries, for garnish

Directions:

1. Preheat the oven to 350°F.
2. In a large bowl, beat the egg whites until stiff.
3. Beat the egg yolks in another large bowl, and add the flour and sugar.
4. Add the butter, lemon juice, lemon zest, and milk.
5. Fold in the egg whites.
6. Pour the mixture into a 2-quart Dutch oven and bake, uncovered, for 40 minutes, or until the pudding is set.
7. Serve with whipped cream and blueberries.

Nutrition:

Carbohydrates – 32.6 g

Fat – 128.9 g

Protein – 4.1 g

Calories – 246

308. Deep-Dish Giant Double Chocolate Chip Cookie

Preparation time: 15 minutes

Cooking time: 30 minutes

Servings: 6

Ingredients:

- ½ cup unsalted butter
- ½ cup light brown sugar
- ½ cup white sugar
- 1 tsp vanilla
- 1 large egg
- 1 cup all-purpose flour
- ½ tsp baking powder
- ½ tsp salt
- 1 cup chocolate chip
- ½ cup chocolate chunks

Directions:

1. Preheat oven to 350°F.
2. Melt butter in Dutch oven over low heat.
3. Add sugars and stir well.
4. Incorporate vanilla and egg, and beat quickly to make sure eggs do not cook.
5. Stir in flour, baking soda and salt.
6. Fold in chocolate chips and chunks and spread dough out in Dutch oven lightly with a spatula to flatten.
7. Bake for 25 minutes until cookie appears browned on top.

Nutrition:

Carbohydrates – 53.2 g

Fat – 21.1 g

Protein – 4.9 g

Calories – 417

309. Gooey Chocolate Fudge Cake

Preparation time: 15 minutes

Cooking time: 25 minutes

Servings: 8

Ingredients:
- 1 cup flour
- ½ tsp baking soda
- 1 cup sugar
- Pinch of salt
- ½ cup vegetable oil
- 3 Tbsp cocoa powder
- ½ cup water
- ¼ cup whole milk
- 1 egg
- 1 tsp vanilla extract

Directions:
1. Preheat the oven to 350°F.
2. In a large bowl, whisk flour, baking soda, sugar and salt.
3. Combine oil, cocoa powder and water in another bowl.
4. Whisk in flour mixture and pour into Dutch oven.
5. Incorporate milk, egg and vanilla into the batter.
6. Bake for 25 minutes, or until edges are set and center is only slightly jiggly.

Nutrition:

Carbohydrates – 38.5 g

Fat – 14.9 g

Protein – 2.9 g

Calories – 290

310. Nutella Brownies

Preparation time: 15 minutes

Cooking time: 50 minutes

Servings: 8

Ingredients:

- 1 cup sugar
- 3 large eggs
- 1 cup all-purpose flour
- ½ cup Dutch cocoa powder
- ½ tsp salt
- ½ tsp vanilla extract
- ½ stick unsalted butter
- ¼ cup half-and-half
- 4 oz chocolate chips
- ½ cup Nutella spread

Directions:

1. Preheat oven to 350°F.
2. Whisk together sugar and eggs in one bowl.
3. Whisk together flour, cocoa and salt in another bowl.
4. In Dutch oven, simmer butter and half-and-half together over low heat.
5. Add chocolate chips and stir until melted, about 2 minutes.
6. Add in Nutella and continue stirring until incorporated. Remove from heat.
7. Pour sugar mixture into chocolate mixture in Dutch oven.
8. Carefully add flour mixture and fold until just incorporated.
9. Bake for 25 minutes, but start checking at 20 minutes. At about 20-22 minutes, you will have a brownie with a fudge-like consistency.

Nutrition:

Carbohydrates – 58,4 g

Fat – 19.8 g

Protein – 6.3 g

Calories – 429

311. Rustic Blackberry Galette

Preparation time: 15 minutes

Cooking time: 45 minutes

Servings: 6

Ingredients:

- 2 lbs fresh blackberries, rinsed and dried
- ¾ cup granulated sugar
- 2 Tbsp fresh lime juice
- 2 tsp chopped fresh basil
- 1 tsp chopped fresh mint
- Pinch of salt
- ¼ tsp cinnamon
- 1 tsp vanilla extract
- 1 package store-bought puff pastry, thawed
- 1 egg white, slightly beaten

Directions:

1. Preheat oven to 375°F.
2. Roll out puff pastry and place in greased Dutch oven. Allow pastry to hang over the sides slightly.
3. Toss together blackberries, sugar, lime juice, basil, mint, salt, cinnamon and vanilla extract.
4. Spread fruit mixture inside pastry dough in Dutch oven.
5. Fold pastry over the berries to cover edges and about ½ way up. Brush egg white over pastry.
6. Place the pot in oven and bake about 40 minutes, until pastry browns.

Nutrition:

Carbohydrates – 44.5 g

Fat – 3.7 g

Protein – 3.3 g

Calories – 211

312. Sweet Cherry Clafouti

Preparation time: 15 minutes

Cooking time: 45 minutes

Servings: 8

Ingredients:

- 1 cup whole milk
- ¼ cup whipping cream
- 3 eggs
- ½ cup granulated sugar
- 1 tsp almond extract
- 2 Tbsp butter, melted
- ½ cup all-purpose flour
- 2 cups cherries, pitted and sliced
- Powdered sugar

Directions:

1. Preheat the oven to 350°F.
2. Whisk together milk, cream, eggs, sugar, extract and butter.
3. Add the flour and whisk gently until incorporated.
4. Lightly grease Dutch oven and heat in oven for 5 minutes.
5. Remove from heat and pour in batter.
6. Scatter cherries all around batter and place in oven.
7. Bake until golden and puffed, about 35 minutes.
8. Dust with powdered sugar.

Nutrition:

Carbohydrates: 61.8 g

Fat: 6.8 g

Protein: 4.5 g

Calories: 326

313. Three Berry Crumble

Preparation time: 15 minutes

Cooking time: 1 hour

Servings: 8

Ingredients:

- 6 cups of fresh mixed berries (blueberries, raspberries), washed and dried
- ¼ cup sugar
- ¼ cup flour
- 1 Tbsp lemon juice
- ¾ cup flour
- ¾ cup brown sugar
- ¾ cup old fashioned oats
- ½ cup chopped almonds
- 1 tsp cinnamon
- 1 stick cold butter, cut into cubes

Directions:

1. Preheat oven to 375°F.
2. Lightly toss the berries, sugar, flour and lemon juice inside your Dutch oven.
3. In a bowl, mix the flour, brown sugar, oats, almonds and cinnamon.
4. Incorporate cold butter with your fingertips into the oat mixture until small clumps form.
5. Pour topping onto fruit and bake for 45 minutes to 1 hour, until bubbles form and top appears browned and crispy.
6. Serve with vanilla ice cream right out of Dutch oven.

Nutrition:

Carbohydrates – 55.9 g

Fat – 15.9g

Protein – 5.7 g

Calories – 387

Appendix – Cooking Conversion Charts

1. Measuring Equivalent Chart

Type	Imperial	Imperial	Metric
Weight	1 dry ounce		28g
	1 pound	16 dry ounces	0.45 kg
Volume	1 teaspoon		5 ml
	1 dessert spoon	2 teaspoons	10 ml
	1 tablespoon	3 teaspoons	15 ml
	1 Australian tablespoon	4 teaspoons	20 ml
	1 fluid ounce	2 tablespoons	30 ml
	1 cup	16 tablespoons	240 ml
	1 cup	8 fluid ounces	240 ml
	1 pint	2 cups	470 ml
	1 quart	2 pints	0.95 l
	1 gallon	4 quarts	3.8 l
Length	1 inch		2.54 cm

Numbers are rounded to the closest equivalent

2. Oven Temperature Equivalent Chart

Fahrenheit (°F)	Celsius (°C)	Gas Mark
220	100	
225	110	1/4
250	120	1/2
275	140	1
300	150	2
325	160	3
350	180	4
375	190	5
400	200	6
425	220	7
450	230	8
475	250	9
500	260	

Celsius (°C) = T (°F)-32] * 5/9

Fahrenheit (°F) = T (°C) * 9/5 + 32

Numbers are rounded to the closest equivalent

Conclusion

Whether you want to treat yourself to a delicious breakfast, hearty main meal, tasty side dishes, or super yummy desserts, you have probably found what you were looking for in this book. Your Dutch oven can help revolutionize the way you cook and prepare your meals. The beauty of the oven is that it can be used in a variety of settings ranging from your kitchen to a campsite. It can also be used to cook a variety of foods from the traditional dry foods such as bread, pita bread, pancakes, and stuffing, to greasy foods such as fried chicken, pizza dough, biscuits, and so much more.

The food cooked in the Dutch oven is often cut into small pieces so that it may fall apart in the end. To make sure the results are wholesome and nutritious, be sure to read the instructions before you start using the Dutch oven.

It is also important that you follow the recipe exactly to ensure a delicious result. In some cases, it is sometimes also nice to experiment a little, to come up with your own unique recipes.

So when you believe you are ready to begin this enjoyable Dutch oven cooking experience, this book is a great place to start with more than 300 sumptuous recipes that will inspire you to cook some of your favorite dishes.

And what is more pleasant about the Dutch oven is that you can use it for cooking indoors or outdoors, you can also take this cookware with you wherever you go because it fits any backpack and you can use it in camps while enjoying with your friends.

Dutch ovens garnered great popularity all over the world, and whether you are new to using the Dutch oven or you are a professional, this cookware will bring the nostalgic taste of the past to your dish and will help you enjoy cooking more.

If you are not familiar with the Dutch oven, this cookbook will make a great start for you. And if you are questioning yourself why you should use a Dutch oven instead of using any other cookware, you will find all the answers you are looking for in this cookbook.

The recipes in this book are healthy and delicious; besides, you will find a recipe that is suitable for each of you. Whether you are a vegetarian or you loveanimal proteins, this book includes a wide variety of recipes that will satisfy all tastes.

Printed in Great Britain
by Amazon

86223778R00194